Addiction

Contributors

H. Dale Beckett
Peter G. Bourne
Carl D. Chambers
Robert L. DuPont
Rinna B. Flohr
Avram Goldstein
Mark H. Greene
Rayburn F. Hesse
Barbara A. Judson
Roger E. Meyer
David F. Musto
Robert G. Newman
Barry S. Ramer
Norman E. Zinberg

Addiction

EDITED BY

PETER G. BOURNE

Special Action Office for Drug
Abuse Prevention
Executive Office of the President
Washington, D.C.

ACADEMIC PRESS   New York   San Francisco   London   1974

A Subsidiary of Harcourt Brace Jovanovich, Publishers

ACADEMIC PRESS, INC.
111 Fifth Avenue, New York, New York 10003

United Kingdom Edition published by
ACADEMIC PRESS, INC. (LONDON) LTD.
24/28 Oval Road, London NW1

Library of Congress Cataloging in Publication Data

Bourne, Peter G   Date
    Addiction.

    Includes bibliographies.
    1.   Heroin habit—Addresses, essays, lectures.
2.   Drug abuse—United States—Addresses, essays, lectures.   3.   Drug abuse—Treatment—United States—
Addresses, essays, lectures.   I.   Title.   [DNLM: 1.   Heroin addiction.   WM288 B775a]
HV5822.H4B68   362.2'93   74-1642
ISBN 0–12–119535–X

Contents

3. **Hypotheses Concerning the Etiology of**
    Heroin Addiction
    H. Dale Beckett

4. **Evaluating the Success of Addiction Programs**
    Carl D. Chambers

5. **Rational Planning for Drug Abuse Services**
    Barry S. Ramer and Rinna B. Flohr

6. **Beginning to Dissect
    a Heroin Addiction Epidemic**
    Robert L. DuPont and Mark H. Greene

7. **Involuntary Treatment of Drug Addiction**
    Robert G. Newman

8. **Three Critical Issues in the Management
    of Methadone Programs**
    Avram Goldstein and Barbara A. Judson

List Of Contributors

Numbers in parentheses indicate the pages on which the authors' contributions begin.

H. Dale Beckett (37), Cane Hill Hospital, Coulsdon, Surrey, England

Peter G. Bourne [1] (1), Special Action Office for Drug Abuse Prevention, Executive Office of the President, Washington, D.C.

Carl D. Chambers (55), Department of Epidemiology, University of Miami School of Medicine, Miami, Florida

Robert L. DuPont (101), Special Action Office for Drug Abuse Prevention, Washington, D.C.

Rinna B. Flohr (63), Division of Special Programs, San Francisco, California

Avram Goldstein (129), Department of Pharmacology, Stanford University, and Addiction Research Foundation, Palo Alto, California

Mark H. Greene [2] (101), United States Public Health Service, Center for Disease Control, Epidemic Intelligence Service, Atlanta, Georgia

Rayburn F. Hesse [3] (187), National Association of State Drug Abuse Program Coordinators, Albany, New York

Barbara A. Judson (129), Department of Pharmacology, Stanford University, and Addiction Research Foundation, Palo Alto, California

Roger E. Meyer (21), Department of Psychiatry, Harvard Medical School, McLean Hospital, Belmont, Massachusetts

[1] Present address: Drug Abuse Council, Washington, D.C.

[2] Present address: Special Action office for Drug Abuse Prevention, Washington, D.C.

[3] Present address: National Association of State Drug Abuse Program Coordinators, Washington, D.C.

David F. Musto (*175*), The Child Study Center and the Department of History, Yale University, New Haven, Connecticut

Robert G. Newman (*113*), Methadone Maintenance Treatment Program, New York City Health Department, New York, New York

Barry S. Ramer [4] (*63*), Division of Special Programs, Community Mental Health Services, Department of Public Health, San Francisco, California

Norman E. Zinberg (*149*), 11 Scott Street, Cambridge, Massachusetts

[4] Present address: 2000 Van Ness Avenue, San Francisco, California

Preface

Heroin addiction has, during the past three years, become an issue of major national concern in the United States. Precipitated primarily by its sudden epidemic spread, its intimate link with rising crime rates, and its unprecedented involvement of American troops in Southeast Asia, concern about the use of heroin has dominated public interest. As with other forms of drug abuse, heroin addiction became both the scapegoat and the symbolic focus for the concerns and fears of a society alarmed about social change and upheaval that was unexplained on other grounds. Such a phenomenon is not new; similar events had occurred around the use of heroin in the early part of the century, but never before had there been such a mobilization of public concern to respond to the problem of drug abuse.

Apart from the emotional reaction to heroin addiction, the late 1960's saw a sudden and very real increase in the use of heroin in America. There were few experts in the field, and many of those who did exist tended to be oriented to different social manifestations of drug abuse that prevailed in earlier eras. The conceptualizations of the addictive process that had been used in the past did not lend themselves to the epidemic of the 1960's in terms of serving as the basis for strategies of intervention. In addition, the historic development of the use of methadone maintenance as a new modality of treatment by Drs. Vincent Dole and Marie Nyswander opened up whole new horizons in terms of the tactics for curtailing the spread of addiction.

One result of the experiences of the past five years has been that enormous amounts of new information have been generated which are only gradually being assimilated into a new conceptual framework by those working in the field. This volume was not designed to be a definitive document on the state of the art in the field of addiction, but rather to provide an opportunity for some of those in the forefront of the conceptual thinking in addiction to express their feelings on key issues that are uppermost in their consideration as the field is presently evolving. There continue to be rapid changes in the manner in which addiction is perceived, but it is hoped that out of the experience and knowledge gained during this recent epidemic sufficient understanding can be gained to prevent effectively in the future a recurrence of the rampant spread of the heroin problem in American society.

This book is geared toward the problem of heroin addiction, and the authors were asked to restrict their contributions to this topic. However, particularly in the area of policy consideration, it was inevitable that the broader field of drug abuse would be considered.

I would like to express my appreciation to Mrs. Jacquelyn Deland whose diligent commitment to this project was indispensable to its success.

Peter G. Bourne

Addiction

1

Issues in Addiction

PETER G. BOURNE

Introduction

Opiate addiction is an affliction of long standing in the United States. Despite the substantial publicity given to this problem in recent years, and hence its seemingly new development, it has been present in our society at varying levels of intensity for more than 100 years. In fact, opiate addiction was so identified with the United States that at one time it was known in Europe as "the American disease." It has in different eras been identified as predominantly a problem of white middle class women, of physicians and other health practitioners, and, most recently, of youth and poor black ghetto dwellers. Yet it is not exclusive to any of these groups, and any understanding of the addictive process must go beyond its transient affliction of any one segment of society.

We know that the spread of opiate use has many of the characteristics of an infectious disease. The epidemic model has proved a useful tool to describe and explain the explosive spread of addiction in widely different communities (Hughes and Crawford, 1972; de Alarcon, 1969). Yet, surprisingly, we know little or nothing about what triggers the sudden onset of an epidemic of addiction. What characteristics define the population at risk and what factors eventually limit the spread of the epidemic and cause it to decline? Our previous explanations of the individual psychological causes for addiction in terms of the so-called "addictive personality" now appear remarkably naive. In fact, except for the need for face-to-face contact with a user, we know little or nothing about what causes an individual to use opiates.

1

In recent years, following the disease model of addiction, we have emphasized the importance of treatment as an essential component in any strategy to control addiction. However, while it is possible to demonstrate beneficial effects accruing to the individual addict as a result of "treatment," we do not know what overall impact, if any, it has on the natural history of an epidemic. It may serve to curtail spread or it may even prolong the outbreak. Our knowledge remains primitive, and while we take certain measures with the hope that they will reduce the use of opiates, we are acting largely on faith, and to date have a scarcity of scientific information to justify our actions.

The epidemic of heroin addiction that has occurred in the United States, and to a lesser extent elsewhere in the world, in the last 6 to 8 years has stimulated the most vigorous attempt to date to analyze the natural history, the epidemiology, and the social cost of addiction and to assess the effects of different approaches to treatment and control. Many of the best studies performed so far have resulted only in the posing of additional questions. However, while we are still far from a definitive explanation of the addictive process, we have reached a level of sophistication in understanding the basic issues that did not exist even 5 years ago. While it would be ideal in a volume such as this to provide a definitive discussion of the phenomenon of addiction, this is not possible, and perhaps the best alternative available is to discuss what appear to be the key issues, resolved or unresolved, as they have become defined in recent years.

Civil Liberties and Addiction

The right of an individual to do as he wishes with his own body is argued to be a fundamental liberty. This assertion holds that the use of drugs in the pursuit of pleasure or the alleviation of pain is within man's basic rights. In its simplest form, drug addiction is a victimless crime (with the possible exception of the user), and laws against the abuse of drugs can be considered an attempt to legislate morality.

The primary argument against this position is that the use of drugs never remains an isolated phenomenon and inevitably involves profiteering from their sale and ultimately the development of a black market, with a rise in the crime rate caused by those addicted attempting to obtain adequate funds to maintain their habits. At the same time, it potentially leads to the debilitation and nonproductivity of a large segment of society. The two extreme reactions to this association of addiction with crime are, on the one hand, to justify treating all aspects of addiction as criminal behavior and a major threat to the welfare of society and, on the other, to suggest that if adequate drugs were available, the association with crime would be eliminated. The idea of government-sponsored heroin maintenance is based on this concept and has recently found strong proponents, particularly among civil libertarians, who feel that the addict has a certain inherent right to his addiction and that society should not penalize him for it.

Both of these positions tend, despite their apparent disparity, to view the use of heroin as a volitional act rather than to see the addict as a sick person in need of treatment. Interestingly, while we often express cursory passing concern for the welfare of those who abuse drugs, this is in general a minor factor in shaping the response of society. Even the establishment of treatment centers is frequently justified as public policy on the basis of the expectation that it will lead to a drop in the crime rate rather than out of humanitarian concern for the addict.

The use of heroin is generally a private act, the transactions necessary to maintain a habit are relatively easy to conceal, and except for secondary acts of crime, the addict population is largely inapparent to the remainder of society. At the same time, society puts vigorous demands on law enforcement agencies to produce tangible evidence of success in interdicting heroin traffic and suppressing its use. As a result, those working in the area of drug abuse law enforcement are obliged to use surreptitious and clandestine methods if they are to have any hope of producing the type of success society demands. As a result, this area of law enforcement has constantly found itself on the borderline between accepted police practices and the invasion of constitutional rights and the infringement of civil liberties.

As long as we believe that society has a right to dictate that the illicit use of drugs is unacceptable and insist that law enforcement agencies produce results, particularly in terms of the number of individuals arrested and the volume of narcotics seized, there will be a tendency for police to resort to wiretapping, questionable searches, and the use of undercover agents and informers. Such practices become almost inevitable when one uses the police in the area of moral or political control. The abdication by the medical profession of responsibility for the addict, accompanied by the demand that law enforcement officials deal with the problem, which occurred in the early part of this century, may well have set us on an irrevocable course that contributed to the major difficulties we face today (Musto, 1973).

The public view of the addict as a moral degenerate has tended to foster the view that he was barely entitled to the protections and due process accorded other citizens and had little grounds for complaint when he had so outraged the public morality. Particularly in the past, narcotic enforcement activities did not enjoy a high stature relative to other law enforcement activities. At the same time, it was considered a field in which there was considerable latitude in terms of allowable practices where police officers were unlikely to be held accountable for mistreating or violating the rights of addicts or suppliers. As one senior narcotics agent has said, "Ours has traditionally been an area of law enforcement where anything goes." The result may well have been to attract a certain percentage of individuals into this aspect of law enforcement who were less sensitive to the rights of the individual citizen, whether an addict or not.

The use of heroin and society's response to the addict are intimately tied to the issue of civil liberties. Addiction has apparently been eliminated in China by imposing the most stringent measures; similarly, the use of heroin, and particularly amphetamines, was largely eradicated in Japan by steps that completely preempted the rights of the addicts. While there are some practical considerations relating to the magnitude of the problem, which might prevent success, it would theoretically be possible to eliminate the problem in the United States if we were willing to take the harsh steps employed in these two countries, such as massive incarcerations without trial or condoning the execution of sellers, even when only small amounts of the drug are involved. Such measures represent such an affront to the American system that few would seriously advocate them. However, it may well be that our desire for the control of addiction must be tempered with our desire to protect the rights of American citizens and that an overzealous commitment to the former will inevitably produce an infringement of the latter.

Heroin Addiction as an Epidemic Phenomenon

As Musto has described elsewhere in this volume (Chapter 10), there has been continuous abuse of heroin in this country since around 1912. Superimposed on the chronic steady utilization, there have been at least three major explosive and sudden increases in the number of users and in the distribution of use. Although the level of documentation varies widely and, in general, is somewhat inadequate, these three epidemic episodes appear to have been from around 1915 to the early 1920's, the late 1950's to the mid-1960's, and from 1966 to the present. The triggering elements allowing these episodes to occur are complex and may have been different in each instance. Why, after many years of containment within a relatively stable subcultural group, should the use of the drug suddenly spread rapidly to involve tens of thousands of new cases?

First use of heroin is almost invariably the result of associating with a user, even one who is himself a relative neophyte. Use of heroin without prior contact with, discussion with, or actual initiation by another individual already using the drug is almost nonexistent. The one exception to this is the group of individuals who become addicted through medical mismanagement. The sudden spread of heroin out of a circumscribed subcultural group where its use is chronic and stable into a much larger segment of the population must involve a shift or disruption of social association patterns.

During the late 1950's and early 1960's, the heroin-using subcultures were for the most part black inner-city dwellers in the major urban centers of the country and particularly highly specific groups such as entertainers and musicians. Social rejection from the larger society diminished contacts outside the group, and intensive law enforcement efforts made users extremely cautious about selling to or initiating individuals with whom they were not closely acquainted. The relatively small numbers of addicts involved in these groups and their chronic use made identification, surveillance, and hence pressure from law enforcement agencies relatively easy to impose. On the other hand, the small size of the addict groups and their relative stability meant that they were hard to infiltrate and that sources of supply were reasonably well protected. For instance, in Atlanta during this period there were between 30 and 40 addicts, nearly all of whom were personally acquainted with each other; a new face as either a user or a seller drew immediate attention and scrutiny, both from the police and the addict group. In effect, a situation of containment existed, with the level of law enforcement effort stalemated or balanced by the ability of the addict subculture to protect itself. The commitment of resources by law enforcement agencies was not enough to significantly interdict the relatively small amount of heroin required to maintain these addicts nor to significantly reduce their number either by driving them into the virtually nonexistent treatment facilities, by incarcerating them, or by forcing them to abandon their habits voluntarily. Similarly, the relatively stable demand and the fact that addicts and street sellers would deal only with people they knew meant that the supply system was controlled and hard to break into. Outside of New York City the potential profits were easily outweighed by the risks of dealing except for the established suppliers and there was little inducement for the free-wheeling hustler involved in other illicit activities such as boot-legging, pimping, numbers, or even for those in more legitimate businesses to get into the heroin market, as happened in later years. In effect, a delicate balance existed that served to maintain the *status quo*.

An additional element in the development of the recent heroin epidemic is identified by some addicts, but has received little attention in the professional literature. Prior to the early 1960's, paregoric was available over the counter in almost unlimited quantities in many states. At the same time it was relatively cheap. In some cities there existed a group of individuals who bought paregoric and went through the laborious process of boiling it down and preparing it for injectable use. These individuals existed on the periphery of the heroin addict subculture, and although they used heroin and other narcotics occasionally, they could not usually afford it, could not count on regular access, and in some instances deliberately avoided becoming heavily involved with heroin because of the pervasive deleterious effects that they observed. While this group associated closely with the heroin-using subculture, they also, in many instances, held jobs and were involved in an integral way with the larger society. Once heavily addicted, the heroin addict had a tendency to turn inward to the addict subculture. Owing to the consuming nature of his habit, he tended to abandon his associations in the outside world, both socially and with regard to employment. The paregoric users, only mildly addicted, if at all, could continue to be a relatively conforming member of the larger society. In many ways they acted as a buffer or as insulation around the hard-core addict community. The nonaddicts they associated with in the larger society were generally resistant to the laborious process and undramatic results of paregoric use and the practice spread very slowly. This changed radically in the mid-1960's when paregoric could no longer be bought over the counter. At that point, many of the mildly addicted paregoric users switched to regular heroin use, their protective role was gone, and they were immediately exposing themselves and their heroin habits to a new, previously unexposed segment of society.

The most critical factor in the maintenance of the phenomenon of containment of the addict groups until the mid- and late 1960's was the manner in which the number of new experimenters was kept to a minimum. New users are for several reasons the key factor in the development of an epidemic because it is they, rather than the chronic hard-core addict, who are responsible for sustaining the momentum of spread and disrupting the balance between supply, demand, and police control. During the first year of use, an addict is more likely to be responsible for contributing to another individual starting to use heroin than at any other point in the course of his addiction. In part, this is because the new user will still be living predominantly outside of the addict subculture, with most of his friends and acquaintances being nonaddicts. As he becomes addicted, he is more likely to move into the addict group, preoccupied with establishing contacts that will help him maintain his habit, and spending less and less time with nonaddict acquaintances. As that happens, he becomes less and less of a threat to the nonaddict population at risk. During the early phases of heroin use, a genuine enthusiasm for the drug may exist which the individual may want to share legitimately with his friends. This is before he becomes aware of the problems of physical addiction or when he still thinks that he can control his use. In some instances, proselytizing for new users may be the result of fear or guilt, with the individual seeking to achieve some peer support through sharing his activities and experiments with the drug.

What happened in the mid- and late 1960's to cause a breakdown in the containment phenomenon and the sudden explosive spread of addiction? What occurred in society to increase the social association of vulnerable nonusers with addicts or caused an increase in the susceptibility of those already exposed?

The social changes of the 1960's, which affected so many areas of American society, almost certainly contributed significantly to the heroin epidemic. It was a time of enormous upheaval when traditional values were consistently challenged and patterns of social association altered dramatically. The civil rights movement may have had a number of significant effects. Not only was there substantially greater face-to-face social contact between blacks and whites, but the generally greater tolerance for drug use among educated white youth almost certainly was communicated to blacks. The white tolerance derived in part from the fact that, in general, they had had no exposure to heroin users, whereas many of the blacks had and continued to do so, and their changing attitude then made them extremely vulnerable. Expectations in the black community also changed substantially during the 1960's. There were more opportunities and substantially more money available from a variety of sources. Not only did many young blacks have money to spend on drugs, but a highly profitable market was created that profiteers were willing to exploit despite the risks. The old distributors no longer held a monopoly and a new infrastructure of distribution developed in the country. As the number of users increased, the demand increased, offering greater profits, which in turn drew more individuals into the market.

The heroin epidemic of the 1960's was predominantly a phenomenon of black America. Particularly outside of New York, distribution systems were through the black communities, and white heroin users tended to be on the periphery of the distribution system. Their drug use was of shorter duration and, during periods of short supply, they were cut off first. Yet the fact that whites were, in the 1960's, associating with blacks sufficiently to learn to use heroin meant that a whole new market was created for black sellers. This increased the volume of the business and provided a significant flow of cash into black communities.

The altered association patterns can explain to a significant degree why young whites began to use heroin in the 1960's in large numbers. What is harder to explain is why a problem, generally retained for many years within a small segment of the black community, should suddenly break out and involve tens of thousands of other blacks who, although they may have had occasional and passing contacts with addicts in the past, had never become heroin users. Perhaps the answer lies in the fact that while we think of the social changes of the 1960's as involving black/white relations, enormous changes occurred within black society itself. Many of the old stratifications broke down and educational and job opportunities available in the past to a thin upper crust of black society suddenly existed at all social levels. Government-funded programs and the opening up of many middle- and lower-level jobs in white businesses infused large amounts of money into lower- and lower-middle-class black families. This meant that many young blacks had money to spend on drugs and other recreational activities that they never had before, and their new affluence gave them opportunities for social associations they had previously been denied.

A suddenly highly fluid economy, with a significant segment of the community "making it," was probably responsible for encouraging a lot of blacks to see drugs as a way of turning a quick profit and maintaining self-respect with regard to those who were making their money more legitimately. Some, however, were not "making it," and the success of others around them heightened their personal sense of frustration and failure. This group, poorly educated, unemployed, and often engaged in petty criminal activities, became particularly susceptible to chronic heroin use.

The age of first use is a figure of particular interest. In Washington, D.C. where the heroin epidemic was in effect exclusively a black phenomenon, DuPont has reported that as the epidemic started in the early 1960's, the age of first use was most frequently in the mid-20's, suggesting that it was in this age bracket that the changing association patterns of a newly vulnerable group with the community's old chronic residual heroin users was first occurring (DuPont and Greene, 1973). Subsequently, as the epidemic gained momentum, the most frequently reported age of first use dropped steadily year by year. This suggested that as the epidemic spread it was transmitted year by year predominantly to a population 1 year younger than the previous year's new users. At the time the epidemic reached its peak in 1971, the year of most frequent first use was age 19. The epidemic subsequently began to decline, even though the year of greatest reported first use continued to become younger still. These facts, supported by data from other cities, suggest that 19 is the age of greatest vulnerability to heroin use and that an individual is most vulnerable to those a year older in terms of close social association or his willingness to be persuaded to start heroin use.

Most cities have reported a ratio of approximately three men to one woman seeking treatment for heroin addiction. Relatively little attention has been paid to the use patterns of women as opposed to men, although it appears that the spread of heroin use as a progressive epidemic phenomenon is a male event. Men induce new heroin use in both other men and women, but the women in general do not encourage other women to become users, and even less frequently does a woman initiate a male user. Use of heroin by a woman is for the most part tied directly to its use by a man with whom she is closely associated. In part, this is due to the traditional male/female roles in initiating any novel or risk-taking behavior and is reflected as much in high school and college drinking behavior as in the use of heroin. Also, women addicts tend either to obtain their supply of the drug from the man with whom they are involved or they gravitate toward prostitution. Women are much less frequently involved in selling heroin than men, and hence they have fewer contacts with new users.

Vulnerability

While social association patterns and availability of the drug are two of the key elements in the spread of addiction, the vulnerability or susceptibility of the individual who is exposed is of equal importance. Prior to the development of the recent heroin epidemic, there were many individuals, particularly in black communities, in large urban cities who were exposed to heroin addicts but did not become themselves users of the drug. At the other extreme, among G.I.'s in Vietnam the use of heroin spread with so little resistance that in some instances almost 100% of the men in certain units became users.

What are the factors that alter vulnerability? The traditional psychiatric view has been that there is a so-called "addictive personality" which predispose individuals to become addicted. Although many of the early descriptions of the personality characteristics of addicts were based on *ex post facto* studies, there is reason to believe that some individuals are more susceptible than others and that this is a manifestation of their psychological makeup.

There are two thresholds affecting individual use of heroin which need to be considered. The first involves the vulnerability to experimental use; the second involves the propensity following experimental use to become dependent whether or not this is accompanied by actual physical addiction. In the past, there has been a tendency to believe that a very high percentage of heroin experimenters subsequently become dependent. However, recent experience has suggested that this need not necessarily be so. It appears that when the level of heroin use in a community is stable, new users tend to be more emotionally disturbed and socially deviant than when there is an epidemic situation. This is in part due to the fact that when there are few users they are more stigmatized and isolated from the large society; hence, those who associate with them will tend, of necessity, to exhibit a high level of deviancy. Under these circumstances, experimental use is likely to result in a very high percentage of dependency. With an epidemic situation and widespread availability of heroin, individual psychopathology becomes much less important in determining the extent of initial experimental heroin use. In this circumstance, those who experiment and have significant emotional disturbance are likely to become dependent. However, many others who become dependent have few problems but have been consistently and repeatedly exposed to chronic users, are subjected to heavy social pressure to become regular users, or are exposed repetitively to high-grade heroin. In its simplest form, this means that when heroin is scarce a greater degree of deviancy and psychopathology is evident among those who become dependent than when heroin is widely available, and that when the drug is scarce there are very few experimenters, whereas when it is abundant, experimentation without psychopathology is widespread.

A recent study has thrown considerable light on the relationship between environment, availability, experimentation, and dependence (Robins, 1974). During 1970 and 1971 heroin use among

American servicemen in Vietnam rose to unprecedented levels. (Use was close to 100% in some units.) The purity of heroin was very high, and many soldiers who were sprinkling the drug in cigarettes or sniffing it unknowingly developed physical dependence. In some parts of the country, heroin was cheaper than Coca Cola and this, combined with a high degree of boredom, made experimentation hard to resist. At the time heroin use reached its peak, a urine-screening program was initiated to identify users as they left Southeast Asia. Those who, on further examination, were found to be physically dependent were detoxified and treated over a 30-day period. On follow-up a year later, only 7% of these individuals were still using heroin. This study substantially refuted the widely held belief that once an individual was addicted to heroin he would always be an addict, repeatedly relapsing and unamenable to treatment and rehabilitation. Particularly it laid to rest the notion that addiction produced irreversible metabolic changes in the user.

The social transitions of the 1960's produced new social association patterns, as has been noted. Other events occurred also, which altered individual resistance to the use, both experimental and chronic, of drugs. The role of Timothy Leary and Ken Kesey is hard to assess, but it is clear that they, together with many others, provided both an awareness and a condonation of drug use among educated white youth which did not exist previously. The "stepping stone" theory of addiction, which held that, beginning with marijuana, an individual progressed through other drugs to heroin, has been the subject of significant controversy. However, the removal of previous psychological and emotional barriers to the use of mind-altering drugs did not make some drugs but not others acceptable. Rather, it opened as a concept for experimentation the full range of drug experience. Obviously, most individuals who smoked marijuana, or even used LSD, distinguished heroin as another order of magnitude and danger which they were not willing to try. However, some were willing, particularly when they perceived the constraints as being largely legal, so that by smoking marijuana they had already broken the law and hence there was no new transgression involved in moving on to heroin.

The net effect of the psychedelic movement of the mid-1960's was to heighten the awareness of youth to the possibility of using drugs and to break down traditional barriers of fear and stereotypic repugnance to drug users as "junkies." The result was an increased vulnerability of youth, which when combined with exposure to many drugs, including heroin, resulted in a greatly enhanced likelihood of use.

The hippie phenomenon and the voice of Timothy Leary would not, however, have spread very far if it had not been for the overwhelming public fascination with drug use and the enthusiastic coverage by the news media. Drugs became, as they had 50 years earlier, a convenient scapegoat for many of the concerns of society, and particularly for the rising crime rate. Every community in America became concerned about drug abuse, and no child in the country escaped being made aware of the range and effects of the drugs that he or she was likely to be exposed to. Geared ostensibly to preventing the use of drugs by young people, there is now little doubt that this massive campaign with movies, printed pamphlets, and specialized teacher-training programs served to advertise the possibilities of drug abuse to hundreds of thousands of young people who otherwise would never have considered using drugs. The dangers described with some drugs were known by young people to be inaccurate, so that the credibility of the entire educational program was often thrown into question. For some the stated dangers of using drugs served only to titillate eager minds looking for new thrills or different risk-taking activity. Above all else, the drug abuse education effort conveyed to young people a message of expectation from the adult world that they either would take drugs or at least were highly vulnerable to doing so. Thus, a self-fulfilling prophecy was made which might never previously have existed. What in fact was a highly effective advertising campaign for drug abuse now in retrospect shows every evidence of having increased the experimental use of drugs rather than diminishing it (Tennant *et al.*, 1973).

The Limiting Factors in a Heroin Epidemic

Once heroin addiction has spread from a small subculture into the larger society, a number of factors may be considered to be crucial to its continuing spread or to its limitation. National policy has considered three approaches to the strategy of limiting the recent epidemic. First, there has been an attempt at several different levels to interdict the flow of heroin into the country, reducing the overall supply and hence its availability on the streets. This approach has clearly been successful. During 1973 there was a clear decline in the availability of heroin, particularly in the eastern half of the country, and not only was heroin hard to get in most major cities, but the purity dropped from a high in 1971 of around 12% to 2% or less in mid-1973. The primary effect of reducing availability is that those on the periphery of the distribution system find it progressively harder to maintain their habits, and they become reluctant to provide any of the drug to new users. Hence the number of new experimenters and new addicts drops sharply.

The second element in the overall strategy is to provide sufficient treatment capacity so that any addict desiring to discontinue the use of heroin has the needed help to do so. The paradigm that has been used is that reduction in supply will drive addicts into treatment and that, conversely, the greater the number of people in treatment the smaller the demand for heroin on the street, the smaller the profit and, therefore, the less traffickers will bring in. In fact, the relationships between supply and demand have proved to be considerably more complex.

There is no doubt that treatment programs have a sequestering effect in terms of reducing the addict pool and hence the potential daily market for heroin in a community. In mid-1973 there were in excess of 100,000 heroin addicts in treatment in the United States who otherwise would have been purchasing heroin on a daily basis. However, most of those who enter treatment programs are users with at least 2 years of involvement with the drug, who for the most part are not the individuals most likely to be responsible for initiating new users and perpetuating the epidemic. In addition, vigorous law enforcement does not have the direct straight-line correlation of driving addicts into treatment that was once believed to exist.

However desirable treatment may be from a humanitarian and crime-reducing standpoint, there is serious question as to what impact it has on the natural history of a heroin epidemic. Major treatment initiatives have often not been fully implemented until the local epidemic had already begun to show a slowing down (Hughes and Crawford, 1972). There is also serious question, despite the relatively high success rate of methadone maintenance programs and their ability to hold a high percentage of their patients in treatment for a year or more, of whether they may not also serve to prolong the epidemic by sustaining many addicts over periods of acute heroin shortage. These individuals, even though they may constitute a minority of those entering treatment, have, in general, been addicted for shorter periods of time, have little motivation to become permanently free from heroin, and use the time in a treatment program to escape the agony and turmoil of the street. Once heroin is again plentiful they drop out, replenishing the addict pool, and serve to sustain and attenuate the epidemic. However, while there may be some validity to this point of view, it is also true that many individuals, once they have spent more than a few weeks in treatment, find a return to the streets unexpectedly difficult because they have lost their old contacts, and the constant pressure to raise money by theft and other illegal activity is even harder to endure. The result is that many treatment programs now see as many returning dropouts as new patients, and frequently a patient who has been out to retaste the hardship of life on the street returns strongly motivated to get help.

The pathology of drug dependence is the result of a complex relationship between individual psychopathology, pharmacological effect, and socially prescribed roles and values. We perhaps have a tendency to put too great an emphasis on the effects of the drug itself and too little on the social and cultural aspects of the phenomenon.

During the 1950's a series of controlled scientific studies were performed to determine the effects of LSD use on student and prisoner volunteers. In general, the subjects experienced psychomimetic effects that were relatively uniform and mild. They did not suffer from the terrifying and violent hallucinatory experiences associated with the "acid trips" of the 1960's. They also did not feel that the drug had any great "mind expanding" capacity, nor did they suffer subsequent "flashbacks." The importance of learning and social ambience in order to enjoy marijuana is clearly recognized by users. Also, in many countries where marijuana is still regarded as a dangerous drug, where the authorities talk of the dire medical, social, and legal consequences of its use, there are frequently well-documented reports of severe psychotic reactions, social disintegration, and a switch to criminal behavior by previously conforming individuals after they have used only small amounts of marijuana.

These experiences suggest that the apparent behavioral effects of an abused drug and the life style that the individual adopts after using various drugs are determined to an overwhelming degree by the concept he has about the implications of drug taking and by his self-concept as a drug user, which is almost entirely prescribed by the beliefs and prejudices of society. Thus, the marijuana user who lives in a society where it is widely believed that smoking cannabis leads to psychosis will have a far greater likelihood of developing a psychotic reaction than a marijuana user in the United States who has little or no concern about this possibility. The outcome, therefore, has little relationship to the pharmacological effects of the drug per se.

The same phenomenon applies to the use of narcotics. The heroin user sees many implications in his act, even though they may be repressed. Most heroin experimenters are convinced at a conscious level that they will not become addicted, yet they have a conceptualization of "the junkie" and the life style that goes with chronic dependence on heroin. The postoperative patient receiving narcotics for pain may be taking larger doses of similar drugs, more frequently, and, at least initially, for a longer sustained period of time, yet he has rarely any concern about becoming dependent and does not perceive any predetermined social and psychological breakdown as a result of his use of narcotics.

As far as treatment is concerned, the old concept of "once an addict always an addict" has not only dominated the thinking of society in this area, but has clearly served as a self-reinforcing statement by convincing addicts that it was true and that they could never recover. Particularly while the number of addicts was stable and the social stigma they endured was great, without access to treatment or jobs, their chances of recovery were slim. Not only a change in the type of individual who has become addicted during the recent epidemic, but also, in particular, a change in the attitude of society toward the addict as one who is capable of recovery has significantly increased the number of individuals who have recovered. This change in attitude more than anything else may have served to make treatment a viable method for reducing the overall addict pool.

The third aspect of the government strategy in seeking to control the epidemic involves prevention through education. The problems inherent in our overall efforts with drug abuse education have been described above. However, if there is one area in which drug abuse education may have had a significant deterrent effect, it is with regard to heroin addiction. The dangers are clearly apparent, and many young people knew from their own experience that what they were being told about heroin addiction was a good deal more valid than what they had heard about LSD and marijuana. Perhaps much more important, however, is that once heroin addiction began to spread widely through most American communities, a sufficient percentage of young people in the vulnerable age groups had been exposed to users, had seen the adverse effects for themselves, and had made a conscious decision not to use heroin whatever their other drug-using habits may have been. It was as though exposure to users, when it does not itself result in experimentation, can have an immunizing effect that helps to limit the spread of the epidemic. The epidemic phenomenon apparently thrives on a naive population, but is eventually limited by forces created by its own magnitude. It will be 15 to 20 years before we again have in the United States a comparable population without exposure to or awareness of heroin addiction. Perhaps in the meantime the present generation will remain significantly immunized to the use of heroin so that another epidemic could not occur in the interim.

The Therapeutic Effects of Narcotic Addiction

We should not underestimate the fact that a significant number of individuals who become addicted suffer from severe psychopathology. There is a higher than average incidence of schizophrenia, and depression clearly antedating the use of the drug is widespread. The fact that heroin, with all its problems, alleviates the suffering that many individuals feel is an important issue to consider. Some schizoid individuals whose disorganized lives left them barely functional found that the structuring of their existence, which heroin addiction forced, was enough to keep them from becoming psychotic. Whether it is external stress and the threat to their survival or the regular demand for an organized existence to relieve the pain of withdrawal on a regular basis is hard to say. However, it is clear that these individuals can function more effectively as addicts than they did previously. Naturally, they tend to do particularly well in methadone maintenance programs, but appear to be the least likely to be able to achieve a completely drug-free existence.

Wurmser (1973) has stressed the importance of heroin and methadone in allowing many addicts to keep affective reactions under control that they would otherwise find intolerable and cause them to become completely dysfunctional. Attempts to treat these individuals with other types of tranquilizing medication have proved unsuccessful, and it is clear that narcotics perform a unique therapeutic function for these individuals.

Tolerance

Perhaps the aspect of addiction that has had the least appreciation and is most misunderstood is that of tolerance. More than any other single element in the phenomenon of addiction, tolerance determines and dominates the behavior of the individual addict and the course of the epidemic. In its most extreme manifestation, tolerance is often the critical factor affecting overdose deaths. The addict is subject to constant change in the tolerance of his body to narcotics.

Sometimes he develops an innate understanding of the phenomenon and can treat himself accordingly. However, many addicts are unaware of its existence except in the most general terms, and it is a constant liability to them. While the addict has some control over his level of tolerance, he has no control over the purity of street heroin, and he must always risk the possibility that incautious use of the drug when unexpectedly pure will far exceed his tolerance and result in an overdose and possibly death. The overdose rate in cities tends to follow the sudden availability of high-grade heroin on the street after a period of shortage. Figure 1 shows the relationship between street purity of heroin and overdose deaths in Atlanta, Georgia. Similarly, many deaths have occurred among addicts when they returned to the street after short-term periods of treatment involving detoxification. Unaware that their tolerance had been substantially lowered, they "shot up" the same dose of heroin they had been accustomed to using prior to entering treatment a couple of weeks earlier. Now with lowered tolerance, they could no longer tolerate the dose and it was frequently lethal.

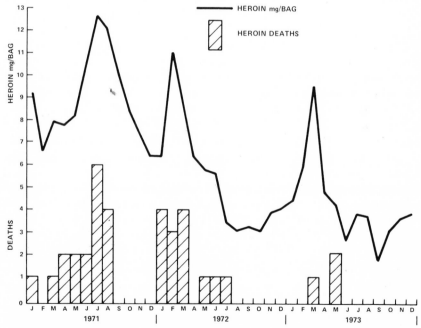

Fig. 1 Heroin overdose deaths and heroin potency, by date (Fulton and DeKalb counties), 1971–1973. Reprinted by permission of Dr. Michael Alexander, Center for Disease Control, Atlanta, Georgia 30322.

The question is often raised as to what brings an addict into treatment. Obviously, there are many factors, including geographical accessibility, the reputation of the treatment program, and so forth. However, the overriding issue in the final analysis is the pain and suffering of withdrawal, with its relentlessly punishing symptoms, which pursues the addict interminably every 6 to 8 hours and all of the anguish that he must go through to keep the pain at bay. The degree to which he suffers is a product of the level of tolerance he has developed, or, in effect, the extent to which he is addicted. This is derived both from his duration of use and the percentage purity of the heroin he has been using. If his tolerance is high, failure to make a contact and obtain heroin on schedule will result in very severe withdrawal symptoms. If his tolerance is low and the quality of heroin on the street is consistently poor, then failure to "score" will result in only mild symptoms. Therefore, because suffering is the primary factor in inducing addicts to seek treatment, more will do so when the quality of heroin on the street is high than when it is low. The optimal situation for driving addicts into treatment is to have a relatively high purity of heroin and then cause an acute shortage to occur, a situation that has been achieved by law enforcement efforts in some cities. However, prolonged and vigorous interdiction of heroin flow results in a diminution of the total available amount of heroin, a decline in the percentage purity as it is cut further and further, and a rise in the price. Over the last 18 months in the major cities of the eastern seaboard the availability of heroin has declined, the purity has dropped from 12% to 2%, and the price has risen from $0.50 per mg to as high as $5.00 per mg. The result is that not only is the new user largely excluded from access to the drug, but even if he can obtain it on a regular basis the effects are mild and it is very hard to build tolerance and, in fact, to become addicted at all. The tolerance of the chronic addict may have declined through a period of enforced detoxification as the purity of the drug went down. If he cannot obtain a "fix" he gets withdrawal symptoms, but they are relatively mild. In addition, the cost of heroin has risen to an exorbitant level even for an addict. Similarly, the individual terminating a treatment program, whether he drops out or is discharged, will find that the shortage and impurity of heroin enormously helps him to stay drug-free.

The decline and termination of an epidemic such as that of the last 5 years is probably manifested by a slow reduction in the availability of the drug and a corresponding decrease in the mean tolerance level in the addict pool. Estimates of the number of addicts in various cities at the height of the epidemic ran into the tens of thousands. In

Washington the estimate was 20,000, in Atlanta it was 6000. Between June 1971 and the present, approximately 3000 addicts have been treated. Another 1000 are serving time in various penal institutions, leaving approximately 2000 who never received treatment. In addition, only 1000 remain in treatment, with the remainder either having completed treatment or dropped out. Of these, approximately 40% on follow-up are no longer using heroin. Although a third of the original addict population never received treatment nor ended up in jail, the epidemic clearly has waned, and one can ask what happened to these people. Apparently, they were, for the most part, the latest users with the shortest period of dependence and probably the least psychopathological. As the supply of heroin became shorter and less pure, they went through a period of involuntary detoxification and eventually reached a point where they were no longer physically addicted. While many apparently continued to use heroin on a sporadic basis, most gradually gave it up and a maturing-out process aided by the shortage of the drug occurred. Thus, the epidemic subsided.

References

de Alarcon, R. (1969). The spread of heroin abuse in a community. *Bull. Narcotics* **21**, 17–22.

DuPont, R. L., and Greene, M. H. (1973). The dynamics of a heroin addiction epidemic. *Science* **181**, 716–722.

Hughes, P. H., and Crawford, G. A. (1972). A contagious disease model for researching and interventing in heroin epidemics. *Arch. Gen. Psychiat.* **27**, 149–155.

Musto, D. (1973). "The American Disease." Yale Univ. Press, New Haven, Connecticut.

Robins, L. (1974). "The Viet Nam Drug Abuser Returns." McGraw-Hill, New York.

Tennant, F., Weaver, C., and Weaver, S. C. (1973). High school drug programs. *Pediatrics* **20**, 863–870.

Wurmser, L. (1973). Methadone and the craving for narcotics: Observations of patients on methadone maintenance in psychotherapy. *Proc. Nat. Conf. Methadone Treatment, 4th, 1972* p. 525.

2

On the Nature
of Opiate Reinforcement

ROGER E. MEYER

An understanding of the etiology of opiate addiction can be pursued at many levels. Large-scale epidemiological studies identifying populations and individuals at risk, clinical research focusing on the treatment of the addict and the use of opiate analgesics in the relief of pain, and basic pharmacological studies in animals and isolated tissues constitute the main sources of our present knowledge. Recent and proposed research in the addictions and related fields suggest that we may be on the threshold of a better definition of the nature of opiate reinforcement. Opiate reinforcement is that property of opiate drugs which leads to compulsive patterns of drug taking by a significant percentage of persons who experiment with (for example) heroin. Analyses of data obtained in two geographically and temporally distant studies (Chein *et al.*, 1964; Robins and Murphy, 1967) suggest that this progression may occur in half of all who experiment with illicit heroin in an economically impoverished community. Obviously, apart from those factors that lead to experimentation, an understanding of the reinforcing properties of the drug may be the most important research question currently being examined in this field.

Hypothetical elaborations on the nature of opiate reinforcement have heretofore been derived from the particular subjective, empirical, clinical, legal, or research experiences of the expositor. Early psychological formulations presumed that opiate reinforcement stemmed from a particular drug–personality interaction in which the drug served to help the individual cope with unpleasant internal or external circumstance. In the 1930's, Edward Glover (1932), an English psychoanalyst, described drug addiction as a defense against sadistic or aggressive impulses. He felt that individuals who became drug addicts tended to become fixated at a prepsychotic level of thinking and behavior. In this formulation the drug served to provide some equilibration while preventing psychic regression. Rado (1933), writing a few years later, saw depression as the painful core affect in drug-dependent individuals. He hypothesized that drug taking was an attempt to ease the pain, while inducing a state of elation. Chein and Gerard (see Chein *et al.*, 1964) saw the problem developing in part from drug availability and sociocultural disorganization. These authors, however, also identified the use of drugs in adolescence as an attempt to cope with internal drives and external unpleasantness. The drug state was seen as syntonic with the unconscious needs of individual addicts. More recent psychoanalytic writers (Wieder and Kaplan, 1969; Frosch, 1970) have postulated that drug choice is specific for an individual where the state of regression obtained in the drug condition is consistent with that person's true level of fixation or internal need. Thus, users of heroin have been described as individuals who suffer from unresolved infantile problems of separation and individuation. The taking of drugs is associated with a sense of fusion, which temporarily serves to alleviate massive separation anxiety. Most of these writers, operating from a psychoanalytic or psychodynamic position, have failed to observe the specific pharmacological effects of the drugs in the patients whom they were treating. They relied instead on the retrospective accounts of the drug experience reported by these patients and on their own formulations of the patients' underlying dynamics. The danger of attributing the etiology of addiction (or the nature of opiate reinforcement in particular individuals) to retrospective reporting has been demonstrated in the field of alcoholism by the work of Mendelson and Mello (1966) and in psychological studies by the work of Schachter (1966). The latter has demonstrated the extreme fluidity and suggestibility inherent in states of autonomic arousal that are pharmacologically induced. Thus, individuals will give meaning to states of arousal and even attribute different affective states to the *same* pharmacologically induced arousal state, depending upon the setting in which the state of arousal occurs and the expectations of the subject.

Mendelson and Mello have observed that, while alcoholics consistently report reduction of anxiety as a function of their drinking experience, in fact, subjective anxiety increases during binge drinking. This failure to recollect subjective states of intoxication during periods of sobriety has been called a type of state-dependent learning (Overton, 1968). The latter characteristic (which also includes a failure of certain memories to be transmitted from the sober to the intoxicated state) may be an important aspect of reinforcement associated with addictive disorders (Overton, 1968).

Apart from the psychoanalytic point of view, a number of psychologists, using standard self-administered psychological instruments, have reported high levels of depression and psychopathic deviancy in hospitalized heroin addicts (Hill *et al.*, 1960). The degree to which these results could be attributed to sampling bias and to the particular environmental stress associated with custodial care in an addiction hospital has never been defined. In general, despite efforts by psychoanalysts and psychologists to define a specific addictive personality, there has been no agreement on the specific constellation of traits that defines these individuals and differentiates them from persons who do not abuse drugs. One experimental study (Beecher, 1959), which has differentiated the effects of opiates in individuals of different psychological traits, suggests that persons who are psychologically more disturbed find morphine more pleasurable than persons who are described as less psychologically disturbed. In general, in this latter study it would seem that the more pleasurable subjective effects of opiates predominate in the former group, while the more unpleasant effects predominate in the latter group.

While research in man has usually differentiated the subjective opiate responses of addicted and nonaddicted individuals (emphasizing the characteristics of the patient or research subject), pharmacological formulations based upon animal research have emphasized the characteristics of the drugs in the genesis of the addiction process. Thus, the development of physical dependence has been considered crucial to the maintenance of opiate-seeking behavior once the addiction cycle has been initiated. Development of tolerance has been deemed responsible for the tendency of opiate addicts to increase their habits with time. Nevertheless, psychopharmacological formulations based upon animal models of opiate addiction have resulted in two distinctly different conceptualizations of the addiction process. On the one hand, compulsive drug taking is seen as an effort to reduce the pain of conditioned or pharmacologically related abstinence symptoms. On the other hand, opiate reinforcement is seen as a primary reinforcement, which is independent of the development of physical dependence (although it is acknowledged that drug seeking may become more intense in the midst of a withdrawal syndrome).

Wikler (1948) first proposed using a conditioning model to understand drug addiction in 1948. In the late 1950's, Nichols *et al.* (1956)

demonstrated that rats found a morphine solution aversive because of taste, but they would learn to seek the drug after being previously injected with daily parenteral doses of morphine and trained to differentiate solutions of tap water from solutions of morphine. In the Nichols paradigm, only previously morphinized animals would choose the morphine solution over tap water in a free-choice oral self-administration paradigm. Wikler *et al.* (1963) showed that rats that have been previously dependent upon morphine will demonstrate wet-dog shakes and other objective signs of abstinence in an environment in which they have previously experienced morphine withdrawal. In other words, by classical conditioning the withdrawal syndrome may be paired to appropriate environmental cues. These observations were further extended by offering solutions of etonitazene * and tap water to rats undergoing withdrawal. In this situation, rats readily learned to prefer the opiate in the environment in which they had experienced abstinence. From these observations, Wikler developed a theory of relapse behavior based upon the pairing of abstinence distress to environmental cues in a classical conditioning paradigm. In other words, a previously opiate-dependent man or animal would become readdicted to opiates in an environment in which he had previously experienced withdrawal because withdrawal symptoms appear in an environment in which withdrawal has previously occurred (Wikler and Pescor, 1967). Recently, Wikler *et al.* (1971) showed that the relapse potential may exist for periods longer than 1 year, and that relapse behavior is not merely a function of the pairing of environmental cues to pharmacological withdrawal. He now proposes an interceptive conditioning process as an explanation of relapse behavior. Other authors (Stolerman and Kumar, 1970; Khabari and Risner, 1972) have demonstrated that animals who have been forced to drink morphine solutions over a period of time will gradually develop a "preference" for (or reduced avoidance of) morphine solutions in a free-choice drinking paradigm. Unfortunately, most of the latter work has not attempted to relate the appearance in time of "preference" for opiate solution to any parameters of physical dependence or tolerance. Our own experience with oral self-administration studies suggests that the difference in drug intake observed in naive versus previously addicted animals is really reduced avoidance of the opiate (rather than preference for the drug) among the latter group. The difference then appears to be due to the persistence of tolerance in previously addicted animals.

---

* Etonitazene is an opioid 1000 times more potent than morphine. It is quite active when given orally. It is an experimental drug limited to animal studies.

It should also be noted that pharmacologists have observed altered responsiveness and physiology for prolonged periods of time in drug-free animals previously physically dependent upon opiates (Martin *et al.*, 1967). This state of "protracted abstinence" has been associated with the tendency toward relapse behavior. In other words, the once-addicted individual seeks to reestablish a state of physiological equilibrium that is now dependent upon continued opiate administration. The state of prolonged abstinence may persist for 6 months or longer.

A second distinct conceptualization of opiate addiction has resulted from the work of Weeks (1961), Yanagita *et al.* (1963), Schuster and Woods (1967), and Thompson and Schuster (1964). A technique for the self-administration of opiate drugs directly into the bloodstream was developed initially by Weeks. Rats and monkeys have been catheterized and studied in both restrained and freely moving situations. In this paradigm, animals are rewarded with a dose of opiate drug upon the performance of a task, usually some type of lever-pressing activity. Using this "self-injection" technique, workers have found that cocaine, amphetamines, nicotine, barbiturates, ethyl alcohol, and the opiates all serve as reinforcers for operant behavior in the monkey. It is of special interest that cocaine and the amphetamines serve as reinforcers, since physical dependence and withdrawal are not generally associated with these drugs. As a general rule, those drugs with a high abuse potential in man are self-administered in the monkey, while those with a low abuse potential in man (for example, phenothiazines) do not act as reinforcers in the monkey. Schuster and Villareal (1968) have observed that when reinforcement is immediate by intravenous injection of an opiate drug, the animal will work to repeat the experience. He feels that it is the positive reinforcement, which is independent of physical dependence, that can account for the total phenomenon of drug-seeking behavior. The development of opiate self-administration in the intravenous paradigm seems to parallel in a number of respects the self-stimulation behavior observed by Olds and Milner (1954). These workers significantly advanced concepts of behaviorism by demonstrating the efficacy of reinforcement unrelated to simple drive reduction (e.g., sex and hunger). Recently, Kornetsky and Nelson (1970) have obtained neurophysiological evidence that morphine acts specifically on the reinforcement center described by Olds and Milner, in a manner that could account for the development of self-administration behavior. In recent work, Schuster (1973) has defined five general and thirteen specific variables that affect drug self-administration:

1. Reinforcement
   a. Delay of reinforcement
   b. Magnitude of reinforcement
2. Antecedent conditions
   a. Deprivation
   b. Satiation
3. Organismic factors
   a. Genotype
   b. Species
   c. Age
   d. Sex
4. Current environmental conditions
   a. Schedule of positive reinforcement
   b. Extinction
   c. Punishment
5. Past history
   a. Pharmacological
      i. Tolerance
      ii. Dependence and withdrawal
      iii. Prior self-administration
   b. Behavioral
      i. Conditioned withdrawal
      ii. Conditioned opiate effects

Although these variables have not been systematically explored with regard to oral self-administration of opiates, a number of these have been studied in the intravenous self-administration paradigm.

Several other related observations bear upon the understanding of opiate reinforcement. Stein (1968) has identified the reinforcing areas of the brain as being norepinephrine-rich. A number of workers (Breese *et al.*, 1971; Arbuthnot *et al.*, 1971) have studied the effects of various biogenic amine manipulations upon self-stimulation behavior. Thus, it is theoretically and practically of interest to observe the effects of biogenic amine manipulations upon the acquisition of opiate-seeking behavior in the monkey and/or the rat and to study the effects of these biochemical alterations upon patterns of established opiate-seeking behavior.

Finally, two distinctly different pharmacological approaches to the treatment of the opiate addict may add significantly to our understanding of the nature of opiate reinforcement. The use of opiate substitution as a treatment modality is consistent with one of the factors in Schuster's list of relevant variables affecting opiate self-administration. Namely, persons on methadone should be satiated to the effects of opiates and, therefore, demonstrate reduced illicit heroin self-administration. Experience in over 70,000 patients suggests that this is indeed the case. More recent work with opiate antagonists suggests that we may be able to differentiate in man between the importance of positive reinforcement versus conditioned pharmacological abstinence in the genesis of relapse behavior and/or in the maintenance of an addiction cycle. The possibility of linking behavioral and biochemical events in the study of relapse and its treatment or prevention suggests that we may be on the threshold of a major breakthrough in our understanding of the nature of opiate reinforcement. One area of exploration currently under way to better define the nature (biochemical, behavioral, and psychological) of opiate reinforcement in heroin addicts will be described in the next section. The experimental program is interdisciplinary and involves parallel studies of opiate addiction in man and experimental animals. The clinical research design permits a systematic analysis of the biological, biochemical, and behavioral variables associated with relapse. Comparative intervention with narcotic antagonists (naloxone, naltrexone, or cyclazocine) and opiate substitutes (methadone or *l*-alpha-acetyl methadol) may help to differentiate the relative importance of conditioned abstinence versus a search for a euphoric experience as the factor most important in generating relapse behavior.

The clinical studies utilize techniques for the experimental analysis of drug acquisition developed by Mello and Mendelson in studies of alcoholics (1970) and recently employed by Mendelson *et al.* (1974) in subacute studies of marihuana acquisition in heavy and casual users. The research ward is set up as a token economy for rehabilitative and research reasons utilizing the experiences of Cohen and Filipczak (1971) at the National Training School in Washington, D.C. The methodology of Mendelson *et al.* (1974) permits the correlation of a number of biological factors (drug metabolism, endocrine homeostasis, catechol amine metabolism, tolerance, physical dependence, and other biochemical and physiological variables) with behavioral observations obtained on addicted subjects during experimental periods of self-determined intoxication and withdrawal. The addition of a treatment modality (narcotic-blocking drugs) on the research ward and at follow-up adds a significant dimension to this design.

General Methodology

Subjects. Male subjects over 22 years of age with a history of multiple rehabilitation failures (including methadone maintenance) will be recruited from two inpatient detoxification programs in Boston. Subjects are recruited four at a time to a research ward for a 60-day period.*

This period is subdivided as shown in the tabulation below.

Entry from detoxification facility	7 days' drug-free baseline	10 days' heroin acquisition	8 days' detoxification	8 days' drug-free	2 days' naloxone 600 mg qid alone
		End of 60 days			
10 days' heroin acquisition but patient is on naloxone	15 days' aftercare planning and shift from naloxone to cyclazocine	Aftercare on cyclazocine with group treatment, crisis counseling, and family treatment			

The experimental design permits each patient to serve as his own control. The token economy system permits some assessment of behaviors for alternative reinforcers (alternative to heroin) as well as a measure of heroin acquisition when the "high" is blocked and when it is not blocked. In the token economy, patients will work for currency by (1) participating in the maintenance of the ward and in personal hygiene, (2) working at specific hospital-based jobs, (3) preparing for educational credits (as high school equivalency), and (4) participating in specific research tasks. During the 10-day periods of heroin acquisition, subjects may earn specific "heroin points" by working at a hand-counter device. Mood assessments carried out throughout the study and prior to and following the acquisition of the drug should provide some indication of antecedent and consequent mood states (associated with drug taking) as well as mood when drug is not available (or is blocked by naloxone). The heroin is to be administered intravenously by a physician on a subject-determined schedule.† Mood assessments will be supplemented by endocrine determinations (serum corticosteroids and testosterone) and 24-hour

---

* Subjects will have a specific absence of the following disease entities as determined by appropriate physical examination and laboratory tests: (a) neurological disease or past history of seizure disorder, (b) hepatic disease, (c) renal disease, (d) pulmonary disease, (e) cardiac disease, (f) gastrointestinal disease, (g) genitourinary disease, (h) nutritional or metabolic disorder. All subjects will be screened for psychiatric disorder by a psychiatrist and subjects with a past history of hospitalization for psychotic illness will be excluded from the study.

† This is, of course, subject to conditions of patient safety as determined by the physician.

urinary catecholamines. Serum determinations of morphine prior to heroin administration should provide some measure of the relationship between the development of tolerance and the tendency to increase the quantity of drug per injection. Morphine assays will be determined by radioimmunoassay (Specter, 1971).

Systematic hourly behavioral observations, daily psychiatric assessments, and automated nursing notes will provide a description of each patient over the course of the study. Observations of daily group therapy and analyses of the verbal interaction patterns by the Bales assessment technique (1950) provide additional data on the subjects during the different phases of the research ward experience and in planning for aftercare. Specific measures of hostility, as described by Salzman et al. (1974), will also be utilized.

Aftercare arrangements including job and residential placement, family counseling, and other services as needed by the patient will begin while the subject is on the research ward and will continue at follow-up. Aftercare data will be supplemented by home visits by a visiting nurse, as well as periodic standard mood and psychiatric assessments and the evaluation of employment status, arrest record, and urine-screening results (for abuse of drugs).

Discussion

It is a striking paradox of research in the addictions that animal research on addictive behavior gained greatest significance and applicability to the human condition when techniques of chronic intravenous self-administration were developed (Weeks, 1962; Yanagita et al., 1963; Schuster and Woods, 1967; Schuster and Villareal, 1968) and the animal was encouraged to determine his own pattern of self-administration. Most pharmacological investigations into the nature of physical dependence and tolerance in man, with the exception of a single study by Wikler (1952), have utilized fixed doses administered at fixed intervals (Himmelsbach, 1942; Fraser et al., 1961; Martin and Fraser, 1961; Fraser and Rosenberg, 1966). Although such schedules of drug administration have been of great value in defining the biochemical and physiological aspects of physical dependence and tolerance, they have been of more limited utility in understanding the nature of drug seeking and relapse. As in the alcohol literature prior to Mendelson's work, most reports on the psychological aspects of drug seeking have been based upon retrospective accounts of the experience by nonintoxicated patients, or upon clinical hypotheses based upon the personality characteristics and psychodynamics of addicted (or previously addicted) individuals (Glover, 1932; Rado, 1933; Wieder and Kaplan, 1969; Frosch, 1970). The limitations of this approach have been detailed elsewhere (Mendelson and Mello, 1966).

While a number of individuals working in a variety of centers have contributed to our knowledge of the pharmacology of opiate dependence in man, the richest contributions have been made by the group at the Addiction Research Center at Lexington, Kentucky. For purposes of this discussion, only a limited number of papers—those with direct relevance to the proposed work—will be cited. Martin and Fraser (1961) found that experienced addicts were generally not able to differentiate acute doses of intravenous morphine and heroin. However, with repeated administration, these patients were readily able to differentiate the two drugs. The results of this study, plus anecdotal reports of A. Wikler (personal communication) and M. Fink (personal communication) suggest that intravenous heroin would be the preferred drug in biochemical studies of heroin addicts. Fraser *et al.* (1963) investigated the effects of chronic intravenous heroin intoxication on motor activity and sleep time. While acute doses caused slight impairment of performance on the pursuit rotor, chronic administration resulted in improvement in performance and increases in total daily activity to drug-free baseline levels. Subjects did spend more time sleeping in their rooms and on the home ward during the chronic phase of the study. This may reflect a response to the conditions imposed by the research setting as much as to the pharmacological effects of the drug.* Martin *et al.* (1967) observed seven former opiate addicts during 34 weeks of chronic morphine intoxication and found persistence of some degree of respiratory depression and constricted pupils throughout the period of intoxication. Systolic and diastolic blood pressure, temperature, and pulse rate were significantly elevated during this period. In the early phase of chronic intoxication there was diminution of caloric intake with an associated weight loss. With the development of tolerance to fixed doses of morphine, caloric intake recovered to baseline levels by week 5 and body weight returned to baseline by week 10. Urinary epinephrine and norepinephrine increased during the initial period of ascending dosage (Eisenman *et al.*, 1969). Tolerance appeared to develop to the effects on epinephrine, but toler-

---

* It is of interest, in this regard, that Gordon (1970) has reported no decrement in performance on reaction time tasks in patients maintained on high doses of methadone. It has also been reported that once tolerance supervenes, these patients are able to function normally at socially productive tasks.

ance was apparently incomplete to the effects on norepinephrine. The urinary excretion of norepinephrine remained elevated above preaddiction levels in subjects maintained on chronic fixed doses of morphine. Levels of hydroxycorticoids in urine were generally depressed during acute administration of morphine, with a return to baseline during chronic administration. During withdrawal there was a significant increase in 17-hydroxycorticosteroid excretion. Urinary levels of catecholamines were not increased over baseline (drug-free levels) during acute withdrawal in man, although the syndrome suggests autonomic arousal. The data on urinary catecholamine excretion are generally consistent with the earlier findings of Weil-Malherbe *et al.* (1965).

The reports of Martin *et al.* (1963), Wikler and Pescor (1965), Himmelsbach (1942), and Sloan *et al.* (1963) tend to confirm a pattern of long-persistent effects subsequent to acute withdrawal, which has been called "protracted abstinence." This is characterized by decreased blood pressure, pulse rate, body temperature, and sensitivity of the respiratory center to CO_2. There are increased urinary levels of epinephrine and norepinephrine suggesting that this is a stressful state or that post-opiate-dependent subjects are "hyperresponsive" to stress. The concept of protracted abstinence, like the theory of conditioned abstinence, has been implicated in the tendency of most ex-addicts to relapse to drug use.

As is apparent from the preceding discussion, much fruitful information has emerged from chronic studies of opiate administration using fixed doses at fixed time intervals. Yet the key behavioral events in the chain of addiction involve progression from experimentation to daily use and from daily administration of modest doses to the insistent demand for greater quantities of drug per injection. It is generally assumed that tolerance is involved in this progression, but tolerance to what specific biochemical, physiological, and/or psychological consequences of opiate use? Clearly, tolerance does not develop uniformly to all effects; what agonistic effects are sought after in the psychological phenomenon of "craving"? At what rate do individual addicts feel compelled to "jack up" blood levels of opiate, and to what degree do they attempt to stabilize these blood levels with repeated injections?

The one major published work that systematically explored the psychological factors involved in a subject-determined cycle of opiate administration was carried out in the late 1940's by Abraham Wikler at the U.S. Public Health Service Hospital at Lexington. In this experiment, one opiate addict was maintained on a self-determined regimen of intravenous morphine injections for a period of 4 months (followed by a withdrawal period of 1 month's duration). At one point this patient was self-administering 115 mg morphine 8 times a day. The results of this study focused on the psychodynamic implications of the addiction in satisfying (or reducing) the basic urges of pain relief, hunger, and sex. The limitations of the research design did not permit other types of analyses.

Finally, the utilization of narcotic antagonists in a treatment and research paradigm adds a new dimension to the study of the addictive states. Apart from their potential clinical utility, narcotic antagonists offer the research investigator the opportunity to explore the theoretical basis of relapse behavior and perhaps to assess the role of conditioned abstinence in this process. Wikler (1965) has argued that an essential component in the treatment of the heroin addict involves a "method for extinguishing both conditioned abstinence and opioid-seeking behavior based on reinforcement through reduction of morphine abstinence." An intervention that blocks reinforcement offers distinct research advantages over opiate substitution in delineating the multifactorial process. Moreover, if blocking drugs can effect extinction of drug-seeking behavior, it is important to observe the behavioral and psychological consequences in individual patients who experience extinction. Viewed from a different perspective, the removal of reinforcement associated with certain behaviors may lead to the unmasking of deeper levels of psychopathology that, theoretically, may have once served as the basis for initial drug experimentation.

ACKNOWLEDGMENTS

This research is supported by National Institute of Mental Health contract HSM-42-72-208 and grants MH 22,999 and MH 19221.

References

Arbuthnot, G., Fuxe, K., Understadt, U. (1971). Central catecholamine turnover and self stimulation behavior. *Brain Res.* **27**, 406.

Bales, R. F. (1950). "Interaction Process Analysis." Addison-Wesley, Reading, Massachusetts.

Beecher, H. K. (1959). "Measurement of Suggestive Responses Quantitative Effects of Drugs," pp. 321–341. Oxford Univ. Press, London and New York.

Breese, G. H., Howard, J. L., and Leahy, J. P. (1971). Effects of 6-hydroxydopamine on electrical self-stimulation of the brain. *Brit. J. Pharmacol.* **43**, 255–257.

Chein, I., Gerald, D. L., Lee, R. S., and Rosenfeld, E. (1964). "The Road to H." Basic Books, New York.

Cohen, H. L., and Filipczak, J. (1971). "A New Learning Environment." Jossey-Bass Inc., San Francisco, California.

Eisenman, A. J., Sloan, J. W., Martin, W. R., Jasinski, D. R., and Brooks, V. W. (1969). Catecholamine and 17-hydroxycorticosteroid excretion during a cycle of morphine dependence in man. *J. Psychiat. Res.* **7**, 19–28.

Fink, M. (1972). Personal communication.

Fraser, H. F., and Rosenberg, D. E. (1966). Comparative effects of (1) chronic administration of cyclazocine (ARC-II-3), (2) substitution of nalorphine for cyclazocine and (3) chronic administration of morphine. Pilot crossover study. *Int. J. Addict.* **1**, 86–89.

Fraser, H. F., Van Horn, G. D., Martin, W. R., Wolbach, A. B., and Isbell, H. (1961). Methods for evaluating addiction liability (a) "attitude" of opiate addicts toward opiatelike drugs, (b) a short-term "direct-addiction test. *J. Pharmacol. Exp. Ther.* **133**, 371–397.

Fraser, H. F., Jones, B. E., Rosenberg, D. E., and Thompson, A. K. (1963). Effects of addiction to intravenous heroin on patterns of physical activity in man. *Clin. Pharmacol. Ther.* **4**, 188–196.

Frosch, W. A. (1970). Psychoanalytic evaluation of addiction and habituation. *J. Amer. Psychoanal. Ass.* **18**, 209–218.

Glover, E. G., (1932). On the aetiology of drug-addiction. *Int. J. Psychoanal.* **13**, Part 3, 298–328.

Gordon, N. B. (1970). Reaction times of methadone treated ex-heroin addicts. *Psychopharmacologia* **16**, 337–344.

Hill, H., Haertzen, C. A., and Glaser, R. (1960). Personality characteristics of narcotic addicts as indicated by the MMPI. *J. Gen. Psychol.* **62**, 126–139.

Himmelsbach, C. K. (1942). Clinical studies on drug addiction: Physical dependence, withdrawal and recovery. *Arch. Intern. Med.* **69**, 766–722.

Khavari, K. A., and Risner, M. E. (1972). *Psychon. Sci.* **26**, 141.

Martin, W. R., and Fraser, H. F. (1961). A comparative study of physiological and subjective effects of heroin and morphine administered intravenously in post-addicts. *J. Pharmacol. Exp. Ther.* **133**, 388–399.

Martin, W. R., Wikler, A., Eades, C. G., and Pescor, F. T. (1963). Tolerance to and physical dependence on morphine in rats. *Psychopharmacologia* **4**, 247–260.

Martin, W. R. (1967). Drug dependence of morphine type: Physiological parameters, tolerance, early abstinence, protracted abstinence. *In* "Problems of Drug Dependence," pp. 4929–4941. National Research Council, National Academy of Sciences, Washington, D.C.

Mello, N. K., and Mendelson, J. H. (1970). Experimentally induced intoxication in alcoholics: A comparison between programmed and spontaneous drinking. *J. Pharmacol. Exp. Ther.* **173**, 101–116.

Mendelson, J. H., and Mello, N. K. (1966). Experimental analysis of drinking behavior of chronic alcoholics. *Ann. N.Y. Acad. Sci.* **133**, 828–845.

Mendelson, J. H., Meyer, R. E., and Rossi, A. M. (1974). Biological and behavioral concomitants of chronic marihuana use in heavy and casual users. Appendix to Report on the National Commission of Marihuana and Drug Abuse (in press).

Nelson, J. (1970). Ph.D. Thesis, Boston University School of Medicine, Boston, Massachusetts.

Nichols, J. R., Headlee, C. P., and Coppock, H. W. (1956). Drug addiction. I. Addiction by escape training. *J. Amer. Pharm. Ass.* **45**, 788.

Olds, J., and Milner, P. (1954). Positive reinforcement produced by electrical stimulation of septal area and other regions of the rat brain. *J. Comp. Psychol.* **47**, 419–427.

Overton, D. (1968). Dissociated learning in drug states (state dependent learning). *In* "Psychopharmacology: Ten Years of Progress" (D. H. Efron, ed.), Pub. Health Serv. Publ. No. 1836, pp. 918–930. US Govt. Printing Office, Washington, D.C.

Rado, S. (1933). Psychoanalysis of pharmacothymia (drug addiction). *Psychoanal. Quart.*, **2**, 1–23.

Robins, L. N., and Murphy, G. E. (1967). Drug use in a normal population of young Negro men. *Amer. J. Pub. Health* **57**, 1580–1596.

Salzman, C., Kochansky, G., and Porrlino, L. (1974). Group behavior: hostility and aggression. *In* "The Use of Marihuana: A Psychological and Physiological Inquiry" (J. H. Mendelson, A. M. Rossi, and R. E. Meyer, eds.). Harvard Univ. Press, Cambridge, Massachusetts (in press).

Schachter, S. (1966). The interaction of cognitive and physiological determinants of emotional state. *In* "Anxiety and Behavior, (C. D. Spielberger, ed.), pp. 193–224. Academic Press, New York.

Schuster, C. R. (1973). Behavioral analysis of opiate dependence. Presented at American College of Neuropharmacology, San Juan, Puerto Rico, 1972.

Schuster, C. R., and Villareal, J. E. (1968). The experimental analysis of opoid dependence. *In* "Psychopharmacology: A Review of Progress" (D. H. Efron, ed.), Pub. Health Serv. Publ. No. 1836, pp. 811–828. US Govt. Printing Office, Washington, D.C.

Schuster, C. R., and Woods, J. H. (1967). Morphine as a reinforcer for operant behavior: The effects of dosage per injection. Presented at the 29th Meeting of the Committee on Problems of Drug Dependence. National Academy of Sciences—National Research Council.

Sloan, J. W., Brooks, J. W., Eisenman, A. J., and Martin, W. R. (1963). The effect of addiction to and abstinence from morphine on rat tissue catecholamine and serotonin levels. *Psychopharmacologia* **4**, 261–270.

Spector, S. (1971). Quantitative determination of morphine in serum by radioimmunoassay. *J. Pharmacol. Exp. Ther.* **178**, 253–258.

Stein, L. (1968). Chemistry of reward and punishment. *In* "Psychopharmacology: A Review of Progress" (D. Efron, ed.), Pub. Health Serv. Publ. No. 1836, pp. 105–123. US Govt. Printing Office, Washington, D.C.

Stolerman, I. P., and Kumar, R. (1970). Preferences for morphine in rats: Validation of an experimental model of dependence. *Psychopharmacologia*, **17**, 137–150.

Thompson, T., and Schuster, C. R. (1964). Morphine self-administration: Food-reinforced and avoidance behavior in Rhesus monkeys. *Psychopharmacologia* **5**, 87–94.

Weeks, J. R. (1961). Self-maintained morphine addiction—a method for chronic programmed intravenous injection in unrestrained rats. *Fed. Proc., Fed Amer. Soc. Exp. Biol.* **20**, 397 (abstr.).

Weeks, J. R. (1962). Experimental morphine addiction: Methods for automatic intravenous injections in unrestrained rats. *Science* **138**, 143–144.

Weil-Malherbe, H., Smith, E. R. B., Eisenman, A. J., and Fraser, H. F. (1965). Plasma catecholamine levels and urinary excretion of catecholamines and metabolites in two human subjects during a cycle of morphine addiction and withdrawal. *Biochem. Pharmacol.* **14**, 1621.

Wieder, H., and Kaplan, E. H. (1969). Drug use in adolescents. *Psychoanal. Study Child* **24**, 399–431.

Wikler, A. (1948). Recent progress in research on the neurophysiologic basis of morphine addiction. *Amer. J. Psychiat.* **105**, 329–338.

Wikler, A. (1952). Psychodynamic study of a patient during experimental self-regulated readdiction to morphine. *Psychiat. Quart.* **26**, 270–293.

Wikler, A. (1965). Conditioning factors in opiate addiction and relapse. *In* "Narcotics" (D. M. Wilver and G. G. Kassebaum, eds.), pp. 85–100. New York.

Wikler, A., and Pescor, F. T. (1965). Factors disposing to "relapse" in rats previously addicted to morphine. *Pharmacologist* **7**, 171.

Wikler, A., and Pescor, F. T. (1967). Classical conditioning of morphine abstinence, reinforcement of opoid-drinking behavior and relapse in morphine-addicted rats. *Psychopharmacologia* **10**, 255–284.

Wikler, A., Martin, W. R., Pescor, F. T., and Eades, C. A. (1963). Factors regulating oral consumption of an opoid (etonitazine) by morphine-addicted rats. *Psychopharmacologia* **5**, 55–76.

Wikler, A., Pescor, F. T., Miller, D., Porrell, H. (1971). Persistent potency of a secondary (conditioned) reinforcer following withdrawal of morphine from physically dependent rats. *Psychopharmacologia* **20**, 103–117.

Yanagita, T., Deneau, G. A., and Seevers, M. H. (1963). Physical dependence to opiates in the monkey, with demonstration. Presented at the 25th Meeting of the Committee on Drug Addiction and Narcotics. National Academy of Sciences—National Research Council, Ann Arbor, Michigan.

3

Hypotheses Concerning
the Etiology
of Heroin Addiction

H. DALE BECKETT

Jellinek's * "The Disease Concept of Alcoholism" was influential in revolutionizing the treatment of that disorder. What more natural than for heroin addiction to be regarded as a disease, of chronic, relapsing type? This concept of the heroin addict as a patient is the basis of the British system of treatment, which has certainly been pretty successful since the treatment centers were started. Its success has been measured by the dramatic slowing of the rate of increase of heroin addicts on the street as well as by the numbers of patients who have given up heroin and have been working and contributing as ordinary members of society.

There is, however, another concept that I believe more nearly fits the facts: that heroin addiction in some is symptomatic of an underlying chronic depression in a wounded personality and in others of a failure of personality development. Thus, the "cures" that have been successful may have been due to each "cured" addict developing personality resources that had hitherto failed to develop. With these new strengths he has been able to deal with his depression and learn how to handle relationships, things, and events. This development is in fact a veritable "adolescence"—growth into an adult.

Let us look at the influences that impel a young person to drug taking.

* Jellinek, E. M. (1960). "The Disease Concept of Alcoholism." College University Press, New Haven, Connecticut.

Society

Our society is changing. It has never changed so much and so fast. This is probably due in part to the urgent impinging on each and every member of society of an increasing quantity of information about what is happening in the rest of the world. This includes information about other people's attitudes. For one thing, attitudes tend to change as a result of the influence of the attitudes of others. For another, it is the attitudes of a society that very largely determine its form, its structure. Thus, our increased awareness of other, different, attitudes elsewhere must lead to an irresistible change in the structure of our society, with resulting instability.

This exogenous change is potentiated by the use in our schools of educational methods that try to show children how to work things out for themselves rather than to teach them in terms of dates, declensions, and correct methods. This has two main effects. First, it conditions children to contribute and to participate in decision making, so that they grow up with a need for a sense of participation in a society that recognizes them as individuals. (It may be said that previously an inherent need to participate used to be conditioned out of children during their school days.) Second, when they become young adults they question things that were accepted unquestioningly by previous generations. Both these factors mean that the existing social structures are under considerable strain and must evolve, particularly at the interface between society and its younger members.

When society is on the move like this there are bound to be casualties. Among these casualties are the drug abusers and the delinquents. Perhaps it is surprising that there are not more of them. Of these two kinds of casualty, the delinquents do more harm to ordinary members of society whereas, in Britain anyway, the harmful influence of drug abusers is more or less restricted to those young people with a predisposition to become casualties themselves.

Adolescents are working through a developmental stage in which the lessons they have learned during childhood are being modified by the attitudes of their peer group, with the final outcome of this interaction not being seen for some years. They are more malleable than adults, more affected by the external environment. If the environment presses in upon them in such a way as to jeopardize their sense of identity and status they are likely to respond in a neurotic way. An example is an adolescent living in overcrowded and soulless conditions in a tower block, on a new housing estate, or in a new town. He may respond by acts of delinquency, vandalism, or hooliganism or by drug taking if opportunities are not available for pursuits and enjoyments which are acceptable both to him and to society.

Counterstimulation

Even if the facilities that are usually regarded as suitable for teenagers are provided by a community, they may not be sufficiently arcane to attract those adolescents who have been badly damaged. Something highly stimulating is needed for them.

The principle of counterstimulation—sometimes called counterirritation—is well known. The application of a strong external stimulus effectively reduces the intensity of internal nervous impulses. Thus, the pain of an alveolar abscess can be relieved by applying a mustard plaster to the face, a sneeze can be aborted by firm pressure on the nasal philtrum, and the urgency of premature ejaculation can be stopped by a hard squeeze of the coronal sulcus.

In the same way, if a disturbed adolescent can put himself into a highly stimulating and unpredictable situation he will find his mental distress quietened. So he will go to the bright lights, the flashing neons, the crowds of people, the frenetic activity, the clanging pin tables. He may put himself in danger by delinquent acts, such as housebreaking, shoplifting, or robbery, for the excitement is stimulus enough to give him a degree of inner peace. The recurrent impulse to steal and drive away fast cars is well recognized. Horror films and horror comics may also be of help. The stimulus of hustling for heroin is of a high order.

The Legacy of Our Past

Our male adolescents are warriors. In the distant past tribes were only safe as long as they were not overrun by neighboring tribes and, in order to preserve themselves, they had to evolve a warrior class, who were the male adolescents. The more reckless and aggressive they were the more likely the tribe was to survive. We still find that our adolescents are generally more reckless than they will be when they grow up (and an adolescent is more likely than an adult to try out drug taking), while the aggression, if it has no external object on which it can be discharged, is directed against "threatening" authority. This antagonism, while apparently destructive, in reality has had the latent effect of preventing stagnation and decay of the species and it can be channeled effectively in many socially desirable ways. If it is not so channeled, these forces of rebellion may be turned harmfully against society. If an adolescent realizes that he can challenge his parents by taking drugs, then it is not surprising if he does so.

Another example of evolutionary pressures that remain operating long after the need for them has gone is the extraordinary interaction between the adolescent and his family. During childhood he or she has been quite charming, but in adolescence he becomes intolerable. Plants usually distribute their seeds widely. As soon as it can manage to fly, a fledgling is pushed out of the nest to make its way in the world. A lion cub is cuffed out of the den by the parent when it can just survive outside. When a manchild is old enough to fend for itself outside the cave, it changes its character and becomes so impossible to live with that it is expelled, being forced to travel some way to set up a home of its own. It is probably largely as a result of this mechanism that man spread over the planet more widely than any other species. This apparent willfulness and unreasonableness may well prompt a normal adolescent to embark on drug use, though not abuse.

The Peer Group

But repeated taking of minor drugs (drug use) is unlikely unless there happens to be nearby a group of people taking drugs who are of his own age and with whom he finds he relates. In any peer group whose members are familiar to him he can feel relaxed and secure. Even though he may realize fleetingly that he does not really want to take drugs habitually, it is hard to break away from this circle of friends spontaneously because of the evolutionarily determined bonds that bind a tribe together, preventing him from deserting them and crossing over to an "enemy" group of non-drug-takers.

Consequently it is the inescapable duty of parents to make sure that their child does not continue to mix with a group that they think is undesirable, no matter what protests their child makes at this apparently high-handed restriction.

The Family

The responsibilities and strains of bringing up a child are considerable—far greater than people care to admit. To do it properly, parents need a close-knit network of relationships for support. Grandparents, although often a trial to the parents, usually are more of an asset than a liability. Friends who live close by and who can be relied on are important too. Such a supportive network of relationships ceases to exist if the family moves to a new area where no one knows anyone else and no one cares much. It may be significant that in Britain many addicts come from this kind of family.

The Present and the Past

Why is there drug taking now but none previously? First, our children are growing up in a drug-oriented society. The adults around him take pills for the relief of stress because the advertisements say they should and most doctors think the same. Maybe psychiatrists prescribe tranquilizers, antidepressants, and so on more than is necessary because we have come to accept these blessed anguish-quelling drugs as right to use. Much heartbreak and intolerable pressures are helped in this way. But it is probably asking too much of a child when we expect him to make a clear distinction between drugs that are medically approved and those that are not, especially when he sees his father cure his hangover with unprescribed tablets advertised on television and his sister goes out to buy pills for her period pains. So the scene is set.

Second, the war years had a bad effect on the present generation of British adolescents. A large number of their parents, if they lived in cities, had to go through the emotional trauma of evacuation at the age of 10 or 11 or so, being wrenched away from their own homes and billeted with parent substitutes who might or might not be good at making positive relationships with the new children and recognizing their emotional needs. Many children below the age of 15 cannot tolerate separation from their parents for an extended period without the development of permanent emotional scars. These scars may prevent them from being able to give themselves emotionally in later years, and so when this generation of children became parents at about age 25, many of their children grew up in an emotionally arid climate. That big evacuation happened 34 years ago and the children of those traumatized children are now themselves in late adolescence. The effect of this emotional deprivation on our present adolescents is likely to show itself, in attenuated form, in their descendents, the ripples eventually dying out unless some other social upheaval starts it all up again.

Third, in the old days, society used to rid itself of nonconformists (and consequently of its potentially socially harmful genes and sprits *) by executing its delinquents. Long before Christ this used to be done by stoning the thief to death, later crucifixion was used, then as civilization matured, transgression such as theft was successively dealt with by burning, decapitation, hanging, transportation, penal servitude, life imprisonment, a shorter term of imprisonment, and now by suspended sentences or probation. With the retention of the delinquent in society, the children he ultimately has are likely to become disturbed adolescents themselves. This disturbance may well show itself in more delinquency or in drug taking.

Fourth, it can be argued that the young people of today tend to be more depressed than those of a generation ago. One reason may be that they have more pressures to contend with. A major kind of pressure stems from overcrowding. Another is daily beamed to them through the television screen. Portraying fact or presenting fiction, the message is the same: You cannot avoid violence. Violence is everywhere—sudden, unpredictable, inevitable. Newscasts and documentaries satellite-bounce into the child's home a message of hate from the whole world. "This is how people are. This is how society should be. These beatings, this distress, this death are not just on the other side of the world but here—all around."

The briefer and less frequent the exposure is to any trauma, the less the damage suffered. Conversely, the longer and more frequent it is, the more the damage. So imagine the effect of this input on the growing child day after day, year after year, while cerebral neurons are developing † and attitudes becoming established. Is it surprising that there should be differences between a child exposed to this kind of conditioning and a child who is not?

Furthermore, this child is not alone. His friends will be conditioned in the same way. In the matrix of his society there is unceasing positive feedback of his learned attitudes, repeatedly reinforcing and fixing them in the shape of a response to (including unconscious defenses against) a violent world. Of these defenses, of course,

* See discussion on page 44.
† See discussion on page 48.

avoidance is one of the most common. It is perhaps not surprising that so many adolescents seem to give up, often quite unexpectedly. These so-called dropouts are usually the ones who have been blessed (or cursed) with a greater sensitivity than others and seek, in rural communes, in meditation, in mind-changing drugs, an escape from what they see as a threatening and oppressive society.

Roads to Addiction

There seem to be two main roads to heroin addiction: one through close contact with an emotionally disturbed peer group in adolescence and the other through involvement in turbulent emotional happenings in childhood.

The first, less common one, is when a school child at 15 or 16 regularly begins to take the "soft" drugs. We are all aware of the importance of school and of the enormous reach of knowledge that is available there to a child. But perhaps of even more importance to him in his maturation are the new proficiencies that he acquires outside the school walls. So he learns not only formal lessons of geography, mathematics, and so on, but he also acquires new attitudes to a whole series of contemporary phenomena and learns the infinitely complex skills of relating to people, solving social problems, postponing pleasure for the sake of future gain, and dealing with painful emotions. He thereby achieves self-respect and consistency by finding an estimable identity. If these lessons, fundamental to his future happiness and success, remain unlearned, the untutored young adult is unable to deal with the ordinary everyday stresses with which life in the twentieth century is provided. So if an adolescent spends much of his time outside school with his mind distorted by any kind of twisting drug, his emotional maturity fails to keep pace with his developing responsibilities. Eventually he realizes that he has not kept up with his non-drug-taking contemporaries. By this time he knows what dramatically "hard" drug to progress to in order to demonstrate to them that he is hard and not soft.

This is true "escalation," but it does not seem to have happened quite like this in the large majority of heroin users. Usually it seems that, as a result of damage during his formative years, a particular individual has found it difficult or impossible to establish proper relationships or to manage his problems efficiently. This failure leads to an increase in the unpleasant state of tension he already experiences. The result is insupportable, so the individual looks around neurotically for some kind of medication to help him, and he starts to take minor drugs: amphetamines, barbiturates, alcohol, LSD, cannabis, methaqualone, cyclizine, glue solvent—whatever he has been told by his friends will help him. Only if he finds that these agents do not give him the answer may he turn to heroin.

As for the major road, it seems that about 85% of British addicts have a background history of poor parental relationships, particularly with the father. The implication is that if there is a good relationship between the father and the child during the child's formative years, with adequate communication between the two, the child is able to make contact with the personality of his father and introject it into his developing psyche. This introjection of the father seems to be a very important part of personality development, laying down a center, an inner core, around which the character of the child crystallizes. This central pith of the father image results in three things. The first is stability in a changing situation. The second is foresight, the ability to think ahead, to foresee the consequences of one's actions. The third is the skill, which should develop in adolescence, of allocating priorities intuitively without thinking twice about them. It is an ability instantly to see the wood in spite of all the trees, to be aware of what is important and what is not so important when arriving at a decision. These two aptitudes, foresight and the allocation of priorities intuitively, together make up that strange facility which goes by the name "common sense." As already indicated, relationships between their fathers and those children who will eventually grow up to be addicts are generally poor. That these British addicts have little common sense is interesting and invites a proper prospective research exercise to compare the eventual development of common sense in a large number of fatherless children with that in suitably matched motherless children.

The relationship with the mother seems to be equally important, although perhaps for a different reason. Evolutionary pressures have made "woman" more accepting and conservative than "man," and in fact parental influences work best when the father knows his own mind and the mother is calm, predictable, and reliably loving. If these archetypal parental attitudes are grossly altered, the introjected parental images will do persistent damage to future relationships.

The Introjection of Sprits

I believe there are three kinds of heredity. The first, the transmission of genetic information by nuclear division, is well researched.

The second, the transmission of cytoplasmic and cell membrane information, has recently been recognized. The third is not perhaps so well known as being a form of heredity. It is what I call environmental, or "sprit," inheritance and has to do with the surroundings of the whole organism as it develops within or without the family.

If a child is in a loving situation he is likely to develop into a loving parent and provide a secure environment for his own offspring. A child whose father is a bully is likely to be a bully to his own children. Progeny of a delinquent family will probably produce a house full of delinquents. It is not that these children carry the genes for loving, bullying, or delinquency; they carry sprits for loving, bullying, or delinquency.

A sprit is a bit of information from the environment, which, programmed into the unconscious, mobilizes a genetic propensity. Webster's Third New International Dictionary defines "sprit" as "a spar that crosses a fore-and-aft sail diagonally from the mast near the tack of the sail to its upper aftmost corner, which it extends and elevates" (cf. bowsprit). The infant craft is launched with a multitude of furled genetic sails with which to navigate. Sprits selectively unfurl them, and angle them to the winds of the times. The greater the number of sprits that become incorporated during development, the more intense will be the experience of life thereafter. Whether the experience will be good or bad will depend much on whether the sprits are consistent or inconsistent with each other. Contradictory sprits make navigation difficult and confusing (viz., the malignant effect of the double bind in childhood, a series of contradictory sprits which may even result in a persistent schizophrenic illness).

A child who is born with a gene for "generosity" may have this propensity modified so that he becomes generous in certain circumstances but not in others, or free with his time and attention but not with his money, or incapable of showing any generosity at all except in rare and surprising situations.

A child who is favored by genes for "practicality" is in a vulnerable situation. If the environment is so shaped, he may find himself equipped with sprits for temporizing, or for lying, or inconsistency.

It is probable that babies are born with different genetic dispositions to particular personality structures, and so to particular ways of behavior. How they eventually behave when they are adults depends on the sprits that have been actively incorporated. It is not that a baby is born with an infinite capacity for all forms of behavior. His potential is restricted in many areas by his genes. All that sprits can do is to enable his genetic potential to be realized. If the environment is particularly poor in sprits, intellectual development is so limited that the individual may be regarded as subnormal. Such is

the case in those few examples of babies who have been reared to
adolescence by wild animals, devoid of contact with human kind.
The only sprits programmed have been those concerned with interaction with a wild environment (which can be seen to a lesser
degree in Amazonian Indians and still less in water diviners).

It is possible that a powerful genetic disposition makes an infant
more receptive to particular sprits and selectively to ignore other
ones. However, the repeated introjection of strong opposite sprits
tends to overcome this genetic selectivity, with distortion of the original genetic disposition.

Although a developing child soaks up the information lapping at
his psyche from all around and puts it out again when he is mature if
the conditions are right, there exists a damping mechanism in the
need to conform with society's standards, which after some years
may nullify a particular sprit.* However, the sprit may be reset, for example, by a colluding spouse who needs a wife or husband with the
sprit in question because of the way his or her own genes were
spritted.

Just as the dimensions of a field cannot be expressed by way of
length or breadth alone, but by the product of the two terms, so the
dimensions of a personality cannot be expressed by way of genes or
sprits alone. The total is not the sum of the terms, but their product.

Guilt

The genes and sprits one inherits from one's father combine with
the genes and sprits from one's mother. The final attitudes are the
resultant of the total forces—internal (genes and those sprits that
have already been programmed in) and external (parental and other
attitudes as well as experience of reward and punishment outside the
home, which are on their way to being internalized as sprits). So a
child of a loveless family who has been to a strict school where child-
ish naughtiness is treated by exemplary punishment is likely to be
programmed with sprits for guilt. He will have a perpetual sense of
foreboding, a feeling of impending doom. Self-medication to relieve
it is natural and drugs are usually about.

When drug taking has become regular, such a person discovers, in

---

* This may be seen for example in schizophrenia that has "burned out" and in the
psychopath who "matures" in his thirties.

common with most other drug misusers, that achievement does not match early ambition. The pessimism and hopelessness that result are in his case potentiated by the malignant presence of these sprits for severe guilt, and the guilt has to be discharged. Heroin addiction offers a way of coping with intolerable despair. But it is more than this. That narcotic addiction is very often a substitute for suicide is borne out by a good deal of evidence. The ritual of mainlining and flushing—that is, pulling blood into the transparent "works," squirting it back into the vein, pulling out another syringe full of blood before squirting that back again, and so on—seems to be a form of stylized bloodletting and to be equated with cutting the throat.

The three most common modes of death in heroin addiction have strong depressive overtones themselves. The most frequent cause of death is overdose. This overdose (which may be of any drug, most commonly heroin, although quite often barbiturates) may be deliberate or otherwise. We cannot know what was in the addict's mind when he prepared his last fatal fix. We can only guess that sometimes the outcome was deliberately contrived, while at others it was the result of a death sprit that at last has found fulfillment. The next is frank suicide, when the addict finds that heroin does not continue to relieve his dreadful problems and he chooses a quick death rather than go on with a slow one. Additionally, of course, it must be remembered that heroin, although it relieves anxiety, is a depressant in every sense of the word.

The third is from some disease that has gained entry by means of an unsterile injection. Hospitals now are quite used to treating addicts with septicemia, thrombophlebitis, lung abscess, endocarditis, and so on, which have resulted because addicts commonly use water from a lavatory bowl to dissolve heroin before injecting it, even when clean water is available. Or the syringe and needle may be dropped on the floor of a stinking public convenience in a puddle of slime and urine before it is picked up and used to mainline with. Or the syringe of a dirty addict living in squalor may be borrowed and used without being cleaned. Who can deny that this kind of bizarre behavior is directed by an unconscious drive to self-injury, self-punishment, and self-destruction? Certainly both before and during their addiction to heroin one finds that the life histories of addicts have been complicated by the most extraordinary incidents, which can only be explained on the basis of a need for self-punishment and failure.

If one has been programmed to guilt, one cannot believe oneself to be deserving of any success. This programming usually has its origins in the home, where the emotional climate is abnormal in one or more important respects. The most noteworthy of these is where the parents seldom or never praise or encourage the child. This malignant atmosphere of constant discouragement is exemplified in the history of one addict whose father, a headmaster, himself had been emotionally deprived as a child. Although the son succeeded in passing a series of examinations during his school days, culminating in obtaining a scholarship, not one of these academic successes provoked the father to any expression of pleasure.

Love Neurons

A disproportionate number of British addicts have a parent who had a stepfather or stepmother. Even where both parents had blood parents themselves, one of them often reports having had an unhappy childhood. The supposition is that if an addict's parent did not get an adequate supply of parental love in his or her childhood, he has not developed the capacity to express love for his own offspring.

Within the past few years some work has been done which illuminates this area. A kitten confined from birth in an upright cylindrical box, the interior of which is banded with vertical black and white stripes, is prevented by a rigid harness from tilting its head. Some months later it is taken out and electrodes are implanted into its visual cortex. If stripes oriented in all directions are then shown to the animal, it can be demonstrated that only the vertical stripes produce electrical impulses. The kitten is blind to all the others. During development of the cerebral cortex, neurons send out dendrites to make contact with neighboring neurons. If impulses subsequently pass, the new connections remain and become consolidated. If, however, no impulses pass, these nerve tendrils retract and contact is lost.

Now it becomes clear why the experience of love is so important to the developing child. I like to think of love neurons, which extend, linking up with each other, in preparation for the experience of love to flow. If no love is received, they atrophy and cannot thereafter easily be reestablished. How then can such a person who has been denied love during his childhood express love to his child? Not only has he difficulty in loving his own child, he has difficulty in loving anyone. The romantic films that end with the girl walking hand in hand into the sunset with the psychopathic male she thinks will change because of her love always end at that point. The sequel could not be shown without making the audience depressed.

That many parents may recognize that they have this particular difficulty and may try to compensate for it is demonstrated by the fact that, as children, many British addicts were plied with all manner of material things and only had to ask for something to get it. At times such spoiling seems to have been so blatantly harmful that an unconscious wish on the part of the parent to damage the child can be inferred. Some parents go on to manipulate their child to take drugs, and then give him money with which to buy heroin. Some have been known to actually go out and score for him themselves if he is sick.

Another feature in the environment of the future addict may be constant blame games played by the parents, who more or less skillfully use the child as a pawn in their strategies. It is not surprising that the child becomes confused and comes to believe that he is to blame for the unhappiness and tension in the household. Every parental scene programs him with more sprits for guilt.

Other addictogenic sprits are produced by constant unfavorable comparison with a sibling. To be informed repeatedly that one is a failure effectively programs one to failure and any experience of the unfamiliar feel of success produces anxiety. The owner of such a guidance mechanism when he becomes adult will be hard put to handle success. Even if, on account of his basic intelligence, he obtains a successful job, he is likely to find himself sooner or later, no less to his conscious dismay than to that of his employer, contriving to knock the pins from under him. Security in failure, familiar failure.

Comfort from failure may well account for the almost universal underachievement of addicts, who are unable to complete an academic course that should be well within their intellectual capabilities. However, failing produces its own discomforts in real terms and, to compensate, the adolescent will probably wistfully fantasize about being a success in some area especially meaningful to him. There arises then the mismatch between achievement and aspiration which typically characterizes the addict in Britain.

We can see then that, as a result of inappropriate programming, the underlying depression is often of some severity and is certainly of considerable chronicity. The setting in which this depression operates, that is, the wounded personality, is itself a very complex one and has its origins in a multiplicity of conflicting sprits. It has already been pointed out that one of the common findings in addicts' life histories is a poor relationship with a parent. There seems usually to have been a failure of communication with the father for any of a number of reasons, as for example, because of his physical absence. Even when the father was physically present, however, he may have constantly ignored his child or have done all he could to humiliate and discourage him. Sometimes this process may have been acted out by physical assault, and one is reminded of the "battered baby" syndrome where the defenseless child suffers from broken bones and bodily bruises. Physical injuries such as these heal with little long-term disability, but the psychic scars of emotional wounds sustained in childhood are more likely to be permanent. A girl's father used to rule his family of five children with a rod of iron (he would beat them with a steel poker), and every evening she used to be called to confess to him why she had been naughty during the day. Depressed, she ran away and became addicted.

Mental Shifts

The human child mind is protected by a homeostatic system of different mechanisms so that in the face of a traumatic environment a child can maintain relative sanity. These unconscious mechanisms can be found to be at work still, either singly or in combination, in every addict. A child may discover that a particular mental shift effectively saves him from the worst of the anxieties and guilts that have been aroused in him by his parents or parent figures. The more intelligent he is the quicker he learns to use that shift, and the more sensitive he is the more he needs to use it.

During his formative years, if a child is insensitive yet intelligent, although he is alert to his environment, traumatic incidents flow off him like water from a duck's back. If he is sensitive yet unintelligent, although appreciating overt threats, he does not perceive the subtleties that really damage. It is the combination of sensitivity and good intelligence that makes a child so vulnerable to hurt, and he may have to deal with recurring problems of enormous magnitude. He is unable to deal with them at an adult level, naturally enough, and his best defense is usually that of magic, which really does work in childhood.

There are a number of ways of using this magic, but two or three examples will suffice. The child can wave a magic wand, as it were, and say, "None of it is true. I am perfectly safe. There is no danger. My father is the best father in the world. I love my mother and she loves me," and so on. This is a powerful magic and has saved many children much distress. But sometimes this simple form of denial is not enough to turn aside terribly dark storms of reality, and an imaginative child may use another kind of magic by putting himself in a fairy tale setting. He weaves a fabric of fantasy with which to clothe himself. Or rather, he grows a rosebush hedge between himself and reality, tending it carefully and cultivating it assiduously, so that it grows dense and impenetrable and he effectively screens himself from the hurtful environment around.

Once these defensive mental acrobatics have been perfected, they usually need to be practiced repeatedly, and they become a reflex response to many different kinds of external or internal stress. They remain instantly available, just as does the learned skill of throwing out a hand when falling.

Let us return for a moment to the child who learned to employ his gift of imagination in shielding himself from hurt. One can begin to understand why it is that, as the child grows up still using this particular mechanism of defense, his contact with reality does not improve and why he believes he is not governed by the laws of reality which apply to other people. He is charmed, just as a fairy prince is charmed. This kind of unfortunate person will go on fantasizing, not only to himself, but also necessarily to others. The result is that when other people find that he does not tell them the truth they lose interest in him, reject and denounce him. But this situation, of course, is unbearably painful to a wounded individual who has been sensitized to just these events and reinforces his realization that reality is hurtful. The only way he can deal with this painful situation is to use again the mechanism of fantasy upon which he has learned to rely. The condition is a self-perpetuating one. It is quite clear how somebody can be a pathological liar and never learn from his experiences to tell the truth. He has been made too afraid of reality and he has grown mentally in such a way as to keep it always at a distance. To tell him to be reliable and truthful is as useful as to tell somebody with a curvature of the spine to stand up straight.

Another example of a mental shift commonly met with in the mind of an addict is that of splitting off as much as possible the painful emotion of guilt. These guilts originate in the home situation and may be rooted, let us say, in the separation of the parents after repeated heated quarrels over the child. It is difficult to do, but eventually, with a lot of practice and persistence, one can achieve a state in which one is untouched by guilt and live a fairly hurt-free life. Unfortunately, although it is possible to dissociate oneself from guilt, the guilts remain in the unconscious, where they are always associated with depression, which they feed and strengthen. But a person who is unable to feel guilt tends repeatedly to do things that ordinarily would have produced guilt, and becomes increasingly depressed unless he can find a way to discharge it, such as expiating it by self-destructive activity.

The sense of guilt is to the psyche what the sense of pain is to the body. It is a warning not to repeat the action that produced the unpleasant sensation. If one twists one's ankle and then tries to walk, the pain makes one limp so as to minimize the pain, thus protecting the injured fibers. If a normal husband on his way home calls in at a betting shop and loses his whole week's wage, he goes on home to his wife feeling guilty and is unlikely to repeat the behavior. However, if he has had to learn in his formative years to shut off guilt, his calls at the betting shop are likely to continue and his wife is going to have a hard time. The husband is not able to comprehend why his wife reacts as she does, and he, reflexly keeping guilt away, blames his wife for not understanding him.

Now it is to be expected that being a heroin addict will be accompanied by guilt on more than one level. In addition to splitting, the guilt can be discharged by load-shedding, which can easily be done by inducing a friend to take heroin. If this operation is successful, one can say with relief, "Joe's a real good guy and he uses, so I must be a good guy too!" Thus, even when there is little economic need to spread the addiction, as in Britain, the addiction is spread.

Projection

To complicate these unrealistic ways of dealing with reality, the very perception of reality may be changed. The unfortunate individual is then doubly handicapped as well as being addicted. This may be found, for instance, when a parent was so unpredictable that the child had to concentrate his whole mental energies in an effort to try to anticipate what his father or his mother was going to do or say next. He had no way of knowing how the disturbed parent would react to anything and was so taken up with keeping a fearful watch for minimal clues that he had insufficient time to attend to many other things that were essential for him to learn if he was to mature. The image of this unpredictable loving or hating, caressing or punishing, tranquil or furious, giving or withholding figure has become impressed on his mind's eye, so to speak, and he projects this image onto everybody he meets who is of the same sex as the abnormal parent, rather as a psychedelic projector in a hippie happening transforms everyone caught in its patterned beams. As he grows up, this masking of the real attributes of the people around him by the attributes of the parental figure causes both himself and others considerable dismay and confusion. If the abnormal parent has been his father, this image is projected onto all male authority figures and, when he reacts in his confused way against the projected image, the real authority figure behind the image tends to react against this reaction. This, of course, only confirms the individual in his false beliefs about authority and strengthens the intensity of the projection. If the mother has been the abnormal parent, when the boy grows up and gets married his wife never stands a chance, and the marriage sooner or later breaks up. Significantly, marriages of heroin addicts are marked by a considerable degree of instability with many separations.

It must be stressed that all along we have been considering normal defense mechanisms of a normal child mind in the setting of an abnormal reality situation. It is easy to assume that dependence on alcohol or other drugs on the part of one of the parents may indicate a genetic inheritance. It is just as likely that it is the relevant sprit that has been inherited.

Cross-Boundary Dependence

The phenomenon of cross-boundary dependence is an interesting one. It appears that there are certain people who, because of their programming, are more prone to drug abuse than others. But it is largely a matter of chance and availability which determines the particular drug that is abused. If that drug for some reason suddenly becomes unavailable, the probability of the drug user substituting it with another drug will be proportionate to his degree of dependence. The change, once effected, may become permanent. (This is seen in Britain where many heroin addicts are purposely switched to methadone, the new pattern of addiction often prevailing thereafter.) The reason a heroin addict may give for starting the drug is an increase in the cost of amphetamines when he was an amphetamine addict or the disappearance of the usual source of supply of marijuana if he was dependent on cannabis.

The Etiological Essence

Of this multiplicity of predisposing elements, one on its own is insufficient to cause heroin addiction. Seed, soil, climate all need to be right at the same time. The seed is the drug and its availability, the soil is the stressed personality, and the climate is the microclimate of opinion about the drug. If all three are right, heroin addiction can take root. If one is wrong, it is almost impossible.

4

Evaluating the Success
of Addiction Programs

CARL D. CHAMBERS

Introduction

At long last, it is recognized that the evaluation of a service or service delivery system is as important as the actual delivery of that service. And of equal importance, evaluation in the drug dependency field has matured beyond addressing the elementary management issues of *what* we are doing with *whom* and *how* we are going about it to include the dynamic issues of how well we are doing and how we could do it better. Given the very explosive nature of drug dependency as a personal and social problem, including the need to deliver service sometimes with only a minimum of planning and with almost nothing but "best judgment" upon which to proceed, such a sequential maturation process was to be expected. But the maturation has occurred and evaluation must occupy the level of attention that its importance warrants.

As an evaluator, I have alternatively been amused, amazed, and frightened at the general lack of concern, absence of understanding and, sometimes, the fear and suspicion of some service planners and deliverers around the issue of program evaluation. For ever so long, evaluators were confronted with the following attitude: "We know evaluation is good but we really are not ready for it and besides we really do not know how to do it." But we *do* know what has to be done and how to do it. This chapter will attempt to describe this what and how. The format is based on questions most often posed to me in my role as an evaluator.

What Is the Goal of Program Evaluation?

Evaluation is that systematic process whereby the information is available constantly to plan, structure, and deliver the most appropriate services in the most efficient manner. Evaluations are analyses, and therefore are best viewed within the analytic method including specifications of objectives and criteria, statement of hypotheses, collection and refinement of data, tests of hypotheses, and conclusions. When derived in this manner, evaluative conclusions become the tools with which decisions are formulated. Evaluation is not a replacement for judgment, but is its foundation. Evaluative analysis, when correctly and rigorously applied, should make explicit the implicit assumptions of policy and action as well as considerably narrowing any uncertainties inherent in the planning, structuring, and delivery of services.

Drug program evaluation is that specific type of analysis that asks the following questions: What is our delivery system? Who is receiving our services? How well are we doing this? How could we be doing this better? What other alternatives for doing this exist? Evaluation may concentrate on a single program, program type, or community, in which case its purpose is for program management, or it may compare the efficacy, effectiveness, and efficiency of several programs, in which case the purpose is alternative program evaluations.

What Have Been Our Mistakes?

At least at the design level, drug program evaluators have made a number of basic mistakes. I believe the most damaging of these mistakes have been those outlined below:

Evaluators have not demonstrated the emotional and intellectual independence necessary to conduct meaningful evaluations.

Evaluators have tended to overlook the highly critical variable of motivation for entering treatment.

Evaluators have been unwilling or unable to separate short-term and long-term program effects.

Evaluators have forgotten that their design must include comprehensive assessments of what the *community* wants (expects) from the program, what the *treaters* want (expect) from the program and its patients, and what the *addicts* want (expect) when they request treatment.

Quite obviously these wants (expectations) differ because each perceives the problem differently and they do vary from community to community, from practitioner to practitioner, and from addict to addict.

I am not in the position to prescribe solutions for these mistakes, but present them as necessary considerations when evaluations are being designed.

What Are the Problems of Evaluations?

No one has ever questioned the need for effective evaluations of addiction programs. However, as with all personal and social intervention programs, there are many inherent problems and risks in developing and using evaluative results, and positive recommendations are hard to derive because numerous conceptual, methodological, bureaucratic, political, and organizational problems have retarded the undertaking of any significant quantity of effective evaluative research. Those who want to perform evaluative research should become as familiar with these problems as have those who want to restrict such research. For example, although the problems confronting the evaluator will not be limited necessarily only to those outlined below, the five that were first delineated by Rossi and Williams (1972) and have been modified for presentation here are probably always in evidence.

Conceptual Problems. Evaluative efforts focused upon personal and social intervention programs are inherently complex and difficult to "control" in any rigorous way. No one has ever suggested that it was easy to describe behaviorally a person or persons in complex social situations.

Methodological Problems. Traditional social science methods and field procedures often are not adequate for producing evaluative results sufficiently sound to warrant their use in the policy planning and action arenas. For example, while social and behavioral scientists faced with evaluation tasks do understand and appreciate the disciplined strengths in statistical measurement, they do not always appreciate the problems associated with not having access to sound experimental design, including designing for experimental and control groups and/or maintaining them over any significant period of time. In most cases, social and behavioral science methodologists have not dealt with the problems of converting multiple variables identifiable with persons interacting within complex personal and social situations into meaningful, measurable terms.

Bureaucratic Problems. Program directors do not like to be evaluated, a process they see as being "graded." I believe this reluctance stems from two situations, both of which are somewhat out of the control of the individual program director they affect. First, program directors must present a "front" that has contradictory components . . . he accepts the state of the art which recognizes that the treatment techniques and procedures we utilize have not by and large been evaluated, but he must present the public, the press, the legislature, and so forth with obvious success. The evaluator, therefore, should not be surprised when program directors attempt to thwart a proposed evaluation or question the validity of a completed study.

Political Problems. All programs supported with public monies—and most drug treatment programs are—are political in the sense that elected or appointed public officials make life and death decisions about them. Drug treatment programs not only have high public visibility, but they also serve a clientele for whom there is usually a more emotional than intellectual reaction, all of which makes evaluation difficult.

Wherein lie the motives for evaluation and what motivates the evaluator? For example, many politicians have "ridden to office on the backs of junkies," but some have done so by creating fear of the "dope fiend," some by promising to reduce crime by locking them up or putting them all in treatment, some by highlighting treatment failures to reduce service and save tax monies, some by advocating no social welfare programs for those who "won't work," etc. Even if the motivation for evaluation and the motivation of the evaluator escape this contamination, it will always be there in some form and any evaluation effort will be affected by it.

Organizational Problems. Comprehensive evaluations of drug treatment programs require a large-scale, multidisciplinary effort demanding high levels of technical, administrative, and organizational skills. There is little in the formal training of social scientists or in the post-training experiences of most social scientists which promotes the acquisition of these skills. These situations result in severe shortages of competent professionals to design, supervise, and perform evaluative studies.

Evaluation research brings together many problems ranging from esoteric statistical concerns and biases, which interest only the sophisticated statistician or methodologist, to the more complicated major bureaucratic and political issues probably perceived in all their potencies and subtleties only by those who have neglected to consider them. Thus, if one is to fully understand the evaluative process, one must have strategies to confront both the methodological and bureaucratic political processes.

Where Were We Five Years Ago?

There is little doubt that five years ago drug program evaluations were all conducted at the preexperimental level. Houston (1972) has described preexperimental design as a procedure for gathering observations that do not permit valid inference regarding program effects. Preexperimental designs are most seductive and do have some descriptive credibility. Unfortunately, they do not permit an analysis that includes the probability that the treatment program had no effect and tend to ignore statistical probabilities entirely.

Five years ago drug program evaluation was at the most primitive preexperimental level utilizing exclusively a *post-test design* only. At this level, a group is exposed to a program and measures are subsequently obtained to characterize the experiences of that group. Thus, a group case study is presented to "demonstrate" the effectiveness of that specific program. As Houston (1972) has indicated, while the evaluator argues that the group is different from how it would have been without the treatment, we have no information as to how it was before the treatment, so there is no basis upon which to agree or disagree with this argument. Further, while the evaluator implies that his group is different from those individuals who were not treated, such differences, if indeed they do exist, might occur because peculiar individuals were selected or because individuals who lacked certain characteristics dropped out of the program prior to the measurements being taken.

At least in the drug treatment field, evaluations during this period of our evolution were typically conducted or at least were under the direction of the persons who were also responsible for delivering treatment services. Not unexpectedly, such evaluations were of limited programmatic and methodological value.

Where Are We Now?

I believe these drug program evaluations have progressed to the second level of preexperimental design. At the present time, most evaluators are at least using a one-group, pretest–post-test design.

Again using Houston's (1972) definition, the one-group, pretest–post-test design is where a group is selected, measured, subjected to a program, and measured again. Since the before and after scores can be compared, it is possible to determine whether any changes occurred between the occasions of measurements.

The minimal components of such a one-group, pretest–post-test design are indicated below:

A group is selected for study. This is usually the total admitted for treatment during a given time period.

All are subjected to the same intake process, including the collection of basic demographic information and comprehensive drug use history. All are given standardized medical examinations, undergo standardized psychological testing, and treatment goals and expectations are assessed.

All are given assignments in treatment based on our most recent findings relevant to "screening patients," and a treatment contract is formulated between the treater and the treated.

All receive periodic status evaluations regarding progress and compliance with the treatment contract. This status evaluation must include careful documentation of services rendered and reactions to these services. Periodic psychological retesting is also employed.

At termination a standardized response to treatment is completed, demographic characteristics are updated, and post-treatment goals and expectations are assessed.

At periodic intervals former patients, both those who complete the defined treatment experience and those who have prematurely left, are located and personally interviewed to determine current personal and social situations.

Needless to say, most critical to the one-group pretest–post-test design are standardization of measurement and the need to follow up our failures as well as our successes. Even with all of these precautions, it is not possible to demonstrate that the group, or its constituent members, have changed independent of the changes that may have occurred in the measurements themselves.

Campbell and Stanley (1966) as well as Houston (1972) have set forth clear limitations to all preexperimental designs. Those which I perceive to be most critical are indicated below:

Events independent of the program occur between the time of measurement which may impact program outcome. For example, new legislation may impose new restrictions on service delivery and impinge upon the process. In general, the longer the time interval between measurements, the greater the danger of impinging events rivaling the program as a plausible cause of change.

Natural maturation does occur in our special group of social casualties. None of us has been able to effectively assess motivation for entering treatment, nor have we been able to identify those persons who will get "better" regardless of what we do to or for them, nor have we been able to identify those who are ready to spontaneously discontinue drug use whether they enter treatment or not.

There are natural limitations to retesting and reinterviewing. Patients *do* become "test wise" and interviewers *do* become more skilled. Given the character disorder nature of some of our patients and the need to demonstrate success by some of our practitioners, these biases become obvious.

Where Do We Go Now?

At a minimum, drug program evaluators must incorporate a comparison group design. Comparisons must be made between groups who were exposed to the treatment and those who were not, with differences being interpreted as program effects. Comparison groups must be selected in such a way that they resemble the treatment groups in as many respects as possible. I believe such comparison groups can be formulated. For example, in various screening programs, such as jail urine surveillance programs, those who accept treatment can be compared with those who do not. I would even suggest that in most communities a comparison group of active addicts can be identified and followed over time. In those communities where there are more addicts requesting services than are available, those who do not meet entrance requirements can be formed into an appropriate comparison group.

Finally, I believe we are at the point where we must consider a controlled experimental design with random assignments. I am no longer convinced that our treatment procedures are so beneficial that we must give them to everyone even at the risk of not being able to determine how effective we are. Without randomization in a controlled experiment, I doubt that we will ever deliver efficient effective service. While I am not advocating long-term denial of service to anyone, I do advocate the need for at least short term denial for some in order to conduct meaningful valid evaluations of our current delivery system.

It would seem we have most of our work ahead of us.

References

Campbell, D. T., and Stanley, J. C. (1966). "Experimental and Quasi-experimental Designs for Research." Rand McNally, Chicago, Illinois.

Houston, T. R. (1972). The behavior sciences impact-effectiveness model. In "Evaluating Social Programs" (P. H. Rossi and W. Williams, eds.) pp. 51–65. Seminar Press, New York.

Rossi, P. H., and Williams, W., eds. (1972). "Evaluating Social Programs." Seminar Press, New York.

5

Rational Planning
for Drug Abuse Services

BARRY S. RAMER
and
RINNA B. FLOHR

Rational planning for drug abuse services requires astute observation and assessment of the political, social, and economic forces that focus on the planning process. No plan can satisfy a community's needs, regardless of how scholarly, erudite, and reasonable it may be, unless it relates to all converging forces (Hall and Bourne, 1973). This chapter will attempt to elucidate these realities and will suggest a positive course of action.

Government's Failure in Crisis Response

Our social system is crisis oriented and responds to the pressures of "brush fires." Initially, society denies that a crisis exists and only rallies after it is out of hand. We often forget proven techniques utilized to control crises. After one has subsided, abortive attempts are made to assess how it began (evaluation and research), but the results of these studies are often irretrievably filed away. The result is that each time the same crisis arises, society responds as if it were a totally new and unique experience. Today's response to our "new" heroin epidemic attests to this inexplicable behavior (Earl and Wolter, 1973; Hartke, 1972; Ramer *et al.*, 1972). Enormous quantities of energy and money are being expended to define this "new" crisis and control it. The needless waste is appalling (Ehrenreich, 1971; Hughes *et al.*, 1972; Rosen, 1971).

Society's failure in the area of planning and prevention stems from diverted attention. As productive answers are being developed to one problem, a new crisis develops, attention is diverted, and interest wanes. There is no excitement or glory in crisis prevention, and the task of developing a major prevention program becomes tedious and uninteresting. It is far more exciting to fight brush fires than to prevent them.

All too often, health plans are conceived in a vacuum far removed from client-recipients or the communities in which they live. "Ivory tower" plans conceived by desk-anchored bureaucrats bear no relevance to an acute crisis or community need. Little wonder that most available treatment modalities have negligible effect on long-term problems (Bowden and Langenauer, 1972; DeLong, 1972: Levy, 1972; Vaillant, 1966).

In its search for meaningful answers to our current heroin crisis, the public has sought out the "experts." Each "expert" espouses his gospel and insists that only his method will achieve "salvation." "Take more drugs." "Take less drugs." "Take no drugs." "Take substitute drugs." "Offer alternative lifestyles." The establishment has selected its experts and counterculture groups have selected theirs. Mythical qualities for various chemical substances have been touted. Street lore abounds (Smith and Luce, 1971). Facts are impossible to uncover.

Alienated and disenfranchised youth have turned away from traditional health care systems and have developed their own in the free clinic movement (Judd and Mandell, 1972; Smith and Luce, 1971; California Medical Association, 1972). Free clinics have become the focal point for drug treatment services, but many of them are staffed by ex-addicts whose only claim to expertise is the fact that they were "immunized" by direct drug exposure. Little evidence exists to support the assertion that merely being an ex-addict confers particular expertise in rehabilitating other addicts.

More recently, narcotics addiction treatment programs have become tools for renovating the cumbersome, intransigent system of government. Each agency head, acting as a baronial fief, dictates policy over his kingdom, uninvolved and uninformed as to other agency activities. They actively protect their fiefdom from the onslaught of other agency incursions, jealously guarding their own and often refusing to cooperate or participate with other governmental groups. Under the onslaught of a heroin epidemic, the present Administration made efforts to end the duplication and political infighting among these bureaucracies. The White House Special Action Office for Drug Abuse Prevention was created, and a mandate was given to its director to coordinate the entire federal government's prevention, education, treatment, and rehabilitation efforts in the areas of narcotic addiction and drug abuse. Unfortunately, the Administration stopped short of providing a truly effective superagency by denying the Special Action Office control over law enforcement activities in the field of substance abuse; hence, this artificial division has only further served to widen the schism between the law enforcement approach and the health care approach to drug abuse problems (Pekkanen, 1973).

In viewing present governmental activity in combating narcotic addiction, two interesting and encouraging side effects have developed. Newly created treatment agencies have hired a cadre of paraprofessionals from the lower socioeconomic strata and created career ladders for their advancement. Large numbers of minority peoples have obtained employment within the treatment systems and have advanced up these career ladders (Deitch and Casriel, 1967). They have learned not only new skills in program administration but also how to cope effectively with bureaucratic game playing.

The second area of encouragement lies in the development of contract mechanisms to expand existing community-based agencies. In its efforts to control and eradicate heroin addiction, the Special Action Office has designed contracts to rapidly expand treatment services. Teams from several federal agencies were sent throughout the country to "buy up" heroin addict treatment waiting lists. Money was pumped directly into existing treatment agencies assuring rapid expansion of treatment capacity.

Health Care System Battles Law Enforcement *

Many psychoactive drugs abused on the street have profound therapeutic effects (Melinger et al., 1972; Passim, 1972). When medically supervised, society seldom contests the use of these chemicals. The basic philosophy of present drug control laws is that it is illegal and evil to self-administer drugs for pleasure or relief from mental disturbance (Kramer, 1972). This medieval thinking is the product of confused minds. Society readily accepts alcohol abuse and even condones the pleasurable "high" achieved from this drug. Those who

* See Winich (1964).

most fervently pursue alcohol's psychoactive effects, most vehe-
mently persecute those who dare to abuse other drugs. They are positive that only illegal chemical substances contribute to social alienation and crime.

Our society will continue to be exposed to a multiplicity of drugs,
many with psychoactive effects. The alienated, the disenfranchised,
and the mentally ill will use psychoactive substances in their quest
to escape unpleasant realities and dismal existences. In a society that
is pleasure oriented, it is inconsistent to condone alcohol abuse
while denying access to other pleasurable, stimulating substances.
We must learn to cope with psychoactive chemicals and to provide
for reasonable alternatives to thrill-seeking behavior. Society's need
to control behavior must be carefully scrutinized as to its underlying
motivations. Individual human rights must be preserved, and the
right to experiment with one's own body must be more carefully
defined (Szasz, 1972). One fact is most certain: Present methods in
controlling drug abuse are ineffective and counterproductive, and
they further alienate a substantial segment of the population from
law and morality (Bowden and Langenauer, 1972; Kramer *et al.*,
1968).

In a society devoted to the hard work ethic, being "stoned" and
nonproductive is defined as "evil" or "sick." If we define drug-abus-
ing behavior as "evil," then clearly those who abuse drugs should be
dealt with through our morality-enforcing system of law. If we determine that the drug user is "sick" (Black, 1969), then his rehabilitation falls into the purview of the health care delivery system. For
the past 60 years the forces for "good" (health) have challenged the
forces against "evil" (law enforcement) as to who has the right to
control narcotic addicts. Perhaps more realistically, these bureaucratic giants are battling for acquisition of the funds society is willing
to invest to modify the substance abuser's perplexing behavior.
Chasing and/or treating "junkies" has become a major preoccupation
of government at all levels. In their scramble for dollars, these giants
have lost sight of client welfare (Deedes, 1969; Einstein, 1970; *Scientific American*, 1970).

Treatment systems indicate that with adequate funding, they can
rehabilitate the heroin addict humanely, effectively, and for less
money than law enforcement agencies. * In this process of "rehabilitation," thousands of former addicts are being hired to care for active

---

* The average cost for outpatient methadone maintenance treatment is $1500 per pa-
tient per year. The average cost for incarceration at California Rehibilitation Center is
approximately $5000 per person per year.

addicts. The major employers of ex-addicts are the health care delivery systems charged with treating drug abusers (Deitch and Casriel, 1967).

The law enforcement complex is not about to be undone by the "do-gooders." They claim that with a larger force of agents, additional money to make drug "buys," stricter laws, and more jail space, they could easily eradicate the problem. Several political leaders have recently expounded plans to "lock pushers away for life." As the law enforcement group grows, peripheral new industries flourish, purveying a myriad of new laboratory tests and sophisticated detection equipment (Einstein, 1970; O'Connor et al., 1971).

Each of these two bureaucratic monsters eagerly applauds the other's failures. Since little evidence exists regarding the effectiveness of either system in controlling the growth and spread of substance abuse, the hue and cry from each camp has taken on an evangelical tone. It is almost impossible to make a rational choice amidst the din. The confused and uninformed taxpayer is in no position to make an educated decision regarding fiscal allocation. His legislative representative, fearing public criticism from one or both camps, follows the motto, "When in doubt, spread it out." The net result of inadequate funding ensures that no treatment or enforcing technique will be successful.

Marginal funding is no longer acceptable in militant minority communities. They are wise in the ways of government and reticent to accept tokenism. All too often they have seen that inadequately funded federal programs fail in their communities. Critics of community-based programs point to these failures as justification to discontinue funding. Community leaders should refuse inadequate funding rather than falsely raise the hopes and expectations of oppressed poverty groups. Poorly funded programs lead to disappointment, disillusionment, and alienation. Tokenism is no longer acceptable in a land that can lavish billions on space exploration (McMearn, 1972).

Although society is eager to rehabilitate ex-addicts, the eagerness is clearly confined to someone else's efforts. Numerous obstacles remain in the way of social reintegration of the addict. Employers refuse the nonusing addict employment and utilize past criminal records to substantiate their fears. The addict himself often lacks skills and is unable to compete in an open labor market. Society's frequent rejection leads to increased anxiety, fear, suspicion, disappointment, unpaid debts, and alienation. All these serve to further immobilize the addict. In an open labor market, what could be more crippling than to be an unskilled minority member, an ex-felon, without friend or employment recommendation, labeled "ex-junkie" (Flohr and Lerner, 1971).

The Drug Scene in San Francisco

Long before the crisis became public knowledge, drugs were already a significant problem in several San Francisco neighborhoods. The Haight-Ashbury area witnessed the arrival of the "flower children" and psychedelic experience purveyors. As thousands of alienated youth arrived in San Francisco, separated from families, friends, and familiar sights, they clustered together in communal living and shared in the psychedelic drug experience. The Haight-Ashbury Free Medical Clinic was established in an effort to deal with the multiplicity of health problems faced by these youngsters (Gay *et al.*, 1972). In addition to the entire range of expected medical problems, these youth were afflicted with typical drug abuse side effects. "Bad trips," infectious hepatitis, malnutrition, amphetamine psychosis, and drug overdose were commonplace in the Haight (Gay *et al.*, 1972; Smith and Luce, 1971).

The community immediately adjacent to the Haight-Ashbury district, known as the Fillmore, is best described as a black ghetto, and contains some of the worst slums and poverty in San Francisco. Narcotic drug usage was rampant in this community. Black community leaders had difficulty comprehending the white middle-class youth's use of psychedelic drugs. They were incensed, unable to understand how white youth could reject good homes, education, automobiles, materialism, and easy living while black society had not even had an opportunity to share in this experience. Black youth were utilizing narcotics in an effort to deal with boredom, depression, poverty, and peer group pressure. To many ghetto youth, school seemed like an endless waste. What purpose did education serve if you were still unable to obtain employment? The only member of the ghetto community who appeared "successful" (as defined by the middle-class ethic) was the "pusher man." He had all the accoutrements of middle-class American success: an expensive apartment, a Cadillac car, flashy clothes, and several women. To a teenage black, the "pusher man's" life seems glamorous. When normal avenues for achieving success are closed, purveying drugs may appear to be the best alternative (Preble and Casey, 1972). Peer group pressure often entrapped alienated youth into narcotics use. What better way to prove one's manliness and courage? Large numbers began to "turn on" to narcotics—the "Cadillac of all drugs."

Across Market Street, in the Latino district of San Francisco known as the Mission, similar social and economic problems exist. Chicano youth along with other Latinos, were actively proving their "macho" by utilization of narcotics. In addition to the usual socioeconomic ills, foreign language further separated them from middle-class society. Likewise in Chinatown, new Chinese youth were arriving daily from Hong Kong. As each successive wave of immigrants arrived in San Francisco, often without English-speaking skills, they were actively exploited by the community. Low income, poor housing, long hours of nonunionized work, and social crowding often led to family breakdowns and social acting out by these ever restless youth.

Sharp divisions exist in Chinatown between young and old, "F.O.B.'s" and the "A.B.C.'s" * Street gangs abound in Chinatown, extorting merchants and beating uncommitted youth. The F.O.B. youth gangs abuse alcohol, while their A.B.C. counterparts consume other chemical depressants (primarily barbiturates). For the most part, Chinese youth steer clear of narcotics.

Not so for their older cousins. Many began smoking opium in China or New York City. Today, best estimates are that more than 800 older narcotic addicts reside in and around Chinatown. These men † control a significant portion of the opiate trade in and around San Francisco.

In the middle-class Caucasian enclaves, school drug abuse surveys pointed toward increased exposure, experimentation, and drug abuse. "Fruit salad" parties were a Saturday night pastime. Admission to these events required a handful of different pills from the home medicine cabinet. Each youth's contribution was stirred in a large bowl and one by one in turn the participants picked and swallowed a pill. Last one remaining conscious was the "winner."

San Francisco's population is unique. Described as "Baghdad by the Bay," almost half the people enumerated in San Francisco's 1970 census were foreign born or the children of foreign-born parents. Foreign stock accounted for 317,000 of the city's total population of 715,000. Approximately 14% of San Francisco's population is of Latin American origin. An equal number are Chinese. Blacks account for 13% of the population. Large numbers of Europeans migrated to California at the turn of the century. Other colonies include foreign-born residents emanating from such diverse places as Germany, Italy, Ireland, Mexico, Central and South America, the Philippines, Samoa, and Japan. (See Table I.)

* F.O.B.'s, Fresh Off Boats (or foreign born); A.B.C.'s, American-born Chinese.
† Among the Chinese, male addicts outnumber females 20:1.

Table I

The Foreign Born [a]

National origin	Number	Percent
Foreign stock total	317,045	100.0
China	48,384	15.3
Italy	29,040	9.2
Philippine Islands	26,645	8.4
Germany	19,610	6.2
Mexico	18,519	5.8
Ireland	16,690	5.3
United Kingdom	14,165	4.5
U.S.S.R.	13,603	4.3
Canada	12,079	3.8
Japan	9,161	2.9
France	5,639	1.8
Poland	5,326	1.7
Sweden	4,724	1.5
Greece	4,285	1.4
Austria	4,145	1.3
Norway	3,335	1.1
Yugoslavia	3,269	1.0
Switzerland	2,795	0.9
Denmark	2,515	0.8
Hungary	1,906	0.6
Czechoslovakia	1,714	0.5
Netherlands	1,450	0.5
Cuba	1,357	0.4
Portugal	1,347	0.4
Finland	1,294	0.4
Rumania	1,187	0.4
Lithuania	825	0.3
All other	62,036	19.6

[a] Almost half the people enumerated in San Francisco during the 1970 census were foreign-born or the children of foreign-born parents. The total number of residents of foreign stock was 317,045, or 44.3% of the city's total population of 715,674.

Each wave of immigrants carved out a colony somewhere in the city and for the most part nurtured their community integrity. Many of these residents do not speak English and continue to use their mother tongue. This presents unique problems for public health or community effort. At a minimum, at least three languages—English, Chinese, and Spanish—are necessary to involve the majority of San Francisco residents. (See Table II.)

As each neighborhood experienced the alarming growth and development of drug-related problems, grass root efforts were created to deal with these problems. Small community-based groups coa-

Table II

Household Foreign Language [a]

Language	Number	Percent
Total population	715,674	100.0
English only	387,587	54.2
Spanish	64,395	9.0
Italian	30,232	4.2
German	26,283	3.7
French	13,219	1.8
Russian	8,549	1.2
Yiddish	5,917	0.8
Swedish	3,797	0.5
Polish	2,986	0.4
Hungarian	1,343	0.2
All other	123,074	17.2
Not reported	48,291	6.7

[a] About 41.9% of San Francisco's population spoke a language other than English in their homes when they were children, according to the 1970 U.S. Census Bureau report. The Census Bureau's breakdown of the population's mother tongue is given in this table. (Chinese was not mentioned in this report, since the Census Bureau did not select Chinese as a major *nationwide* language.)

lesced in order to cope with drug problems in an attempt to fill the vacuum while awaiting government action. In each colony, native language and ethnically diverse programs sprang up. Drug programs were organized in the Mission by Spanish-speaking youth, in the Haight-Ashbury by the "hippie subculture," in Chinatown by Chinese youth, in the Fillmore and the Bayview-Hunters Point communities by black self-help groups, and in the middle-class Sunset community by a counter-culture group called Huckleberry House for Runaways.

In the beginning there was chaos, paranoia, suspicion, jealousy, rivalry, and broken communication. In this amorphous state, drug programs rose and fell. Many were so entrenched in their own philosophical approach that they were unable to share or exchange vital information. The fiscal crumbs cast among this group were avariciously snatched up, but no single group had enough money to implement an effective program. Each organization was busy "doing its own thing." Many well-meaning groups were established primarily to provide social service. Other agencies were set up in an effort to provide self-aggrandizement for their leaders. Still other makeshift organizations were put together by social "do-gooders." Our local government, under pressure from parents and the media, began to mobilize limited treatment resources to cope with the burgeoning problem. A few beds were set aside at San Francisco General Hospital for detoxification. Detoxification as a sole treatment modality served only to facilitate a "revolving door." Addicts would enter the hospital, spend 5 to 7 days receiving decreasing doses of methadone, and would then be discharged as "drug-free." Within a few days they were back on the streets using narcotics to an even greater extent.

Bedroom suburban communities remained smug in their complacency. Drug abuse was a big-city problem. Middle-class youth would never be affected. However, the sparks of crisis soon settled in the suburban communities and they learned an important lesson. Even their communities were not immune from the blight of drug abuse. At first these communities actively denied that they had a problem. Once the realization occurred, panic ensued. A hue and cry for action was heard in Washington and at state legislative levels. After months and years of inactivity, the ponderous and cumbersome system of government began to formulate needed programs.

As public awareness grew regarding the magnitude of the drug abuse epidemic, the first action was that of repressive police activity (McMearn, 1972). The general public was led to believe that by stricter laws, more police, and greater enforcement, defined deviant behavior would cease. To everyone's surprise and dismay, the problem did not evaporate, nor was it controlled. The law enforcement complex, bewildered by its impotence, called for stricter and stronger legislation. Fault was placed on lenient judges and lenient laws. However, the increased law enforcement activity met with dismal failure. The problem was still there and more severe than ever (Stachnik, 1972).

School administrators issued ultimatums: "Stop abusing drugs or face expulsion! " Scare tactics were used as an educational approach. Narcotics officers were brought in to the schools to elucidate the bad physiological effects and criminal penalties for drug use. In general, these school assemblies had no demonstrable effect on student drug consumption. Now totally out of control, both teachers and administrators experienced panic. New rules were rigidly enforced, and the students complained of mass victimization. Subsequent inconsistent enforcement of rules caused further confusion and the crisis exploded.

Distorted and grossly exaggerated stories of massive student drug abuse led to fears of violence and overdose death. Youthful drug arrests covered newspaper headlines. In desperation, health workers were called upon to establish crash pads in several schools. When these health workers opened the crash pad doors, they found their jobs ill defined, their skills unrelated to the school needs, and an absence of a genuine medical crisis. When clients failed to appear for service, the health workers turned their attention toward reforming the educational system, now defined as the root of the drug abuse evil. Before long, the students learned that they could obtain permission to visit the crash pad and did so during opportune times, i.e., to avoid examinations, unpopular classes, gymnastics, and so forth. The pass issued for admittance to the crash pad was used instead to play truant from school. Students would feign drug overdose to obtain admittance into the crash pad. When they appeared alert and awake, the school administrators ordered them back to class rather than have them participate in a therapeutic process (Flohr, 1972).

Fanning the hysteria was the lay press. Horror stories covered the front pages of local papers (*Journal of the American Medical Association*, 1971; Louria, 1972). Children of prominent citizens were being led away by the "Pied Piper" of drug abuse. As the epidemic spread and engulfed even middle-class youth, the cry for more stringent laws abated. Suddenly, numerous legislative hearings were convened to investigate this "new" societal blight. No one honestly wanted to send their children to prison for drug abuse. The drug pusher often turned out to be the boy next door. Society redefined its goals as humane medical treatment and alternatives to incarceration (Smith and Gay, 1972).

In San Francisco, drug program administrators were called upon to provide testimony and comment on new bills pending before federal, state, and local legislative bodies.* Many of these program administrators provided significant information to the general public about pending legislation that would affect treatment and funding. Special news bulletins, television interviews, newspaper and television editorials, radio talk shows, and public addresses were used to build public support and awareness. In addition, magazine articles, speaking engagements before prestigious community groups, and involvement in community planning meetings helped crystallize public thinking and action. As public awareness grew, people demanded more information on actual treatment programs and their philosophical goals. As programs developed, more critical attention was given to budgets and fiscal accountability.

---

* Testimony of the San Francisco Drug Program Administrator can be found in House of Representatives Committee on the Judiciary, 1972: Investigation of Treatment and Rehabilitation of Narcotic Addicts, Vols. 1 and 2, State Hearings on California Senate Bill 714. Federal Hearings on Drugs in School by the House of Representatives Select Committee on Crime; Federal Hearings on Amphetamines, etc., 1972.

San Francisco Coordinating
Council on Drug Abuse *

A degree of sophistication developed in San Francisco when several community-based programs decided to meet and communicate. They recognized that duplication existed in some service areas, while a total absence occurred in other areas. Thus, in 1969 the San Francisco Coordinating Council on Drug Abuse was conceived. A small group of private and public organizations met in an effort to define common goals. Each agency expressed a need to communicate difficulties, share experiences, avoid duplicating efforts, and develop new programs. Early meetings were frustrating, long, and, heated. Discussions centered around financial problems, dogmatic allegiances, condemnations of various treatment approaches, and public confusion (which seriously interfered with fund-raising efforts). The group wanted to facilitate public awareness, understanding, and community education. However, limited funding pitted private agencies against each other in their bid for community support.

At first, some Council members recommended that the organization remain autonomous, elitist, clannish, and avoid contact with other programs not already members of the Coordinating Council. They recommended restrictive bylaws that would keep numerous agencies out of the Council. Through careful planning and group education, the membership was encouraged to define broad qualifications for new member organizations. Rather than exclude any community agency, all were encouraged to join the Council. The expanded scope of the Council assured significant input from all communities and their ethnic minorities.

Initially, the organization membership primarily represented treatment agencies. Any action taken by the Council would be meaningless without the participation of local police, the probation department, parole officers, and the schools. These agencies were invited to join the Council. The Police Department remained skeptical and sent as their representative a low-ranking patrolman who was not empowered to vote or speak on behalf of the Department. Since the Council initially had no official sanction from the city fathers, the higher-echelon police officers were reluctant to become associated with this group. After all, the Council was constituted from "ragtag longhair people, hippies and troublemakers." Continued efforts to solicit police participation were of limited success.

* More information on the development and operation of the SFCCDA can be obtained through their office, 121 Leavenworth Street, San Francisco, California 94102.

In addition, there was considerable antagonism between publicly and privately operated groups. Private agencies were suspicious of government's incursion on their territorial expertise. A great deal of suspicion was directed toward professionals by paraprofessional street workers who were reluctant to share the field with middle-class, highly educated professionals.

It soon became evident that neither professional training nor street drug experience *alone* was adequate for designing, operating, and maintaining successful treatment programs. Physicians found themselves uninformed and unfamiliar with the life style of lower socio-economic groups and addicts. Many of them expressed frustration in their inability to communicate with alienated youth and drug abusers.

The former drug addict experienced a similar difficulty in his lack of therapy skills. Merely being exposed to drug use and living through the dreadful experience was not sufficient to provide thera-peutic know-how. Many of them expressed anger and frustration in their inability to effect change in other drug abusers' behavior. They often recommended punitive treatment approaches, utilizing humil-iating and dehumanizing "games" in an effort to deal effectively with the drug abuser's antisocial behavior.

In order to maintain a balance between public and private groups, professionals and paraprofessionals, the Coordinating Council de-fined broad representation on its governing board. A Special Council (Board of Governors) was created with thirteen positions: six for pri-vate agency members, six for public agency members, and a thir-teenth member elected from the community at large. This member was required to be a consumer of services (former addict).

The ordinary level of participation within the Coordinating Coun-cil is through General Council membership. Each member agency appoints or elects a single representative to the General Council. Each agency is permitted to cast one vote at a General Council meet-ing. At present, more than 100 agencies are actively participating in Council functions, each with its single vote.

Elections are held annually, and the Council members divide themselves into a public and private forum, held in separate rooms. Both the public and private segments elect six representatives to the Special Council. These twelve members then call for election of the thirteenth member from the membership at large. The thirteen Spe-cial Council members act as a Board of Directors for the Coordinat-ing Council and, through a secret ballot, elect the Executive Com-mittee consisting of a President, First and Second Vice-Presidents, Secretary, and Treasurer.

The San Francisco Coordinating Council on Drug Abuse is incorporated as a nonprofit agency in the state of California and holds a tax-exempt status with the Internal Revenue Service. The Council meets twice a month. On the first Friday of each month, the thirteen-member Special Council meets to discuss policy decisions and to create an agenda for the General Council meeting held the third Friday of each month.

When federal funds became available to develop a comprehensive drug abuse program, the private agencies coalesced and the public versus private competitive rivalries reawakened. The publicly operated Methadone Maintenance Treatment Program was seen as a threat to small private agency survival. It was felt that the Methadone Program, governmentally operated and administered, would usurp all available federal funds, and an attack was launched against it.

When it appeared that there would be sufficient funding for all local agencies, competition markedly decreased. Community-based services agreed to cooperate with each other and discontinued their attack on public agencies. Public agencies, with their mantle of respectability, would serve as the funding intermediary between federal government and community-based agencies. Furthermore, since internal strife and feuding would adversely affect the entire community's ability to obtain treatment funds, every program's survival was dependent on a strong partnership between the public and private sectors.

San Francisco's Plan

One of the earliest actions undertaken by the Coordinating Council was the development of a citywide plan. Three program areas were described: existing services, proposed services, and future planned services. By surveying and listing all existing services, the areas of additional needs became apparent. The community agencies, under the sponsorship of the Council, defined the following immediate needs:

Comprehensive 24-hour emergency and crisis telephone service
Inpatient detoxification services
Central referral system
Expanded methadone maintenance treatment
Expanded therapeutic community services

Creation of youth advocacy services and crisis beds
Establishment of an evaluation, research, and patient tracking
system
Drug education and prevention
Vocational rehabilitation and legal services

Several of the better organized and more effective private treatment groups prepared descriptions of their proposed programs and financial needs. These were incorporated with the public agency program and fund needs, and the package submitted to the Narcotic Addict Rehabilitation Branch of the National Institute for Mental Health as a Drug Abuse Special Project.* At long last it appeared that the community was moving toward the common goal of funding a comprehensive community drug program. Shortly after the grant was submitted to the NIMH, new and foreseen problems developed.

Before the plan was developed, many community agencies considered the Coordinating Council an oddity. These groups were skeptical of the Council's ability to coordinate and even more skeptical regarding its ability to obtain funds. When it became apparent that the Council might achieve success in its funding efforts, many heretofore unknown groups stepped forward, demanding to be part of the city-wide plan. They launched their attack stating that the plan was far from comprehensive. They insisted that it did not provide a means of linking all the various efforts throughout the community in a productive manner. There were no special services for youth, or for the aged, nor were their considerations to provide drug abuse services for other special groups, including the psychotic, the mentally disturbed, and the pregnant addict. Proposed treatment sites were not well distributed geographically, and the special needs of various ethnic groups had been poorly considered.

In reality, many of these criticisms were valid. Little thought had been given as to how individuals would be transferred from one facility to another. The problems of prevention, education, and long-term rehabilitation were not fully discussed. Once again, the abstinence versus methadone maintenance controversy was reignited. The community demanded to know how much of the comprehensive plan funding would be for methadone maintenance and how much would be earmarked for other treatment modalities. Since money was the basic issue, a compromise was found. Therapeutic communities would accept patients from the methadone maintenance program as residents, and both treatment modalities could then support each other, coexist, and provide even more meaningful services.

* NIMH Grant No. 1 H80-MH01085-01, September 1972–1980.

This compromise was achieved only after methadone maintenance treatment teams recognized that medication alone was not sufficient to rehabilitate addicts. Additional community rehabilitative services were necessary to integrate the addict into the community. Secondly, since methadone maintenance could only be used after addicts had tried some other treatment approach,* these other treatment approaches would have to be developed. Attitudes within the therapeutic communities were also changing and it was no longer considered necessary for an addict to suffer abstinence withdrawal as proof of his motivation for help. Patients actively participating in a methadone program were also eligible for therapeutic communities if residential treatment was indicated. Lastly, a referral system was created to divert those ineligible for methadone maintenance treatment into therapeutic communities.

The San Francisco Coordinating Council on Drug Abuse has secured a $34,000 grant from the Law Enforcement Assistance Act (LEAA), enabling them to support a full-time staff consisting of a planner, a coordinator, and an administrative secretary. The Special Council has expanded to fifteen members in order to reflect the increased membership of law enforcement agencies on the General Council. Eight committees and task forces are active. The current Council conflict is pitting the law enforcement system against the health care system, as manifested by the severe criticism leveled toward the development of a Treatment Alternatives to Street Crime (T.A.S.C.) proposal. Also, the focus of the Council has changed. Although once action oriented, today it is primarily information gathering and sharing. This assures a forum for the exchange and debate of various conflicting ideas, philosophies, and viewpoints related to drug abuse. The Council is now charged with initiating and developing a regular planning process to prepare a yearly comprehensive plan for drug abuse service. The planning process is not static, but is dynamic and constantly changing. As services are implemented, new needs arise and new community priorities will emerge. The Comprehensive San Francisco Drug Plan is rewritten each year, and the planning process takes approximately 6 months. The Council has conducted an arduous series of forums to redefine community needs each year. A list of current priorities follows.†

---

* California Methadone Regulations and Food and Drug Administration Regulations.

† Adopted by the San Francisco Coordinating Council on Drug Abuse's Full Council, 1972.

First Priority

1. Increase reentry and follow-up services to those in rehabilitation programs, including job development and placement for rehabilitated drug abusers
2. Divert adults and juveniles from the criminal justice system *at the time of arrest*, when charges are for personal possession of drugs
3. Expand drug detoxification services, both within the community and in its jails
4. Provide nonjudgmental, objective education to the general public to (a) increase their awareness of the difference between users, traffickers, and dealers, (b) provide information on available treatment and support programs, (c) define social, economic, and political factors that contribute to drug abuse, (d) describe the effect of drugs on body function, (e) list legal services already available for the addict

Second Priority

1. Increase the number of residential treatment facilities
2. Provide ongoing education and training for professionals and paraprofessionals to (a) increase their understanding of individuals and types of individuals who use drugs, (b) expand their awareness of services, roles, and problems of others who provide drug abuse services (police, doctors, lawyers, judges, counselors)
3. Increase availability of crisis assistance for acute drug-related problems
4. Provide educational experiences that help preschool and elementary school students and their parents increase self-awareness and emotional development
5. Expand legal services to (a) provide community-based criminal legal assistance to youth and adults charged with drugrelated offenses, (b) increase legal services in the city prison and county jail
6. Increase interagency communication to (a) increase the responsiveness of the San Francisco Coordinating Council on Drug Abuse to its drug abuse agencies, (b) develop program responsiveness to community needs through peer agency review, (c) develop a communitywide forum for the ongoing

discussion of a strategy to identify problems related to drug abuse and methods to solve these problems

7. Develop controls on mass media drug advertising that tends to promote chemical solutions for all problems
8. Provide for analysis of street drug samples and widely disseminate test results
9. Establish training programs for those providing drug abuse services
10. Expanded services for pregnant addicts

Realistic and achievable goals must be defined, and although goals may vary from community to community, uniform and common denominators could include (Senay and Renault, 1972):

1. Cessation of illegal drug abuse
2. Cessation of criminal activity associated with drug abuse
3. Obtaining gainful employment
4. Self-support and support for the family constellation
5. Reentry into the community and reestablishing community ties

To coordinate and implement a community program, an administrative staff must be employed. Depending on resources, administration may include:

1. Public health physicians and nurses
2. Epidemiologist
3. Special consultants
4. Program developer
5. Coordinator
6. Developer and supervisor of contracts
7. Public education unit
8. Referral unit
9. Public relations unit
10. Director of business affairs
11. Accountants
12. Personnel officer
13. Procurement officers
14. Data processing personnel
15. Researcher and research assistants
16. Program evaluators

Developing a Rational Plan

The planning process for local drug programs varies greatly with each community, depending on their sophistication and prior exposure to similar problems. A community under stress will eagerly welcome a drug abuse treatment program and define unrealistic goals for the agency. When the agency fails to eradicate all vestiges of the community's problem, it may lead to disillusionment and disappointment. Some communities perceive drug treatment agencies as magnets for addicts and respond with hostility. They oppose the arrival of a drug program and take their complaints to the local legislative body.

Legislative hearings serve as an excellent forum for educating the public (Le Dain, 1972). They are usually well attended by the press and are directed by citizens empowered to make the necessary legal changes in society's attitudes. Any individual charged with community planning for drug abuse prevention and treatment must make a concerted effort to participate in this legislative process. It may necessitate frequent trips to the legislative body, admittedly an inconvenience, but certainly a worthwhile endeavor. Although legislative members seldom understand or recognize the complexity of drug problems, most of them seem eager for education. Frequently, the outcome of this educational process is informed, compassionate, and meaningful legislation.

A more insidious form of destructive behavior occurs in the so-called sophisticated community where everyone agrees that addict treatment is necessary, but not in their neighborhood. Benevolently, they agree wholeheartedly with the treatment concept and are eager to place treatment centers *on the other side of town*. The planner is faced with a critical decision: Would it be better to quietly open a drug treatment center in their neighborhood, thus risking public indignation and a flight afterward, or attempt community education and enlightenment prior to the establishment of the program? The risk in the latter approach is that the program may be prevented from opening by community antagonism, ignorance, and misunderstanding (Coon, 1969).

The program planner must sell his program to the public. He is often placed in the position of making promises to the community, promises of diminished criminal behavior, increased employment, decreased welfare rolls, and greater human productivity. Salesmanship requires active politicking, utilizing all means of media exposure. Merely appealing to the benevolent nature of the public, hoping that support for the program will be forthcoming for altruistic reasons, is self-deluding. The general public's concerns relate to their own personal safety, preservation of their material possessions, and decreased tax payments. If a program can relate to one or more of these areas, it will certainly receive substantial public support.

Another method used to influence public reaction and activity is to produce supporting statistics. Such statistics are initially sought to substantiate the size of the drug abuse problem before any program can be planned. Many program administrators guess at a figure. There are means of more accurately estimating the addict population (Hughes and Jaffe, 1971). First, an estimate of the number of addicts in a geographic area should be made in comparison with the total population (Nurco *et al.*, 1971). This should be done not only for narcotics, but also for other depressants, stimulants, and hallucinogens. These estimates are difficult to determine, but they can be made by surveying local medical and hospital authorities. The number of reported cases of actual drug addiction can be culled from medical records. Medical conditions secondary to drug abuse may also be surveyed in hospital records. In addition to a community-wide survey of hospitals, physicians, and medical societies, drug-related deaths can be supplied by the coroner's office.

Law enforcement agency data can be used as an indirect measurement of the problem's magnitude. The number of drug arrests and convictions may yield relative answers. Figures should be obtained on burglaries involving physicians' and dentists' offices and cars, pharmacies, hospitals, and pharmaceutical warehouses. The police keep records that include the number of cases of illegal possession and sale of narcotics and other dangerous substances. Federal, state, and local law enforcement agencies may also have valuable information as to the scope of the problem.

Survey the community's active drug treatment programs for the number of addicts currently in treatment, the number presently on waiting lists, and their estimate of the number either unable or unwilling to seek treatment. New surveying techniques using sophisticated statistical analysis can yield highly accurate estimates of the number of addicts in a community. Such a method is being developed in our program by the Director of Evaluation (Earl and Wolter, 1973). It can be shown that the estimation of the size of a (sub)population whose members are inaccessible to conventional random sampling procedures may be achieved by sampling in a manner that imposes upon the sample(s) properties that are a function of the population size to be estimated. These properties are then utilized to estimate the population size in question.

The method of "trapping by lots" is a random sampling technique that overcomes classical estimation difficulties in determining prevalence by:

1. Guaranteeing the anonymity of the addict
2. Employing very large samples and stratified sampling procedures
3. Employing a cross-validated drug jargon questionnaire to screen out nonaddicts posing as addicts
4. Imposing properties upon the samples that are a function of the parameters to be estimated

Once the size of the population is estimated, the available service resources must be determined through an exhaustive survey. Before developing new programs, efforts must be made to utilize existing services, and, if necessary, redirect existing agency priorities to meet the needs of the newly identified service population. If existing services are not sufficient, new services should be developed, based on priorities established with community input.

Since the public has come to depend on polls, surveys, and statistics as gospel truth, these unsubstantiated "facts" may well contaminate solicited community input. As any scientist knows, statistics can substantiate any desired result. Furthermore, when they are printed, they are accepted as fact. Bureaucracies often use "statistics," "facts," and other "scientific data" to support their program and expenditures.

Obstacles and Pitfalls

The planner, attempting to make rational decisions in this totally irrational endeavor, will be faced with numerous obstacles and pitfalls. An entire book could be written on the administrative intricacies and maneuverings involved in implementing a comprehensive drug program. We will attempt to elucidate a few of these major stumbling blocks, including press relations, ethnicity, funding, contracts, and subcontracts.

PRESS RELATIONS

The press should never be overlooked as a means of obtaining a public forum. Although the press endeavors to create sensational stories that sell copy, most reporters have an honest sense of curiosity and an eagerness to provide the truth to their readers. The planner or planning agency should never pass over an opportunity to meet with the press and describe their endeavor. Although not often possible, the right of editorial review might ensure that facts are conveyed accurately to the reader. While few drug abusers actually read traditional periodicals, their parents do. It is just as important to educate parents as it is to educate the drug abuser himself.

Before engaging in media saturation with educational programs, the planners and programmers must decide what population they are attempting to reach. Obviously, if the intent is to reach a group speaking a foreign language, there is no point in putting public information spots on traditional English-language radio. Educational programming should be translated into as many languages as possible. Every foreign-language station should be encouraged to broadcast public information messages in their native tongue. Often media exposure can be obtained at no cost. Federal law requires that radio and television stations carry a certain number of public service and "free speech" announcements. These should be factual and carefully presented in a meaningful and interesting manner.

When attempting to reach youth in counterculture groups, the media campaigns should be geared to their radio stations, underground newspapers, and magazines (Judd and Mandell, 1972). Often spot announcements on "rock" stations reach a far greater audience than the local newspapers, and the message should be geared to the listener's interests. Another approach we are investigating is displaying short drug abuse information films in selected community movie theaters. These films will either be displayed immediately preceding or immediately following the feature film. With wide enough distribution, most members of the community will be exposed to these informational messages.

Every large urban center supports a cadre of newspapers reflecting the composition of ethnic minority groups. In San Francisco, numerous Chinese-language newspapers illustrate that several hundred thousand Bay Area residents speak Chinese as a primary or secondary language. When minority populations reach a size large enough to support two or more papers, these papers reflect different political or social philosophies. The Spanish-speaking community has several newspapers published in the Bay Area. Black newspapers and radio stations reflect the ethnic consciousness of this racial minority group. Since drug problems are a major concern of minority groups, their newspapers will give excellent coverage and exposure to drug issues.

ETHNICITY

Interpretation of "minority" is important, and careful judgment should be used to describe a specific minority, whether racial, ethnic, poverty, political, or geographic. Another crucial question is: Who is the minority group's spokesman? Numerous factions exist, and often no one person can speak for the entire group. Spokesmen reflect their own personal opinions and are unable to speak for other members of the group. Unfortunately, we are frequently distracted by the loud rhetoric of militant, outspoken members of a group. They espouse the sentiments of only a few. The planner should be well versed in the mechanics of community politics and not be led astray by radical fringe elements. Planners are often caught in the cross fire between the militant left and the reactionary right.

After careful assessment, the planner begins negotiating the development of services and the implementation of a program. As soon as the plan is completed, other groups appear and insist that this plan is not responsive to their needs. Furthermore, they charge that they were not consulted in the planning process. The planner then accedes to their demands and begins the arduous and tedious planning process again. Since no plan will ever satisfy all elements in any community, rational planning seems impossible.

Several nonviable courses of action may result. In total frustration, the plan may be discarded. More significantly, the *community* and its needs may be deserted. The politician, unable to ascertain which group, agency, or community to support, avoids making a decision and does nothing but make conflicting promises.

Another pitfall exists in the cultivation of "ethnic consciousness." We are told that by encouraging ethnic consciousness, group self-reliance, and recognition of cultural differences, we bring about a meaningful identity to oppressed populations. Fostering these differences is divisive and does not allow the community to coalesce in a common cause. By encouraging minority differences, we reinforce the myth that whites are unable to help or understand blacks; blacks are unable to relate to the Chinese; and the Chinese are incapable of comprehending the problems of whites. By erecting racial and ethnic barriers, we have effectively cut off communication between community groups.

It is necessary to recognize that cultural factors directly affect treatment outcome, and we must learn to appreciate the cultural influences upon human behavior. Therapist and patient should mutually and jointly share in the problem of communication. Both should share and exchange value systems with the expectation that, for the patient, higher orders of organization will evolve. The patient can utilize the therapist as a role model for effecting change in his behavior (Hsu and Tseng, 1972).

Staffs delivering health care services should reflect the ethnic composition of the communities they serve. The Chinese immigrant unable to speak English avoids traditional sources of medical treatment and experiences anxiety when dealing with middle-class whites who cannot comprehend ethnic and cultural differences. Recruiting a Chinese treatment team, when possible, is the most meaningful way to reach them.

In theory this is an excellent ideal. In our experience, however, we have had significant difficulty recruiting qualified ethnic minorities. Difficulties encountered include the lack of traditional education, clinical skills, and facility in the use of English. These characteristics are impediments to passing Civil Service examinations. Many programs have sought to liberate themselves from traditional government control by establishing a nonprofit corporation or foundation. This facilitates a significant degree of employment flexibility. Indigenous people can be given job credits for street experience, facility in a foreign language, or special job skills outside the realm of Civil Service requirements.

Our greatest difficulty occurred in hiring minority professionals. Their services are in such demand that they can literally name their own salary. The lure of private practice offers significantly more than the limited benefits of government service. Public servants seldom earn salaries commensurate with those who are employed in private practice and industry. Many of these professionals have struggled all their lives to be liberated from poverty and the ghetto and are reluctant to return to them.

We have attempted to maintain an ethnic ratio that reflects the community composition immediately adjacent to our treatment facility. After congratulating ourselves on our ability to hire substantial numbers of minority peoples, we were attacked by Caucasian community members who accused us of reverse discrimination. "No employee may be discriminated against on the basis of race, creed, or national origin." Now caught in a bind, we are faced with an impossible choice. If we select employees from traditional Civil Service examination lists, our staffs will reflect a middle-class, college-educated Caucasian majority, subject to the community criticism of being "lily white." Reserving positions for minorities involves reverse racism and violates civil rights.

THE ISSUE OF CONFIDENTIALITY

All treatment agencies are extremely concerned about the issue of patient record confidentiality. Grass-root private agencies are exquisitely sensitive in this area. They firmly believe that their clients would not utilize necessary medical services if there were any possibility of breaking record confidentiality. Counterculture groups abhor computerization and fear that their clients, once labeled, may be susceptible to future repressive government efforts and indiscriminate incarceration. Although their fears initially appeared irrational, recent events have reenforced their predictive powers (Buckley, 1970). Several government leaders are calling for lifetime incarceration of "drug pushers."

Many community-based agencies advertise that they keep no records and any attempt to enforce a patient tracking system meets with total opposition. The addicts themselves fear that any breach of confidentiality may lead to their incarceration for past criminal activities. It is a widely held belief that free services with "no strings" encourage addicts to seek help.

Recognizing the complexity of these issues, Section 408 of the Drug Abuse Office and Treatment Act of 1972 (21 U.S.C., 1175) mandates protection of drug abuse patient records. The rationale underlying the policy of Section 408 is simple and compelling:

Drug abuse in our society, at least with heroin, inevitably involves unlawful possession of drugs as a minimum criminal complication, and the very high cost of the heroin required to maintain a full-blown habit leads in many instances to a pattern of crimes against property. Socially, there is no more crushing stigma than to be known as a "junkie." If society is to make significant progress in the struggle against drug abuse, it is imperative that all unnecessary impediments to voluntary treatment be removed. There is clear agreement among drug abuse treatment program operators that their ability to assure patients and prospective patients of anonymity is essential to the success of their program. The identification of a person as a patient of a general practitioner or hospital clinic is not ordinarily of great significance, but the identification of a person as an enrollee in a narcotic treatment program can, in and of itself, have profoundly adverse consequences.

Law enforcement agencies are totally unable to comprehend how drug abuse can be controlled, or treatment yield success, without adequate records, addict registries, and computerized patient tracking systems. Accepting federal money requires that fiscal accountability be assured, that adequate medical records exist, and that tracking systems be developed to ensure unduplicated services. Any community seeking public funding must recognize that indigenous agency distrust and suspicion will be reawakened during the implementation of a federally funded drug treatment program.

Many meetings must be held with these community-based treatment agencies to reassure them on reporting requirements. We developed a compromise solution that was feasible, although it did not meet with everyone's satisfaction. No patient would be identified by name. Instead, each would be assigned a sequential number from our Central Referral office. This number is used throughout the tracking system and represents the unique identifier in the data system. The code matching client name and number is maintained by the community agency, and when referrals are made to other agencies, only the number is utilized in all communications and correspondence.

The test of credibility will occur early in the development of a program. As if it were staged, some law enforcement agent will demand confidential client information and all community attention will be trained on the drug treatment program. If a breach of confidentiality occurs, all credibility is lost.

FUNDING

Early in our program's growth, we utilized the voluntary services of the San Francisco Advertising Club to create public awareness and recognition of our drug abuse curbing efforts. At no cost to us, the Advertising Club developed a community-wide fund appeal. Some donations were forthcoming, but unfortunately they were small and infrequent. A full-page advertisement in *Newsweek* magazine distributed to several thousand homes in the Bay Area failed to develop more than a few hundred dollars in contributions. We were also able to secure over 100 huge billboards throughout the city, describing our needs and requesting donations to "Check Heroin." We received a few checks from families who had experienced a drug abuse crisis; e.g., the mother of a deceased young black girl who had overdosed with heroin, sent us a contribution to honor her memory. Several clubs also donated graciously.

Although efforts to raise cash through billboards, magazine ads, streetcar displays, and radio-TV appeals yielded less than $2000, the advertising served to dramatize our financial needs and educated the public as to the significance of the drug problem in our community. It also mobilized citizen action, and local political leaders were encouraged to provide financial support.

Since every community is determined to reduce street crime, we linked crime reduction to treatment program expansion. Tax savings, lower insurance premiums, and safer streets were the stated benefits of increased treatment activity. Care should be exercised so that in the effort to "sell" a program unrealistic promises are not made. The program's reputation may be the only asset an addict has in obtaining community acceptance and employment.

Pilot studies were funded with existing resources obtained from internal program priority shifts. When a project showed merit, we sought public support for additional funds. Since most politicians are loath to spend money on addicts, human resource planners are well advised to demonstrate the cost benefits of a new program.

Community foundations may be very helpful in bridging financial gaps. They may supply the starting power for a new project or new community need. Once established and operative, larger and more stable forms of funding may be sought.

Most federal treatment funds are provided by the National Institute of Mental Health, Narcotics Addiction Rehabilitation Branch. Five grant mechanisms exist which are summarized in Table III. The Drug Abuse Service Project provides funds for staff and operating expenses. Comprehensive Treatment Center grants only provide support for professional and technical salaries. Initiation and Development Projects provide a maximum of $50,000 to develop a comprehensive community plan and grant application. The Demonstration and Survey Projects grant is awarded to administer new, effective treatment modalities. The new Special Treatment Projects grant provides federal support for total program operation in an effort to expand existing treatment capability and is under the direction of the Special Action Office for Drug Abuse Prevention.

CONTRACTS AND SUBCONTRACTS

It was our intention to employ and expand all existing community-based treatment agencies rather than create new publicly operated treatment programs that would actively compete with private agencies for limited funding. We encouraged many private groups to develop treatment proposals and submit them to our agency for future funding.

We negotiated fee-for-service contracts at agreed upon fixed rates. For each service rendered, the contractor bills our agency. The fee-for-service contract stimulates an agency to provide maximum service. The more service units provided, the larger the payments received. However, there are hazards. Unless the subcontractor is capable of accepting a full patient load on the first day of contract operation, he will find himself with insufficient income to pay his expenses. This obstacle may be partially resolved by providing "front money," an advance payment equal to approximately 2 month (one-sixth) of the total contract yearly allowance. The advance can be utilized to make down payments on property, to purchase insurance

Table III

Selected Principles Governing Drug Abuse Grant Projects [a]

Program Name	Drug Abuse Services Projects (Treatment H80)	Comprehensive Treatment Centers (Treatment H19)
Legislative basis	CMHC Act, Part D, Section 256 as added by P.L.91-513	CMHC Act, Part D, Section 251 as amended by P.L.90-574, P.L.91-211, and P.L.91-513
Legislative and management requirements	Must be public or private non-profit agency	Must be public or private non-profit agency
Applicant eligibility and other legislative requirements reviewed by program and management staffs and Ad Hoc Review Committee, as appropriate	Provides federal support for % of total operations costs	Provides federal support for professional and technical salaries only
	Matching funds are required	Matching funds are required
	Provides for 8-year support	Provides for 8-year support
	No federal funding maximum	No federal funding maximum
	Provides advantageous federal funding support for poverty areas	Provides advantageous federal funding support for poverty areas
	Service to be provided narcotic addicts and other drug-dependent persons	Service to be provided narcotic addicts and other drug-dependent persons
	Applications submitted through state for comments	Application submitted to state for comments
	Grants awarded in accordance with criteria designed to provide priority to states or areas within states having the higher percentages of population who are drug abusers	Grants awarded for provision of comprehensive services in one or more CMHC catchment areas
		—
	Projects to provide treatment only through detoxification services and/or institutional services and/or community aftercare services	—
	By administrative determination federal funds may be used only to supplement the level of state or local effort and may not replace non-federal-funding support	Federal funds may be used only to supplement the level of state or local effort and may not replace non-federal funding support
Program requirements Program proposals required by program staff and Ad Hoc Review Committee	One or more of the 3 treatment services as indicated under legislative requirement above	Five essential services: emergency; inpatient; intermediate care; outpatient; community consultation and education

Initiation and Development Projects (Planning) D20	Demonstration and Survey Projects (may include Treatment Service) H81	Special Treatment Projects (Treatment) Tentative as of 11/13/72
CMHC Act, Part D, Section 261c as added by P.L.91-211	CMHC Act, Part D, Section 252c and d, as added by P.L.90-574 and P.L.91-211	Drug Abuse Office and Treatment Act, Section 223 and 410 (P.L.92-255)
Must be public or private agency	Must be public or private agency	Must be public or private agency
Provides federal support for total operations cost	Provides federal support for total operations cost	Provides federal support for total operations cost
Matching funds are not required	Matching funds administratively required	Matching funds administratively required
Provides 1-year support	Support administratively limited to 5 years	Support administratively limited to 8 years
Maximum federal support of $50,000	No federal funding maximum	No federal funding maximum
Up to 100% federal support for all projects	—	Advantageous federal support for poverty areas administratively authorized
Not a service program	Treatment service may be provided drug abusers	Service to be provided drug abusers
Maximum use must be made of qualified professional persons in the community	—	—
Preliminary plans and protocols for the project must demonstrate sound methodology and provide reasonable assurance that a viable treatment program proposal, including financial support, will be developed at the conclusion of the project, if such a proposal is determined to be warranted	— — —	Provisions must be made for referral of patients to other agencies, as appropriate. Provision must be made for continuity of care. Services must be available on a 24 hour a day basis, where required
Projects are encouraged in accordance with treatment need priorities	—	Projects are to be located in areas consistent with the Legislative Requirements above
—	—	—
Application submitted to state for comments.	Application submitted to state for comments	Application submitted to state for comments

Table III (cont.)

Table III (cont.)

Program Name	Drug Abuse Services Projects (Treatment H80)	Comprehensive Treatment Centers (Treatment H19)
		—
	—	Other optional services may be funded
	Provision must be made for referral of patients to other service agencies, as appropriate	Provision must be made for referral of patients to other service agencies, as appropriate
	Provision must be made for continuity of care	Provision must be made for continuity of care
	Services must be available on a 24 hour a day basis, where required	Services must be available on a 24 hour a day basis, where required
	Projects to be located in areas as indicated under Legislative Requirements above	Projects to be located in areas with a high civil commitment rate under NARA, a high prevalence of drug abusers, and few, if any, treatment facilities
	—	The services, or parts of services, to be funded must be new or reflect a new method of delivery not used before in the community
	The use of methadone in the treatment program must be in accordance with the regulations of the FDA and BNDD and the guidelines of NIMH	The use of methadone in the treatment program must be in accordance with the regulations of the FDA and BNDD and the guidelines of NIMH
	The rights and welfare of the patient must be protected in accordance with laws of the community, and, where appropriate, through the utilization of groups composed of competent professionals convened to resolve ethical or related issues	The rights and welfare of the patient must be protected in accordance with laws of the community, and, where appropriate, through the utilization of groups composed of competent professionals, convened to resolve ethical or related issues
	Confidentiality of patient records must be maintained	Confidentiality of patient records must be maintained
	Community participation must be obtained to the greatest extent possible	Community participation must be obtained to the greatest extent possible
	The geographic area to be served must be established on a reasonable basis	The geographic area to be served must be established on a reasonable basis and is catchment area related

Initiation and Development Projects (Planning) D20	Demonstration and Survey Projects (may include Treatment Service) H81	Special Treatment Projects (Treatment) Tentative as of 11/13/72
Treatment service area to be defined during course of project	Grants awarded to demonstrate new or relatively effective or efficient treatment methods and to survey adequacy of existing programs to determine ways to improve, extend, or expand them without regard to service area requirements	Grants awarded under Section 223 may either parallel Part D, Section 252 authorities or supplement or expand treatment capability where there is an exceptional need or where existing programs are determined to be exceptionally effective or determined by SAODAP. Section 410 authorizes treatment grants without qualification. Service area must be appropriately defined in accordance with administrative requirements. By administrative determination federal funds may be used only to supplement the level of state or local effort and may not replace non-federal funding support
—	—	
—		
—	—	
Assessment of need for treatment programs must be based upon sound community survey techniques and procedures	Services may be provided which are compatible with the project design and assure sound treatment for those patients enrolled in the project	Treatment projects must provide comprehensive services where no services exist or fill the gaps in existing networks of service
—	—	—
—	—	—
—	—	—
Community participation must be obtained to the greatest extent possible	—	Community participation must be obtained to the greatest extent possible
The planning area must be established on a reasonable basis and is catchment area related	—	The geographic area to be served must be established on a reasonable basis

Table III (cont.)

Table III (cont.)

Program Name	Drug Abuse Services Projects (Treatment H80)	Comprehensive Treatment Centers (Treatment H19)
	Innovative treatment methods consistent with sound medical practice are encouraged	Innovative treatment methods consistent with sound medical practice are encouraged
	Program evaluation may be funded	Evaluative research may be funded
	Affiliation agreements and other contracts must be properly established and executed	Affiliation agreements and other contracts must be properly established and executed
	Persons indigenous to the community, including ex-addicts, should be used to the greatest extent possible	Persons indigenous to the community, including ex-addicts, should be used to the greatest extent possible
	Inservice training must be provided	Inservice training must be provided
	Services may not be denied on the basis of ability to pay. Fees may be charged when possible	Services may not be denied on the basis of ability to pay. Fees may be charged when possible
	Model Cities endorsement must be obtained, where necessary	Model Cities endorsement must be obtained, where necessary
	Community resource analysis required	Community resource analysis required
	Program-Budget Matrix analysis required including adherence to cost guideposts or acceptable justification of deviations	Program-Budget Matrix analysis required including adherence to cost guideposts or acceptable justification of deviations
	Grant award contingent upon decision as to relative need when compared to needs of other communities	Grant award contingent upon decision as to relative need when compared to needs of other communities

[a] Funded under Narcotic Addiction Rehabilitation Branch, National Institute of Mental Health.

and equipment and to provide money for training and other start-up costs. In addition, it is utilized to pay salaries until the first regular contract payment is made. The advance is reimbursed to our agency on a pro rata basis in equal, deductible installments over the remaining course of the contract life.

In our attempt to ensure quality service and fiscal accountability, we carefully defined various units of service and their fee equivalent. The contracts were developed to ensure clinical responsiveness and adequate professional supervision.

Initiation and Development Projects (Planning) D20	Demonstration and Survey Projects (may include Treatment Service) H81	Special Treatment Projects (Treatment) Tentative as of 11/13/72
Innovative treatment methods consistent with sound medical practice are encouraged	—	Innovative treatment methods consistent with sound medical practice are encouraged
—	—	Program evaluation may be funded
Affiliation agreements and other contracts must be properly established and executed	Affiliation agreements and other contracts must be properly established and executed	Affiliation agreements and other contracts must be properly established and executed
Persons indigenous to the community, including ex-addicts, should be used to the greatest extent possible	—	Persons indigenous to the community, including ex-addicts, should be used to the greatest extent possible
—	—	Inservice training must be provided
—	—	Services may not be denied on the basis of ability to pay. Fees may be charged when possible
Model Cities endorsement must be obtained, where necessary	—	Model Cities endorsement must be obtained, where necessary
—	—	Community resource analysis required
—	Program-Budget Matrix analysis required including adherence to cost guideposts or acceptable justification of deviations	Program-Budget Matrix analysis required including adherence to cost guideposts or acceptable justification of deviations
Grant award contingent upon decision as to relative need when compared to needs of other communities	—	Grant award contingent upon decision as to relative need when compared to needs of other communities

Some of our contract requirements included:

Proposed program and staff description
Description of professional supervision
Acceptance of technical assistance
Periodic evaluation of staff performance
In-service training
Evaluation of services, goals, and treatment
Provision for data collection
Protection of confidentiality

Description of program administration
Cost-benefit relationships
Participation in the Central Referral system
Participation in the Evaluation Unit's patient tracking system
Adhering to local housing codes
Provision of proper liability and malpractice insurance
Required facility maintenance
Descriptive line-item budgets
Proper bookkeeping and audit trails
Independent audits
Description of reimbursement rate for services rendered
Requirement regarding nondiscriminatory hiring practices
Conditions of contract cancellation

If contracts remain nonspecific and general in their content, it is a disservice to the community-based program and to the funding agency. Only by specifying each and every requirement within the contract can we anticipate fulfillment of our expectations. The more specific the contract, the less likely the possibility of misunderstandings, arguments, accusations, alienation, and communication breakdown. Although contract specificity may to some degree limit flexibility of treatment approach, our experience has shown that the agencies most capable of meeting our high expectations were best equipped to provide the desired services.

Flat rate fee-for-service contracts may not provide adequate funds for actual operating costs. For example, during the start-up period of a new program, expenditures may exceed income. Costs incurred during the early treatment process are disproportionately high, since they include initial laboratory studies, physical examinations, extensive histories, treatment planning, and intensive professional supervision. The greatest rate of treatment failure and dropout occurs immediately following the period of greatest energy and fund expenditure. Several of our agencies have complained that their costs far exceeded revenues and have requested renegotiation of their contracts. It was their wish to be paid a higher fee that more accurately reflected actual expenditures, early in the treatment course.

Conclusion

Rational planning for drug abuse is a frustrating, thankless, and exhausting experience. The planner is continuously subjected to vicious attacks by the community, his clients, his staff, politicians, and the media. The entire field of drug abuse is submerged in irrationality, hysteria, and political rhetoric. Competitiveness, jealousies, and rivalries abound. Today's hero is tomorrow's scapegoat. Drawn to this endeavor are a number of highly dedicated, energetic, and idealistic individuals, who find that achieving success is also fraught with danger. Drug treatment programs define their goals as reducing the incidence and prevalence of drug abuse and diminishing human suffering. If the planner is successful, the crisis will cool, public interest will wane, funds will cease to flow, and finally, his program will terminate. Perhaps the only consolation comes from the knowledge that needy, disenfranchised, alienated, and suffering human beings have come closer to reaching their full human potential.

References

Black, P., ed. (1969). "Drugs and the Brain." Johns Hopkins Press, Baltimore, Maryland.

Bowden, D. L., and Langenauer, B. J. (1972). Success and failure in the NARA addiction program. *Amer. J. Psychiat.* **128**, 568–572.

Buckley, W. F. (1970). No knock. *Nat. Rev.* **22**, 220.

California Medical Association, Bureau of Research and Planning (1972). Free clinics in California. *Calif. Med.*, **116**, 106–111.

Chien, I., Gerald, D. L., Lee, R. S., and Rosenfeld, E. (1964). "The Road to H." Basic Books, New York.

Coon, C. (1969). Drug dependency—a community responsibility. *Community Health* **1**, 101–105.

Deedes, W. F. (1969). The politics of drug dependence. *Community Health* **1**, Sept./Oct., 90–94.

Deitch, D., and Casriel, D. (1967). The role of the ex-addict in treatment of addiction. *Federal Probation.*

DeLong, J. V. (1972). Treatment and rehabilitation. In "Dealing with Drug Abuse," p. 173. Praeger, New York.

Earl, R. W., and Wolter, D. G. (1973). Sampling methods in the estimation of drug abuse prevalence. In preparation.

Editorial (1971). Just who has copped out? ed. Hugh Hussey. *J. Amer. Med. Ass.* **216**, No. 4, 668–669.

Ehrenreich, B. (1971). New York City tries a new model. *Social Policy* **1**, No. 5, 25–34.

Einstein, S. (1970). Be careful: More than drugs are being sold (articles on prevention and control). *Int. J. Addict.* **5**, 593–594.

Flohr, R. B. (1972). The San Francisco school crash pad program. In "Drugs in Our Schools" (Hearings before the Select Committee on Crime, House of Representatives, Ninety-Second Congress, Second Session, San Francisco, California, Sept. 28–30; San Francisco, California), pp. 1580–1597. US Govt. Printing Office, Washington, D.C.

Flohr, R. B., and Lerner, S. E. (1971). Employment characteristics of heroin addicts in three treatment programs and employer attitudes. *J. Psychedelic Drugs* **4**, No. 2, 148–153.

Gay, G. R., Newmeyer, J. A., and Winkler, J. J. (1972). The Haight-Ashbury free medical clinic. *In* "It's So Good, Don't Every Try it Once" (D. E. Smith and G. R. Gay, eds.), p. 126. Prentice-Hall, Englewood Cliffs, New Jersey.

Glasscote, R. M., Sussex, J. N., Jaffe, J. H., Ball, J., and Brill, L. (1972). "The Treatment of Drug Abuse: Programs, Problems, Prospects." Joint Information Service of the American Psychiatric Association and the National Association for Mental Health, Washington, D.C.

Hall, A. L., and Bourne, P. J. (1973). Indigenous therapists in a southern black urban community. *Arch. Gen. Psychiat.* **28**, Issue 1, 137–142.

Hartke, V. (1972). The narcotics problem. *J. Drug Issues* **2**, No. 3.

Hearing. (1972). "To Establish A Special Action Office for Drug Abuse Prevention and to Concentrate the Resources of the Nation Against the Problem of Drug Abuse," Public Law 92–255, 92nd Congress, S. 2097. US Govt. Printing Office, Washington, D.C.

Hsu, J. and Tseng, W. S. (1972). Intercultural psychotherapy. *Arch. Gen. Psychiat.* **27**, No. 5, 700–705.

Hughes, P. H., and Jaffe, J. J. (1971). Heroin epidemic in Chicago. *Proc. World Congr. Psychiat., 1971.*

Hughes, P., Senay, E., and Parker, R. (1972). The medical management of a heroin epidemic. *Arch. Gen. Psychiat.*, **27**, No. 5, 585–594.

Jaffe, Jerome (1972). Available therapy: aim of opiate abuse plan. (Extracted from a talk.) *Hosp. Trib.* October 16.

Journal of the American Medical Association (1971). Just who has copped out? (Editorial). **216:**668–669.

Judd, L. L., and Mandell, A. J. (1972). A 'free clinic' patient population and drug use patterns. *Amer. J. Psychiat.* **128**, 1298–1302.

Kramer, J. C. (1972). A brief history of heroin addiction in America. *In* "It's So Good, Don't Even Try it Once" (D. E. Smith and G. R. Gay, eds.), pp. 32–44. Prentice-Hall, Englewood Cliffs, New Jersey.

Kramer, J. C., Bass, R. A., and Berocochea, J. E. (1968). Civil committment for addicts. The California program. *Amer. J. Psychiat.* **125**, 816–824.

Le Dain, G. (1972). Drugs and society; what can a public inquiry do? *Addictions* **19**, No. 2, 19–26.

Levy, B. S. (1972). Five years after: A follow-up of fifty narcotic addicts. *Amer. J. Psychiat.* **128**, 868–872.

Louria, D. B. (1972). "Overcoming Drugs: A Program For Action." Bantam Books, New York.

McMearn, J. H. (1972). Radical and racial perspectives on the heroin problem. *In* "It's So Good, Don't Even Try it Once" (D. E. Smith and G. R. Gay, eds.), pp. 119–124. Prentice-Hall, Englewood Cliffs, New Jersey.

Melinger, G. D. *et al.* (1972). Patterns of psychotherapeutic drug use among adults in San Francisco. *Arch. Gen. Psychiat.* **13**, 384–394.

Nurco, D. N. *et al.* (1971). The feasibility of locating addicts in the community. *Int. J. Addict.* **6**, 51–62.

O'Connor, G., Wurmser, L., Brown, T. C., and Smith, J. (1971). The drug addiction business. *In* "The Drug Abuse Centennial," Vol. 1, pp. 3–12.

O'Connor, G., Wurmser, L., Brown, T. C., and Smith, J. (1972). The economics of heroin addiction: A new interpretation of the facts. *In* "It's So Good, Don't Even Try it Once" (D. E. Smith and G. R. Gay, eds.), pp. 86–96. Prentice-Hall, Englewood Cliffs, New Jersey.

Passim (1972). Drug abuse not due to mis-prescribing, surveys show. *Geriatrics* **27**, 120.

Pekkanen, J. (1973). The President's drug fighter. *Hum. Behav.*

Preble, E., and Casey, J. J., Jr. (1972). Taking care of business: The heroin user's life. *In* "It's So Good, Don't Even Try it Once" (D. E. Smith and G. R. Gay, eds.), pp. 97–118. Prentice-Hall, Englewood Cliffs, New Jersey.

Ramer, B. S. (1972). Have We oversold methadone? *Proc. Nat. Conf. Methadone Treatment, 4th, 1972*, pp. 97–98.

Ramer, B. S., Zaslove, O. and Langan, J., (1971). Is methadone enough? The use of ancillary treatment during methadone maintenance. *Amer. J. Psychiat.* **127**, No. 8, 1040–1044.

Ramer, B. S., Smith, D. E., and Gay, G. R. (1972). Adolescent heroin abuse in San Francisco. *Int. J. Addict.* **7**, 461–465.

Rosen, S. M. (1971). Change and resistance to change. *Social Policy* **1**, No. 5, 3–4.

Scientific American (1970). Addiction, medicine, and the law. (Editorial) **223**:50.

Senay, E. C., and Renault, P. F. (1972). Treatment methods for heroin addicts: A review. In "It's So Good, Don't Even Try it Once" (D. E. Smith and G. R. Gay, eds.), pp. 148–163. Prentice-Hall, Englewood Cliffs, New Jersey.

Smith, D. E. and Gay, G. R., eds. (1972). "It's So Good, Don't Even Try it Once." Prentice-Hall, Englewood Cliffs, New Jersey.

Smith, D. E., and Luce, J. (1971). "Love Needs Care." Little, Brown, Boston, Massachusetts.

Stachnik, T. J. (1972). The case against criminal penalties for illicit drug use. *Amer. Psychol.* **27**, 637–642.

Szasz, T. S. (1972). The ethnics of addiction. *J. Drug Issues* **2**, No. 1, 1–42.

Time Magazine (1970). No knock drug bill. (Editorial.) **95**, 11–12.

Vaillant, G. E. (1966). Twelve-year follow-up of New York narcotic addicts. 1. The relation of treatment of outcome. *Amer. J. Psychiat.* **122**, 727–737.

Wald, P., and Hutt, P. B. (1972). The drug abuse survey project. In "Dealing with Drug Abuse" p. 21. Praeger, New York.

White, G. (1971). Hysteria, the cause of the drug craze. *Med. J. Aust.* **2**, 1257.

Winich, C. (1964). Drug addiction: Enforcement and/or treatment. *In* "Mass Society in Crisis" (B. Rosenberg, F. Gerver, and F. W. Howton, eds.), pp. 401–405. Macmillan, New York.

6

Beginning to Dissect
a Heroin Addiction Epidemic

ROBERT L. DUPONT
and
MARK H. GREENE

Millions of Americans think drug abuse is one of the nation's most serious domestic problems—ranking it ahead of inflation, unemployment, race, and poverty. President Nixon labeled it "public enemy number one." Reflecting this concern, major national, state, and local efforts are under way to deal with drug abuse, particularly heroin addiction, the most deadly form of drug abuse.

The District of Columbia's attack on heroin addiction began in February 1970 with the establishment of a large-scale treatment program, the Narcotics Treatment Administration (NTA). On January 5, 1973, more than 3800 people were in active treatment for addiction in Washington. On that date there were 25 treatment centers located throughout the city. Twenty of these centers treating 3400 patients were operated by the city. NTA spent at the rate of $7.5 million a year during 1972 and offered a full range of treatment opportunities to heroin addicts including methadone maintenance, detoxification, and drug-free programs in both residential and outpatient facilities. Over 13,000 of the city's heroin addicts were treated by NTA in the 2 years between 1970 and 1972 (DuPont and Katon, 1971; DuPont, 1971; DuPont and Piemme, 1971).

However, treatment is only part of the total approach to heroin addiction. Law enforcement has been in the forefront of this country's attempts to deal with addiction since the enactment of the Harrison Narcotics Act in 1914. Since then, these efforts have been targeted on the individual drug user because law enforcement agencies reported the number of drug arrests they made each year as the primary measure of their success. In recent years there has been a growing awareness by law enforcement officials that their most effective role does not involve any relationship with the individual addict. He is better handled by treatment programs. However, law enforcement does have a major role to play in reducing the supply of heroin through vigorous enforcement of laws against manufacture, importation, and distribution of heroin. In early 1972 the District of Columbia was selected for maximum impact of this new strategy, which was jointly handled by the Office of Drug Abuse Law Enforcement, the Bureau of Narcotics and Dangerous Drugs, and the Metropolitan Police Department.

Thus, in the District of Columbia, the new law enforcement strategy aimed at reducing the *supply* of heroin was combined with a treatment program aimed at decreasing the *demand* for heroin. Together, it was hoped, these approaches would end the heroin addiction epidemic in the city.

In addition, a major national and international effort was developed to prevent heroin availability in American cities. This ranged from a 1972 agreement by the Turkish government to stop cultivating poppies to the elimination of clandestine laboratories and the seizure of large quantities of heroin all over the world.

The efforts to reduce both the demand for and the supply of heroin reinforced an antiheroin cultural attitude, which emerged in 1971 and 1972 in the District of Columbia and other major cities. This attitude shift also reinforced the efforts of treatment and law enforcement.

Was this massive mobilization in the District of Columbia to provide treatment for heroin addicts and to reduce the supply of the drug a success or a failure? How can the available data be used to understand the progress, or lack of progress, in dealing with the heroin epidemic? It is obvious that counting addicts in treatment, or addicts arrested, or program dropout rates are not in themselves adequate measures. These indices are useful in following the course of a single individual, but they can be dangerously misleading when generalized to large, urban populations of heroin addicts.

Several specific examples will set the stage for an evaluation scheme based not solely on individual patient successes or failures but on an understanding of the epidemic characteristics of heroin addiction.

Case I

C.N. was a 19-year-old high school dropout who first entered a specialized NTA residential youth treatment program in 1970. He had been using heroin daily for 3 years with the exception of a 2-week period of incarceration in a juvenile detention facility 1 year before entering treatment. While in the treatment center he took methadone in low doses (up to 30 mg per day) for 6 months. He stayed with the program for a year and at the same time returned to high school to complete his junior year. After a year of residence he returned to heroin use and dropped out of the program. Six months later he was arrested for possession of heroin and sentenced to 2 years of probation on the condition that he return to treatment. He chose to come back to the same residential center and took decreasing doses of methadone for 3 months before becoming completely drug free. Six months after his return to the center he was asked why he had left the program and had returned to daily heroin use a year earlier. He said, "I don't know, I just felt under too much pressure at the house." He said he did not come back voluntarily because he would have had to wait 2 weeks after applying before he could get in. C.N. described his arrest as "the best thing that happened to me in the last year because it got me back into the program." He is now finishing his senior year of high school. Several times during the last year C.N. was frustrated and disappointed. He wanted to try heroin again but found it much less available and decided "it wasn't worth the trouble—and besides that stuff never really helped me."

Case II

R.S. was a 30-year-old man who had used heroin regularly for the last 12 years with the exception of 3 years he spent in prison on a robbery charge and 2 years he was in an NTA methadone maintenance program. He first entered treatment in 1970. He took methadone every day and stopped using heroin except on rare occasions. For the first 6 months of treatment he supported himself in the same way he had earlier supported his habit, by shoplifting. He was arrested and spent 60 days in prison awaiting trial before his charge was dropped. He returned to methadone treatment and got a job as a laborer with a construction firm. After a year of successful methadone maintenance he detoxified, became drug free over a 6-month period, and left the program abstinent. He was readdicted within a month and returned to methadone maintenance voluntarily after 2 months of active addiction. R.S. said, "I felt like I was a traitor to myself and to all black people when I used heroin—I was hurting everyone so I've quit it now forever."

Case III

T.B. was 18 when he entered the NTA program as an outpatient receiving daily doses of methadone. He detoxified over the course of a year of treatment and left the program. Three months later, he returned to treatment after again beginning heroin use. He was detoxified in 3 weeks and left the program again despite his counselor's attempt to persuade him to enter a residential treatment program. Four months later he was apparently doing well in a job that he liked. His parents said he never "looked or acted better" when he went out to a party with some friends. He was found dead from a heroin overdose the next morning in an alley. His friends said he shot up his usual dose of heroin. However, because his body then lacked tolerance to the drug, the dose was fatal.

These three stories, each slightly modified from actual case histories, are representative of literally thousands of unique personal experiences in the city during the last 3 years. They reveal the complex interaction of treatment programs, efforts to decrease the supply of heroin, and major attitude changes. Are these stories of success or failure? What can be learned from them about the city's heroin addiction epidemic?

Recognizing the dynamic nature of heroin use in a community, we have developed a model that is subject to quantitative study (see Fig. 1). It is based on the concept of a census of heroin users or, in the language of the public health physician, the point prevalance rate of heroin use. It is not designed to replace the earlier approaches to evaluation, but to extend them so that the problems of whole populations can be evaluated and treatment can be seen as one among many aspects of the solution to the problem of heroin addiction in a community. In these calculations, individuals who have used heroin less than 10 times in their lives are considered never to have been addicted and are included with "nonusers."

To make the model more easily understood, the date June 1, 1972, was picked for a hypothetical census. Some of the numbers in this census are based on actual count (e.g., the treatment figures and the District of Columbia population), some are based on reasonable estimations (e.g., the number of former users in the prisons and the number of active users in the community), and others are simply guesses (e.g., the number of former users in the community). On June 1, 1972, there were 4400 heroin users in treatment. Two thousand five hundred were in maintenance treatment, 1000 were in detoxification treatment, and 900 were in abstinence treatment. Other studies have shown that there were about 18,000 people in the District of Columbia who had used heroin regularly at some time during the last 5 years (DuPont and Piemme, 1973). Subtracting this user

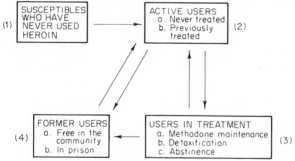

Fig. 1. A schematic model for analyzing the status of heroin abuse in the community.

figure from the total District of Columbia population of 751,500 leaves 733,500 people who have not used heroin (98%). Since 4400 of the 18,000 users were in treatment on June 1, 1972, a total of 24% were then in treatment. In addition, 2000 (11%) were estimated to be in prison on that day. It was also estimated that 4000 (22%) of the 18,000 users had not used heroin during at least the 2 weeks prior to June 1, 1972, and were at that point in time "former users in the community." Thus, 7500 (42%) of the city's recent heroin users were estimated to be actively using heroin on June 1, 1972.

The summer of 1972 was picked for this census because it was the period of peak demand for heroin addiction treatment in Washington, D.C. The following 7 months saw a progressive decline in the demand for treatment, which was part of the pattern of evidence indicating that the city's heroin addiction epidemic was ending (DuPont and Greene, 1973).

The entire District of Columbia population can be divided into four mutually exclusive categories on the basis of heroin use: (1) never used, (2) active users, (3) users in treatment, and (4) former users. The hypothetical totals for the four groups on June 1, 1972, were 733,500, 7500, 4400, and 6000. The categories can be further subdivided so that category 3 specifies those individuals in abstinence, detoxification, and maintenance treatment, and category 4 reflects the fact that some of the former users were in prison and some were free in the community. Category 2 can also be subdivided to show that some active users had received treatment for their addiction while others had never been treated.

These four basic categories can also be applied to the three case histories. Collectively over the last 5 years these three individuals spent 15.7% of their time in category 1, never used; 41.4% of their time in category 2, active users; 31.9% in category 3, users in treatment; and 11.9% in category 4, former users. All three began heroin use prior to the widespread availability of heroin addiction treatment in the District of Columbia. During the existence of NTA, these three individuals spent nearly two-thirds of the available time in active treatment and an additional 8% abstinent in the community. Thus, for these three individuals, the antiheroin efforts in the city succeeded in moving them from category 2 to categories 3 and 4 for about 70% of the available time. Expressed differently, the efforts failed to move these people either out of prison or active use for 30% of the available time. Prior to the availability of treatment, these three individuals would probably have spent virtually all of the last 2½ years either in prison or in active use (see Table I).

Using this design, it is possible to develop techniques to measure the point prevalence of the various states of heroin use in a community and, even more importantly, to assign social, economic, and personal costs and benefits to each state. It is also possible to develop rates of movement between the various categories and to subdivide the individuals in each of these global states for more precise analysis.

For example, it is possible to determine the annual rate of movement from the never used, to the active use. Similarly, this framework suggests some approaches to influencing the movement between categories.

For example, the movement from never used to active user will be slowed by a decrease in the availability of heroin, so that those individuals who are most likely to use heroin for the first time will not find it easily available. This is one of the areas where supply-reduction activity will have the greatest effect. It is also obvious that re-

Table I

Heroin Use during the Last Five Years: Case History Examples

Category	Case 1 (months)	Case 2 (months)	Case 3 (months)	Total (months)	Total as % of time in last 5 years
1. Never used	12	0	16.25	28.25	15.7
2. Active user					
a. Never in treatment	23.5	18	24	65.5	36.4
b. Formerly in treatment	6	2	1	9	5
3. Users in treatment					
a. Abstinence	9	0	0	9	5
b. Detoxification	9	6	12.75	27.75	15.4
c. Maintenance	0	19	0	19	10.5
4. Former users					
a. In the community	0	1	6	7	3.8
b. In prison	0.5	14	0	14.5	8.1
Total	60.0	60.0	60.0	180.00	99.9

ducing the number of active addicts, and the average amount of heroin used by them, will decrease the spread of their patterns of addictive behavior, as described by Hughes *et al.* (1972). Other, less obvious ways to reduce the rate of movement from nonuse to use include giving the susceptible nonuser more information about the dangers of heroin use, developing antiheroin cultural attitudes, and decreasing the psychological distress of the susceptible nonuser population.

The data available for the 13,000 people treated by NTA for heroin addiction shows that between 1966 and 1972 the number of new users each year was: 1966, 755; 1967, 1222; 1968, 2574; 1969, 2847; 1970, 1846; 1971, 741; 1972, 260. These data on incidence of heroin use are among the most convincing evidence that the heroin epidemic in Washington is ending (DuPont and Greene, 1973). See Fig. 2 for similar data on the incidence of new addiction.

More generally, it can be seen that society is attempting not only to reduce the movement from nonuse to use, but to shift the users out of category 2 and into either category 3 or 4. Much more needs to be learned about the relative costs and benefits associated with

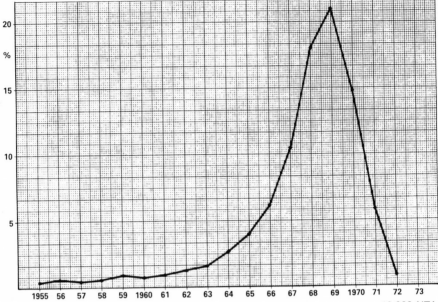

Fig. 2. Incidence of heroin addiction: year of first heroin use among 13,000 NTA patients.

membership in either of these two categories, but there is already ample evidence that the social cost in either category is far less than that associated with active heroin use.

Overdose deaths present a special problem. It appears that active users are less likely to overdose than are either nonusers or former users who do not have tolerance for opiate drugs. Individuals receiving daily doses of methadone have the lowest risk of dying from an overdose after they have taken methadone for a week or two and established tolerance. The nonusers who begin use may be frightened of the drug and therefore use relatively little. However, the former user who renews use after a period of abstinence may use a dose similar to what he used while previously addicted. Without tolerance, this previously benign dose can be fatal. Therefore, as the number of individuals in category 4, former users, increases, the number of overdoses may increase. Since this category has increased more rapidly than any other category in the District of Columbia in the last 2 years, it is possible that the rate of overdose deaths could increase even though the number of individuals actively using heroin decreased. This anticipated rise in overdose deaths would not occur, however, if the purity of heroin available on the street dropped sharply so that lethal doses were no longer available. This appears to have happened in the District of Columbia during the last half of 1972 when the heroin overdose death rate fell dramatically at the same time that large-dose packages (containing greater than 30 mg) of heroin virtually disappeared from the illicit market (DuPont and Greene, 1973).

Understanding the trends in overdose deaths is also complicated by the progressive improvement in the capacity to identify these deaths. Since July 1971, when the Medical Examiner's Office was established, the District of Columbia has had one of the most sophisticated systems for narcotic death investigations in the nation. Overdose deaths in the District of Columbia before July 1971 were undoubtedly greatly underreported.

Examining the deaths from July 1971 through December 1972 shows a progressive decline in heroin deaths from about 8 per month to a total of only 2 in the last 6 months of 1972. Methadone deaths showed a different pattern, peaking in January and February 1972 at about 7 per month and falling to about 3 per month by the end of 1972. The total overdose deaths in the city (including methadone, heroin, and deaths associated with both drugs) showed a progressive decline over this 18-month period. (See Fig. 3.)

The relationship between the rate of heroin use and the rate of

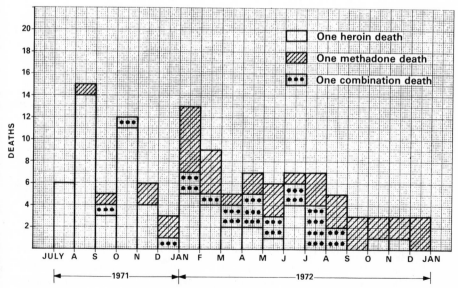

Fig. 3. Acute opiate overdose deaths in the District of Columbia from July 1971 to December 1972.

crime in the District of Columbia must also be considered specifically. The active users, category 2, account for the majority of the criminal activity of the heroin-using population (i.e., criminal activity is the exception in categories 3 and 4, while it is a daily necessity for individuals in category 2). This group, the active users of heroin, probably committed as much as 75% of the total serious crime in the District of Columbia during the peak of the heroin epidemic in 1969. The rate of heroin-connected crime in an area is related to the amount of money needed to support the addicts' habits. Prior to the introduction of widespread treatment, the active addict in the District of Columbia had almost no alternative but to continue to escalate his heroin use until he was hospitalized or incarcerated. Today, with ready access to treatment, when an individual addict finds that his habit is too great he can enter treatment and eliminate his need for heroin. This has profound social benefit in terms of decreased criminal activity.

The rate of reported serious crime (murder, rape, robbery, aggravated assault, burglary, larceny over $50, and auto theft) has progressively declined in Washington from a peak daily average of 202 in November 1969 to 94 in December 1972. (See Fig. 4.) This parallels the decline in both the incidence (rate of creation of new users) and prevalence (total number of active users) of heroin addiction in the District of Columbia over the same time frame. (See Fig. 2.)

Using this public health analytical framework, what changes occurred in the District of Columbia in association with the introduction of treatment on a relatively massive scale and the more recently launched law enforcement effort? What will be the likely state of heroin use in the city in the summer of 1974? (See Table II.)

The estimates for 1968 represent an early state in the city's heroin addiction epidemic, which began in 1966 and peaked in early 1970. January 1970 was selected because it was an early point in the treatment mobilization. June 1972 represented the peak of treatment activity.

The epidemic declined dramatically during the last half of 1972. Assuming that this downward trend continues, it can be anticipated that by 1974 the heroin epidemic in the city will be over.

The most striking changes from January 1970 to June 1972 were the relatively small increase in the number of total users (16,100 to 17,900), the sharp rise in the number of people in treatment (from 120 to 4400), the large increase in the number of individuals who were former users in the community (2000 to 4000), and the drop in the number of active users (14,000 to 7500). These shifts were associated with a sharp drop in the crime rate, and a decrease in the enlistment of new addicts.

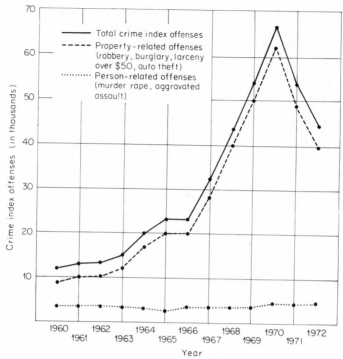

Fig. 4. Crime-index offenses in Washington, D.C. from 1960 to 1972. (From the District of Columbia Metropolitan Police Department.)

Table II

Estimate of Population Changes in Heroin Use in the District of Columbia, 1968–1974

Category	July 1, 1968	Jan. 1, 1970	June 1, 1972	July 1, 1974
1. Never used	740,500	735,500	733,600	733,200
2. Active users				
a. Never in treatment	9,000	12,000	4,000	100
b. Formerly in treatment	0	0	3,500	300
3. Users in treatment				
a. Abstinence	0	20	900	200
b. Detoxification	0	50	1,000	200
c. Maintenance	0	50	2,500	1,000
4. Former users				
a. In the community	1,000	2,000	4,000	15,700
b. In prison	1,000	2,000	2,000	500
Total users in the previous 5 years	11,000	16,100	17,900	18,300

The projection to the summer of 1974 calls for an even more dramatic decrease in the number of active users (7500 to 400), a decrease in the number of individuals in treatment (4500 to 1400), and a large increase in the number of former users in the community (from 4000 to 15,700). This should be associated with a further drop in the crime rate and the rate of new addiction.

Although many of the numbers presented in this preliminary analysis are based on educated guesses rather than empirical evidence, they suggest the data that will be needed before it will be possible to determine whether the current combined treatment and law enforcement approach to urban heroin addiction is succeeding.

Until hard data covering entire urban populations are available to those of us working in this field, we must rely on our everyday experiences with individual heroin users. These experiences, and the fragments of data now available, strongly suggest that success (as measured by a sharp drop in both the number of untreated heroin users, and in the rate of creation of new addicts) has been achieved in the District of Columbia. Until absolutely convincing data are available, however, we will also endure the chaotic ups and downs of headlines and investigative reports that are based on the often misleading results of glimpses of the problem of dealing with the urban heroin addiction epidemic in America.

References

DuPont, R. L. (1971). Profile of a heroin addiction epidemic and an initial treatment response. *New Eng. J. Med.* **285**, 320–324.

DuPont, R. L., and Greene, M. H. (1973). Monitoring a heroin addiction epidemic—the decline of heroin abuse in Washington, D.C. *Science* **181**, 716–722.

DuPont, R. L., and Katon, R. N. (1971). Urban crime and the rapid development of a large heroin addiction treatment program. *J. Amer. Med. Ass.* **216**, 1320–1324.

DuPont, R. L., and Piemme, T. E. (1971). Evolution of an urban heroin epidemic and influence of a drug treatment program. *Clin. Res.* **29**, 573–576.

DuPont, R. L., and Piemme, T. E. (1973). Estimation of the number of addicts in an urban area. *Med. Ann. D. C.* **42**, 323–326.

Hughes, P. H., Senay, E. C., and Parker, R. (1972). The medical management of a heroin epidemic. *Arch. Gen. Psychiat.* **27**, 585–591.

7

Involuntary Treatment
of Drug Addiction

ROBERT G. NEWMAN

One weapon against today's narcotics "epidemic": Lock up drug
users while they undergo treatment. The idea is picking up support—and opposition. (1)

Introduction and
Semantic Considerations

Controversy surrounding the complex issues involved in the compulsory treatment of addicts is by no means new. As the gap closes
between demand for treatment and available services, it is inevitable
that the debate will become more intense. Unfortunately, as with
many other controversies in the field of addiction, the polarization of
opinion which exists stems at least as much from semantic confusion
as from substantive disagreement. For this reason, a careful consideration of precisely what is and what is not meant by "voluntary treatment" is a prerequisite to any meaningful discussion of the principles that are involved in forcing people to accept therapy against
their will.

Voluntarism is not precluded by the existence of outside pressures.
Rather, voluntary ". . . implies the exercise of one's free choice or
will . . . whether or not external influences are at work" (2) (emphasis added). The difficulty, of course, is determining what constitutes
"free choice." However unappealing the alternative presented, the

addict nevertheless always retains the option of choosing the sanction associated with *not* entering a treatment program. One could thus argue that there are only voluntary patients and those others punished for failing to volunteer, but no involuntary patients. To avoid such abstract arguments, it is necessary to define voluntarism pragmatically by describing the relationship that exists between patient and practitioner.

Voluntary treatment describes a therapeutic relationship in which the primary responsibility of the clinician is to the patient. In an involuntary treatment setting the clinician's primary responsibility is to some third party. An obligation to report patient attendance, progress, or termination to an outside individual or agency defines the relationship as involuntary, even if patients are induced to sign, in advance, open-ended authorizations for such reports.

The physical environment in which treatment is forced on people is immaterial to the underlying principles. Whether a facility is behind bars, in a locked residential setting, or in a neighborhood storefront serving ambulatory patients is to a large extent determined by the modality that is favored in a particular instance. Endorsement of involuntary commitment to a drug-free encounter group lends equal support for enforced enrollment in a methadone maintenance clinic, in a religious community, or in any other program—ambulatory or residential—that may exist. Furthermore, the decision regarding which form of treatment is indicated will generally be based more on subjective prejudices than on objective assessment of need.

The Rationale for the Involuntary Treatment of Addicts

The principle is, that the sole end for which mankind are warranted, individually or collectively, in interfering with the liberty of action of any of their number is self-protection. That the only purpose for which power can be rightfully exercised over any member of a civilized community, against his will, is to prevent harm to others. His own good, either physical or moral, is not a sufficient warrant. He can not rightfully be compelled to do or forbear because it will be wise, or even right. These are good reasons for remonstrating with him or reasoning with him, or persuading him, or entreating him, but not for compelling him, or visiting him with an evil in case he do otherwise. (3)

Compulsory treatment of addiction has been justified on the basis of society's need to protect itself and/or on the grounds that it is in the interests of the unwilling addicts themselves. Regarding the former contention, there can certainly be no argument over the need for laws designed to protect individuals against infringement of their rights by others. Sanctions against those who violate such laws, however, must be equitable, reasonable, and imposed only after determination of guilt. These safeguards of our due process system are critical; the terminology used to describe the punishment that is meted out is essentially irrelevant.

It is inconsequential that penal institutions have been renamed "correctional facilities," and that guards have assumed the title "correction officers." These and similar euphemisms only take on a sinister quality when used to justify the abridgment of constitutional rights. Sanctions applied against addicts for the protection of society may be labeled "punishment," "treatment," or "rehabilitation"; but they must be reserved for persons convicted of a criminal violation, must be applied to all people equally, and must be neither cruel nor unusual according to accepted standards.

In acknowledging the right of society to protect itself, it must also be recognized that our traditional use of incarceration has failed to achieve this goal. Data on recidivism rates following release from prison would suggest that jail sentences might actually be counterproductive. More humane and effective alternatives must be explored, and no proposed innovation in dealing with lawbreakers should be arbitrarily dismissed. The one constant, however, *must* be that constitutional rights are not abridged.

It is significant that the constitutionality of involuntary commitment laws has *not*, in fact, been based on the rationale that society must protect itself at all costs. Rather, it has been stated that due process safeguards apply only to the prosecution of criminals and have no bearing on the treatment of the sick. As suggested by a presidential Commission on Law Enforcement and the Administration of Justice, the only condition imposed on compulsory treatment is that it be effective: "It is essential that the commitment laws be construed and executed to serve the purpose for which they were intended and by which alone they can be justified. This purpose is treatment in fact and not merely confinement with the pretense of treatment" (4). This sentiment is also expressed in a recent New York judicial decision: "The extended period of deprivation of liberty which the statute [New York State's Narcotic Control Act] mandates can only be justified as necessary to fulfill the purpose of the program . . . If compulsory commitment turns out in fact to be a veneer for an extended jail term and is not a fully developed, comprehensive and effective scheme, it will have lost its claim to be a project devoted solely to curative ends . . . and the constitutional guarantees applicable to criminal proceedings will apply in full measure" (5).

Whether the key criterion of effectiveness is in fact met is highly questionable. Reports on the results of involuntary treatment have been consistent in the grim picture they present of extremely high recidivism rates (6). Furthermore, in practice, this critical demonstration that compulsory programs are "fully developed, comprehensive and effective" is left to those responsible for the programs' operations. This is a weak foundation indeed upon which to permit and encourage the deprivation of liberties of tens or hundreds of thousands of citizens.

The underlying premise in the assumption that addicts should be forced to undergo treatment for their own good is that they are sick and thus in need of the treatment that we wish to impose against their will. Since there is no universally applicable *physical* ailment, the illness we purport to "cure" must be mental, and the addict is essentially powerless to refute the diagnosis. In fact, protestations are considered further confirmation of both the psychopathology that is said to exist and its severity, since it is a well-known adage that inability to recognize and accept one's own illness proves just how sick one really is!

The process of labeling addicts mentally sick, and the conclusion drawn from this generalization, is summed up as follows: "In recent years, professionals, nonprofessionals, and groups best designated unprofessionals, have taken to viewing drug abuse as a symptom of psychopathology—necessitating verbal and/or chemotherapeutic intervention . . . The main point is that once we view the drug abuser as being sick, we automatically fall into the trap of assuming and recommending 'treatment' for him. The choice between traditional and avant garde modalities is but a minor one once our initial perception is set of the person and his 'problem' " (7).

Generalizations applied to addicts are particularly suspect, since the addicted universe itself is so ill-defined. People are deemed addicts on the basis of laboratory tests that give an indication only of recent (as opposed to habitual) drug use. This "objective" measure is then supported by medical examination, which is generally cursory and inconclusive, and by a past social–medical history, which is notoriously unreliable when the patient–practitioner relationship is not voluntary. Nevertheless, physicians who accept the notion that all addicts are psychologically ill are at no loss for specific diagnoses of individual patients. One study of 91 women addicts, for instance, reported every single subject to be suffering from either brain syndrome, psychotic disorder, psychoneurotic disorder, personality pattern disorder, personality trait disorder, or sociopathic personality disorder (8).

Empirical evidence, however, such as the well-documented success of methadone maintenance treatment of heroin addicts (9), refutes the contention that addiction must be associated with some form of psychopathology. Most methadone maintenance programs, in assisting a large proportion of their voluntary patients to return to a productive role in society, supplement the medication itself with pragmatic counseling aimed at *external* problems, such as housing, employment, and legal cases, rather than with psychotherapy (10).

Nevertheless, there is considerable appeal in attributing the growing use of illicit drugs to psychological illness of the addicts themselves. Indeed, "blaming the victim" (11) is a traditional response to social ills (the classic example of this approach is the conclusion that malnutrition among the poor is due to the fact that ". . . low income families place less value on food than we think") (12). Political realities explain the attractiveness of seeking both the cause and the cure for addiction within the addict himself. As difficult as may be the task of rounding up drug addicts against whom one imposes nominally therapeutic measures, it is far easier than attempting to change the socioeconomic and other external factors that play a role. Compulsory treatment, by focusing on real or imagined shortcomings within the addict, serves to draw attention away from these environmental problems, and the result must inevitably be counterproductive.

The addict, of course, is not impressed with the argument that he is being deprived of his liberty for his own good. He generally perceives "treatment" as simply another form of punishment, if indeed he believes there is any distinction whatever; proponents of compulsory treatment acknowledge this, and cite it as an argument for, rather than against, depriving the addict of a choice (13):

C. You say that we are using a euphemism when we call that secured setting a rehabilitation center, while you opt for the label of a jail, prison or correctional facility. Now there is quite a difference between the structured environment of a civil facility and that of a jail or state prison.

N. . . . you said earlier that the person who has the most at stake in the decision is the addict who is about to be committed. He is the most concerned about the differences, and yet the addict himself puts these aside and evaluates the options by one criterion: where will I spend the least time? If he could spend two years in one of these very nice rehabilitation treatment facilities, and only one year in one of those disgusting jails, my impression and experience is that 95% will take the one year. So whatever the differences, they are not that impressive to the addict.

C. They might not be impressive to the addict, but he has certain ends in mind which, as enunciated by the legislature, happen to be contrary to the will of society.

N. Freedom is the end in his mind.

C. No, the end in his mind is to be irresponsible.

The addict's perception that he is being punished, rather than helped, seems to be shared by the lay press, as evidenced by phraseology such as the following: "4 ESCAPE YONKERS NARCO CENTER—*Police* yesterday were seeking four *inmates* who *escaped* Sunday night from the . . . Rehabilitation Center in Yonkers . . . A fifth was *captured* by a *guard* at the Center shortly after the *break"* (14) (emphasis added).

Success: Potentially More Ominous than Failure

In arguing against the desirability of involuntary treatment, it is tempting to dwell on the voluminous literature that demonstrates the widespread failure of this approach to addicts. To do so, however, would detract from the thesis that effectiveness, or "success," is a potentially far worse consequence for the unwilling subject. By definition, the involuntary patient enters the enforced therapeutic relationship rejecting that which the clinician sees as the desirable objective. Cure and rehabilitation therefore become synonymous with achieving that which the addict does not want, and this can be accomplished only by changing values and attitudes along with behavior. The all-powerful clinical director, acting for society, is the sole judge of what is healthy and appropriate.

The following excerpt from a military medical journal is an example of psychiatrically defined success, which in medical terminology could be classified as iatrogenic psychosis (in plain language, medical intervention that has destroyed an individual's ability to perceive and appropriately respond to reality) (15):

. . . Fear of Flying: A 26-year-old SSgt AC 47 gunner, with 7 months active duty in RVN, presented with frank admission of fear of flying. He had flown over 100 missions, and loss of several aircraft and loss of several crews who were well known to the patient, precipitated his visit. He stated he would give up flight pay, promotion, medals, etc., just to stop flying. Psychiatric consultation to USAF Hospital, Cam Ranh Bay, resulted in 36 days hospitalization with use of psychotherapy and tranquilizers. Diagnosis was Gross Stress Reaction, manifest by anxiety, tenseness, a fear of death expressed in the form of rationalizations, and inability to function. His problem was worked through and insight to his problem was gained to the extent that he was returned to full flying duty in less than 6 weeks. This is a fine tribute to the psychiatrists at Cam Ranh Bay (633 Combat Spt Gp Dispensary, Pleiku AB).

It is unclear from this case history whether the sergeant was a voluntary or involutary patient, although it would appear that he presented his superiors (and the doctors) with a firm decision to stop flying rather than with a symptom of illness for which he sought help. The conflicts inherent in attempting to modify behavior, however, are *always* present when practitioners relate to addicts compelled to accept their services: The clinician defines the disease and makes the diagnosis; the clinician decides on the therapeutic goals and implements the procedures he hopes will achieve these goals, although they are openly rejected by the patient; and, finally, the clinician measures the effectiveness of treatment. Should he decide that the therapy is not sufficiently successful, it is the patient who pays the price of continued, unwanted treatment.

It is naïve to assume that the power which is given the practitioner over the involuntary patient will not be applied to its fullest degree. The following candid statement outlines what society expects its agents—the clinicians—to accomplish: "From the addict's point of view, he properly perceives that the therapist is, in fact, trying to engage him in a conventional life, which will often mean low pay and prestige, continued insecurity, and poor access to the goals of our affluent society. This conformity, *which society demands of the addict*, is neither respected nor valued when it is achieved" (16) (emphasis added). Like the Air Force sergeant who, understandably, did not want to fly again but returned to flying duty after "treatment," these patients are considered "successful" when they are willing to accept whatever grim reality is considered by others to be appropriate.

Drug abuse is the activity which, by being labeled an illness, forms the spurious medicolegal rationale for permitting unwanted treatment to be forced on the addict. The objectives of the "rehabilitation" process, however, will almost invariably be far broader than simply eliminating the illicit use of drugs. All other forms of behavior that the clinician believes, on the basis of his own and society's prejudices, to be pathological will also be dealt with. Thus, the addict who is a homosexual may well find his sexual preference a focus of the therapist, while the nonaddict homosexual (despite the acknowledged burdens which society imposes) cannot be deprived of his liberty or forced into undergoing therapy in most states. The same is true of the involuntarily committed addict who belongs to a bizarre religious sect, who is a member of a radical political group, or who engages in any other activity that does not have the blessings of the general population and is thus classified as "deviant" and an additional component of the "symptom" complex. Some proponents of compulsory treatment define the broad nature of their goals quite explicitly: "To alter, where indicated, the attitudes and behaviors of the addict in the areas of: (a) work, (b) friendship and heterosexual relationships, (c) family responsibility, (d) leisure-time activities, (e) criminality" (17). It goes without saying that the *clinician* decides when changes are "indicated," and the involuntary patient is compelled to acquiesce, as a prerequisite to discharge.

The Clinician's Role in Compulsory Treatment

In the Therapeutic State toward which we appear to be moving, the principal requisite for the role of Big Brother may be an MD degree (18).

Legal experts may argue over the constitutionality of involuntary treatment of addicts. Politicians and the lay public may weigh the desirability and the dangers of such treatment. Economists may enter into heated debates over its absolute and relative cost-effectiveness. But the clinician who accepts patients rendered powerless to refuse his services by legislative fiat (as opposed to medical incapacity) must be viewed in the role of persecutor. Rationalizations cannot obfuscate the issue: in dealing with an unwilling subject, a doctor is by definition striving to bring about a change in behavior, which the patient does not wish, but which the government has mandated. He accepts payment from society in order to work against the perceived self-interest expressed by the patient; in such instances, the concepts of treatment and cure lose all meaning.

There are legal restraints against an internist who, in his professional wisdom, may be tempted to imprison a diabetic who fails to adhere to a prescribed diet. A surgeon, recognizing the inevitable consequences of ignoring a malignancy, is nevertheless restrained by professional as well as legal sanctions from operating on a cancer patient without informed consent. The seemingly self-evident nature of these examples would indicate that the medical profession has made considerable progress since the late 1930's, when a physician performed tubal ligation (sterilization) on 62 teenage inmates of a Kansas reformatory as retribution for disorderly behavior (19). Any difference in the ethical repugnance of these real and hypothetical cases, and of the compulsory treatment of the illicit drug user, is in degree only. As Szasz (a psychiatrist) has pointed out: "Physicians who interfere with the medical patients' autonomy by treating them involuntarily are guilty of an offense, punishable by both civil and criminal statutes. Why should this not apply to similar offenses against mental patients?" (20) Szasz does not condition his condemnation in any way on treatment outcome: "Treating patients against their wishes, even through the treatment may be medically correct, should be considered an offense punishable by law . . . Let us not forget that every form of social oppression has, at some time during its history, been justified on the ground of helpfulness toward the oppressed" (21).

Involuntary Treatment as an Alternative to Criminal Justice

I'll make him an offer he can't refuse (22).

"Diversion" of addicts from the criminal justice system to a treatment setting is an increasingly common practice in many states. This approach, which purports to deal with addict-offenders as "patients" rather than as criminals, has been heralded as an enlightened, humane alternative to an expensive and ineffective prison stay.

In general, all of the problems already discussed apply to this particular brand of compulsion: there is no rationale for assuming that the label of drug addict is synonymous with "illness," let alone illness that can or should be treated; there is no evidence to suggest that treatment provided addicts under coercion will be effective, and there is a basis for concluding that "success," even when attainable, may be more undesirable than "failure"; the all-powerful role of the physician and other staff members creates a very dangerous potential for abuse.

Diversion from the criminal justice system also entails additional inconsistencies. For example, while the rationale is that the addict-offender is "sick," the period of compulsory treatment is determined less on supposedly medical grounds than on the nature of the *criminal* offense that brought the addict before the court. Generally, addicts convicted of misdemeanors are committed to "treatment" for shorter periods of time than those convicted of felonies (23), ". . . a differential which smacks of penal rather than therapeutic aims" (24).

There are several mechanisms by which the criminal justice system forces addicts into treatment. In many situations the court, upon conviction of an addict, may *impose a sentence* that specifically mandates a term in a treatment facility in lieu of prison. Such terms can extend either for an indefinite period of time, depending upon the "progress" perceived by the clinician, or for a minimum duration, which frequently exceeds the longest sentence possible for the criminal act itself (25).

The other commonly used diversion technique offers a "choice" to the addict: either stay in prison, or "voluntarily" request release, which will be conditioned upon entering and remaining in a specified treatment program. This practice is particularly invidious when it is applied (as is increasingly the case) to the pretrial addict-prisoner whose alleged offense is compounded by his inability to obtain bail money. Frequently, the prosecutor's agreement to the release of defendants is reserved for those persons whose charges are relatively minor (i.e., misdemeanor and low-degree, drug-related felonies). Those involved, therefore, are primarily poor people, arrested on charges of which they are presumably innocent under the law, and which even upon conviction would carry comparatively short sentences. They are "offered the opportunity" to enter a treatment program they may or may not want or need, and which will in any event provide society with the means of observing and controlling their activities for an extended period of time. Such coercion of legally innocent detainees is possible since overcrowded court calendars and other delays inherent in the judicial process make virtually any alternative more attractive than continued incarceration while awaiting trial. Incredibly, it is in precisely these cases that advocates embrace diversion as an especially humane and appropriate expedient.

A problem inherent in all of the diversion schemes is that the officials of the criminal justice system are put in a position of abrogating their appointed responsibilities, while simultaneously accepting roles for which they are not qualified. Judges, probation officers, and parole officers have a primary obligation to protect society at large, and in exercising this obligation they must place consideration of the *community's* well-being ahead of all others. They cannot, and should not, have their roles redefined as therapists, any more than physicians should attempt to make decisions regarding the need for incarceration of criminals.

Distinguishing between the functions and responsibilities of criminal justice personnel and clinicians does not imply a value judgement. The point is simply that the functions *are* different, and that both groups must retain their own priorities if they are to achieve their respective goals. Physicians, just like lawyers and priests, will be rendered totally impotent if they attempt to serve society *at the expense* of their clients. Similarly, judges and probation and parole officers will not be able to meet their obligations to those who elect or appoint them if they lose sight of their primary responsibility.

Neither role is easy. Those who work in the criminal justice system, for instance, are inevitably plagued by the knowledge that while prisons do not as a rule "correct" anybody, simply releasing convicted criminals without punishment is not feasible. The tempting middle road with addict-defendants is to force them, under *threat* of imprisonment, to enter a treatment facility with the assurance that the clinical staff will promptly report absconding or continued involvement in "antisocial" activities. The attractiveness of such an approach is that it seems to offer something to everyone: the problem of ineffective and overcrowded jails is addressed; the judge is reasonably secure in the belief that the treatment facility staff will closely monitor the addict's behavior; the addict has been permitted to escape, at least temporarily, prison confinement for a more subtle (though perhaps longer) punishment; and finally, the treatment center frequently welcomes the added "business" and often believes that it will be more successful in dealing with what amounts to a captive population.

In fact, this type of program is a perversion of the role of all the parties concerned. The *judge* engages in inequitable justice by providing different punishment to different people convicted of the same offense, merely because one happens to be an addict and is deemed "treatable" and the other is not. Also, the judge imposes as the primary criterion of continued release attendance at a facility that may or may not offer society (let alone the addict) any benefits. The basic premise underlying such conditional release is that there is an inherent value in being in a treatment program; this assumption is as invalid as the belief that there is an inherent virtue in being a member of a particular religion, political party, or any other group. Finally, the judge is left with the task of deciding which type of treatment program should be required, a decision for which he is usually totally unqualified, and which will depend more on personal bias than on objective determination.

The addict-defendant is forced to accept "treatment," which he generally does not want, for an "illness" that he more often than not believes is nonexistent. The addict who has not yet been tried or convicted forfeits the opportunity to prove his innocence by accepting treatment in lieu of prosecution and the attendant pretrial incarceration.

The clinical staff, in agreeing to share the responsibilities of the criminal justice system, cannot meet its primary obligation to the patient. It thereby severely compromises its ability to serve *either* patients *or* the community. Clinical judgement is also compromised, since *medical* decisions (to terminate treatment, for instance) can and generally do lead to inevitable *criminal* sanctions against the client.

Consequences of Abandoning
Involuntary Treatment

It would be wrong to assume that arguments against involuntary treatment in any way denigrate the value and importance of *voluntary* services. Although a law mandating treatment of everyone over a specified weight would be unthinkable, people who are obese should have access to medical assistance for weight reduction.

Continued counterproductive and inhumane incarceration of addicts is *not* an inevitable consequence of eliminating coercive referrals for treatment. The number and type of people imprisoned is purely a reflection of the orientation and emphasis of enforcement agencies, prosecutors, and the judiciary. Rounding up drug users and imposing long jail terms for charges of possession of "dangerous drugs" is admittedly no more rational or productive than sentencing such people to therapy. Such a practice also reflects the contradiction in the ruling of the Supreme Court when it stated that ". . . addiction, devoid of an overt act, is merely a status of craving which should not be criminally punished" (26), without simultaneously precluding penalties for use and possession of drugs, which addiction entails.

Furthermore, the arguments against compulsory treatment of addicts in no way undermine the concept that the criminal justice system retain alternatives to incarceration, such as parole and probation. Rather, they are directed only against the *use of parole and probation to coerce people into accepting therapy.* In fact, as pointed out previously, such practice is counterproductive of the goals of these alternative means of protecting society.

If compulsory treatment as a form of punishment is to be eliminated, this would simultaneously preclude the addict-defendant from pleading illness as a justification for crime, or as a rationale for avoiding the usual penalties that the court imposes on nonaddicts for similar offenses. Equal *severity* of the law is no less a principle than the corollary of equal *protection*. The proposition that incarceration of convicted criminals serves no useful purpose may well be correct; whatever alternatives are suggested, however, should not distinguish between people on the basis of drug abuse.

Finally, in contemplating the impact of eliminating involuntary treatment of addicts, it is well to consider the insignificant role this practice plays in two countries where addiction seems to have been contained: England and Japan.

England, although reputedly dealing with addiction as a medical rather than criminal problem, does not compel anyone to enter treatment. Nor is the addict offered a "choice" of therapy in lieu of pretrial detention, or as a condition of release from jail after conviction. Thus, removing criminal sanctions from the state of addiction per se does not require a concomitant policy of forcing drug abusers into treatment.

In the case of Japan, the 1963 Narcotics Control Law did provide for compulsory hospitalization. At the same time, however, this statute heralded a massive enforcement effort against narcotics importation and trafficking, which was launched by a police department with a reputation for absolute incorruptability. These factors, and others, in the ensuing 6 years resulted in a decline in the estimated number of heroin addicts from 40,000 to a few hundred (27). The role of involuntary hospitalization in this achievement was insignificant: during the 6-year period only 593 people were forced to accept treatment, and it is relevant to note that in Japan treatment of addicts is *never* a substitute for prosecution or incarceration (28).

Conclusion

Ignorance, of itself, is disgraceful only as far as it is avoidable. But when, in our eagerness to find "better ways" of handling old problems, we rush to measures affecting human liberty and human personality, on the assumption that we have knowledge which, in fact, we do not possess, then the problem of ignorance takes on a more sinister hue (29).

Whatever the terminology and whatever the means by which coercion is applied, compulsory treatment of addicts is void of benefits and counterproductive of the goals that form the rationale for depriving people of their liberty. The interests of society cannot possibly be protected by ineffective attempts to force attitudinal and behavioral change on resentful and unwilling subjects; the rights of *all* Americans are severely threatened when the principle is established of ignoring safeguards of our criminal justice system. The assertion that compulsory treatment is in the interests of those who are forced into therapy is equally spurious; such efforts have been proven a costly, unsuccessful error in the past, and they are doomed to fail in the future.

There is little doubt that proposals such as the following will become more common as the addiction problem remains unsolved: ". . . [a prominent New York City politician] has called for a crackdown on violent crime by interning hard-core narcotics addicts in treatment camps . . . 'if that's what they need' " (30). Concern over such proposed "solutions," which are as inevitably self-defeating as they are radical, should not obscure the fact that the more subtle forms of compulsory treatment are an even greater danger.

The causes of drug addiction are as complex as society itself, and they must be faced directly. The analogy is frequently made between drug addiction and contagious disease. In that context, it should be noted that even where a readily defined illness exists (which is not the case with addiction), and even where that illness can be effectively cured by appropriate treatment (which also is not the case with addiction), elimination of the problem from a community generally requires far broader measures. Thus, tuberculosis was brought under control not by the introduction of chemotherapeutic agents, but by a substantial improvement in living conditions; in areas where that improvement has not occurred, the disease persists despite the medication that is available. Venereal disease is widespread throughout the world, even though each individual patient can be readily diagnosed and cured. Similarly, we must recognize that addiction is a social problem, which will never be eliminated by measures that are imposed on the addicts themselves, and until this is understood our effectiveness in dealing with drug abuse will remain severely limited.

References

1. *U.S. News World Rep.*, Sept. 11, 1972, p. 76.
2. "Webster's New World Dictionary of the American Language" (1964), p. 1636. World Pub. Co., Cleveland, Ohio.
3. Mill, J. (1926). "On Liberty and Other Essays," p. 13. Macmillan, New York.
4. President's Commission on Law Enforcement and the Administration of Justice (1967). "Task Force Report: Narcotics and Drug Abuse," p. 16.
5. *Fuller v. People* (1969). *24 N.Y. 2d 292, 300 N.Y.S. 2d 102.*
6. Brecher, E. and the Editors of Consumer Reports (1972). "Licit and Illicit Drugs," Chapter 10. Little, Brown, Boston, Massachusetts.
7. Einstein, S. and Garitano, W. (1972). *Int. J. Addictions* **7**, No. 2, 324.
8. Chambers, C., Hinesley, R. K., and Moldestad, M. (1970). *Int. J. Addictions* **5**, No. 2, 274.
9. Gearing, F. (1972). *Proc. Nat. Conf. Methadone Treatment, 4th*, p. 157. NAPAN.
10. Joseph, H. and Dole, V. (1970). *Federal Probation* **34**, No. 2, 44.
11. Ryan, W. (1971). "Blaming the Victim," Pantheon Press, New York.
12. U.S. Department of Agriculture, quoted by E. Drew. *Atl. Mon.* Dec., 1968, p. 55.
13. Civil commitment of heroin addicts—a panel discussion (1972). *Contemp. Drug Prob.* **1**, 576–577.
14. *Daily News*, Sept. 7, 1971.

15. *PACAF Med. J.* (1967). **11**, No. 8, 5.
16. Brill, L., and Lieberman, L. (1969). "Authority and Addiction," p. 57. Little, Brown, Boston, Massachusetts.
17. Brill, L., and Lieberman, L. (1969). "Authority and Addiction," p. 112. Little, Brown, Boston, Massachusetts.
18. Szasz, T. (1968). *Med. Opinion Rev.*, p. 35.
19. 2 *Kansas Law Review* 174 (1953–1954), pp. 176–177.
20. Szasz, T. (1963). "Law, Liberty and Psychiatry," p. 253. Macmillan, New York.
21. Szasz, T. (1963). "Law, Liberty and Psychiatry," pp. 185, 253. Macmillan, New York.
22. Puzo, M. (1969). "The Godfather," p. 39. Fawcett, Greenwich, Connecticut.
23. *N.Y.S. Mental Hygiene Law*, §208.
24. Kittrie, N. (1971). "The Right to be Different," p. 246. Johns Hopkins Press, Baltimore, Maryland.
25. DeLong, J. (1972). *In* "Dealing with Drug Abuse—A Report to the Ford Foundation," p. 186. Praeger, New York.
26. *Robinson v. California*, quoted by Kittrie (Ref. 24, p. 239).
27. Japan Ministry of Health and Welfare (1970). "A Brief Account of Narcotics Abuse and Countermeasures in Japan," p. 7.
28. Japan Ministry of Health and Welfare (1970). "A Brief Account of Narcotics Abuse and Countermeasures in Japan," p. 7.
29. Allen, F. (1967). quoted by Aronowitz, D., *Columbia Law Review* **67**, No. 3, 405.
30. Leone, S., quoted in *The New York Times*, Dec. 12, 1971, p. 27.

8

Three Critical Issues
in the Management
of Methadone Programs

AVRAM GOLDSTEIN
and
BARBARA A. JUDSON

The data and clinical impressions to be reported in this chapter are based on 3 years of experience in the Santa Clara County Methadone Program. In this period of time, 926 patients have been admitted to 5 clinics geographically dispersed over a county with a population of about a million. Patients were assigned randomly and concurrently to comparison groups of 20 each. All dosages (given in the mornings) were single-blind, i.e., the nurses knew the doses but the patients did not. All addicts meeting the following criteria were admitted in the order of application: (1) documented history of at least 2 years of narcotic addiction; (2) at least one documented detoxification with subsequent relapse; (3) at least 18 years of age; (4) evidence of current narcotic use (positive urine) except for patients accepted directly upon release from jail or penitentiary. Neither multiple drug abuse (including alcoholism) nor diagnosis of psychosis was cause for exclusion.

Evaluation criteria included the following: (1) A 42-item questionnaire administered by a counselor at the time of admission (before starting methadone) and repeated at weeks 3, 5, 9, and 13 and quarterly thereafter. This instrument is reproduced verbatim elsewhere (Goldstein and Judson, 1973). It deals largely with physical symptoms, but also seeks information about employment, criminal activities, mood, and drug abuse. (2) Urine test results based on random sampling 1 day in 5, with additional tests as required to ensure a sample collection at least once weekly. Urine was collected under direct observation by a staff member, was kept thereafter in a locked box, and was transported to the laboratory under strict conditions of security. Failure to give a urine sample called for by the random list (generated by computer) resulted in an automatic "dirty," i.e., positive for opiates. All urine samples were analyzed for opiates and methadone. Analyses for amphetamines and barbiturates were carried out at least once monthly. For the first 2 years the urine analysis was performed by standard thin-layer chromatography (Dole *et al.*, 1966; Mulé, 1969), in the third year by the free-radical (FRAT) procedure (Leute *et al.*, 1972). (3) Clinic attendance. (4) Time spent in jail.

Additionally, in certain experiments special questionnaires were administered weekly, on Monday morning, to assess symptoms ascribed to withdrawal ("feeling sick"). These were relied on heavily in the studies with *l*-methadyl acetate (*l*-α-acetyl methadol, LAM), where the critical question was whether or not the effects of the medication lasted effectively for 72 hours over the weekend. On Monday questionnaires, patients were also asked to express an opinion about the adequacy of their dose.

All the data referred to above were entered in a computer file, from which they were retrieved for the various analyses.

Critical Issue 1: Is There an Optimal Dosage?

Most drugs are administered in order to obtain a definite effect, the characteristic agonistic effect of the drug. For example, diphenylhydantoin is given to suppress epileptic seizures, digoxin to improve the efficiency or alter the rate of the failing heart, penicillin to kill infectious microorganisms. In such cases, there is a threshold dose or concentration that must be exceeded to obtain an optimum effect, and a toxic level that must not be exceeded if adverse actions are to be avoided. With methadone the situation appears to be quite different (Goldstein, 1972a). The agonistic effects are the typical actions of an opioid narcotic—analgesia, tranquilization, suppression of anxiety, pupillary constriction, constipation, and so on. Since the drug is given by mouth, the acute "high" or "rush" is not readily obtained, but otherwise its actions are much like those of heroin or morphine.

In methadone treatment of heroin addiction, these agonistic effects are considered undesirable. The drug is therefore administered initially at low dosage, and the dosage is increased gradually as tolerance to the agonistic effects develops. Since a very high degree of tolerance can develop to all the opiates, including methadone, it is possible slowly to increase the dosage to a level many times what would have been lethal at the outset. The immediate result is to suppress all withdrawal symptoms that would otherwise occur upon discontinuance of heroin use, and thus to permit the smooth substitution of methadone dependence for heroin dependence on an ambulatory basis. After stabilization at a moderate or high level of tolerance, the cross-tolerance to other narcotics ("blockade") is thought to play an important part in discouraging heroin use by abolishing the positive reinforcement associated with such use. Finally, methadone is said to abolish "narcotic drug hunger" (craving), although this action is controversial (Dole and Nyswander, 1967; Goldstein, 1972b).

If it were true that complete tolerance developed to all the agonistic effects of methadone, one might argue in favor of a very high dose. Even on this assumption, however, there are objections to high dosage. We have come to believe that the best dose of methadone is the lowest dose that is effective, for the following reasons:

1. With all narcotics, withdrawal is easier, the lower the level of dependence, i.e., the lower the maintenance dose (Andrews and Himmelsbach, 1944). The patient's freedom, and his feeling of freedom, is closely related to this fact. A patient may wish to withdraw for a variety of reasons, including disenchantment with program rules or staff, desire to leave the area, or a decision to attempt abstinence. Furthermore, a patient may have to withdraw abruptly, and sometimes without benefit of effective detoxification, if he is arrested and incarcerated, or if he becomes ill or suffers a serious accident. There is no doubt that, from this point of view, a patient on a low dose is in a far better position that one on a high dose.

2. As long as any methadone leaves the clinic, the community is better protected, the lower the dose. This applies most forcefully to the hazard of accidental ingestion by a child. It also applies to the illicit diversion of take-home methadone. Indeed, high doses encourage diversion, once the patient discovers he can get along with less methadone than he is given. And high doses in the street can be extremely hazardous, since even heroin users may have insufficient tolerance to protect against the lethality of high methadone dosage. These dangers are documented in the history of accidental methadone deaths in children and adults over the past several years (Dole

et al., 1971; Cranley and Haddow, 1971; Aronow *et al.*, 1972; Blatman and Lipsitz, 1972).

3. Finally, the assumption that tolerance develops to all the effects of high methadone doses needs to be examined critically. It is generally recognized that constipation persists for a very long time after dosage stabilization has been achieved. What about other agonistic effects? And are there side effects to which tolerance does not develop at all? If tolerance to any troublesome actions of methadone is incomplete or absent, it follows that low but adequate doses should be preferable to high doses.

Our earliest experiments sought to compare the effects of 30, 50, and 100 mg daily. We were surprised to find virtually no difference on any of the criteria between patients on 50 and on 100 mg; and although the 30 mg dose appeared to be marginal in some respects, even it was remarkably effective in most of the patients (Garbutt and Goldstein, 1972). Subsequently, we conducted blind dose comparisons of 40 and 80 mg, and of 40, 80, and 160 mg. We also carried out blind dose increases to as high as 200 mg, and decreases from high levels to a standard 80 mg dose. Finally, we reduced dosages from 80 to 50 mg in hundreds of patients simultaneously. The data from some of these experiements are reported elsewhere (Goldstein and Judson, 1973) in detail. Space does not permit their repetition here, but the results may be summarized as follows.

Very large dose differences yielded little or no difference in effects, as judged by all the criteria cited at the outset of this chapter. We have found, in general, that most patients do as well at 50 mg daily as on higher doses. Moreover, slow changes of dose (e.g., 5 mg once weekly) are in nearly all cases undetectable by the patients. Patients who are still using heroin at a methadone dosage of 50 mg daily do not necessarily cease using if the dose is raised slowly, even to very high levels. Patients using heroin at high methadone doses may stop using when the dose is reduced, if additional counseling effort is expended. These conclusions, however, which are based upon group comparisons, do not exclude the possibility that some fraction of all patients may indeed require more than the standard 50 mg dose. Establishing this requires long experimentation with individuals, involving repeated slow increases and decreases of dosage, to establish conclusively the relationship between dose and the patient's condition and behavior. Experiments of this kind require close adherence to a double-blind design, since psychological factors play such an obvious role in the patient's sense of well-being or of "feeling sick." That a 50 mg daily dose may not meet the needs of some patients is made plausible by our recent unpublished findings on methadone plasma levels. At constant dosage, the steady state lowest plasma level (24 hours after the daily dose) varied between patients over a range of nearly 50-fold. From the standpoint of efficient program management, the advantages of low dosage (cited above) can be achieved in the great majority of patients by administering the standard dose of 50 mg daily. Apparent exceptions should then be confirmed individually, by objective methods and double-blind design, before accepting the necessity of a higher dose.

Critical Issue 2: Is Urine Testing Useful?

The cost of urine testing represents a major expenditure in any methadone program. In addition, the procedures associated with urine collection may have a number of detrimental effects on the program as a whole. The basic question is whether urine testing has any positive therapeutic value, and if so, how its efficiency can be improved.

First, we shall discuss the procedures themselves, in order to lay the groundwork for the later discussion about their usefulness. How often should urine be collected? This question was analyzed in a previous publication (Goldstein and Brown, 1970), in which it was shown how different average sampling frequencies affected the probability of detecting sporadic use of narcotics or a shift from abstinence to regular use. A random procedure is absolutely essential. One can, of course, collect urine at each clinic visit, and then decide by a table of random numbers or other random device which urines are to be sent to the laboratory and which are to be discarded. A disadvantage of this procedure is that the supervised collection of urine samples is both time consuming and unpleasant for the staff and patients. We have argued that, without direct supervision, urine data are meaningless—that one might just as well accept the patient's word about his drug use as accept an unsupervised urine sample.

We suggest the following procedure. A computer-generated random list of numbers is generated for each day, consisting of enough numbers to represent one-fifth of the patient population. If patients are numbered sequentially, the simplest list will consist of two single-digit numbers, where each represents the final digit of a patient's serial number. For example, if the list for a given day consisted of the numbers 3 and 8, patients with numbers terminating in 03, 08, 13, 18, and so forth would be required to give a urine sample.

Hundreds of single-day lists like this are produced in advance, on separate slips of paper, and kept in an envelope in the dispensing room. The first patient each morning is asked to draw out a slip, and this becomes the list for the day. The purpose of transferring control of the random process to the patients is to reduce suspicion and paranoia about how the lists are chosen. Only patients whose numbers appear on the list are required to produce a specimen (or be marked down as "automatic dirty"); thus the work load for staff is reduced by four-fifths, as compared with daily urine collection. On the average, each patient is sampled once in 5 days. If a patient's number appears on the list on a day he does not attend the clinic, he is obliged to give a specimen on the next day he does attend. In addition to this random procedure, all patients who have not been sampled in the previous 7 days are added to the next list, in order to comply with the FDA requirement of a urine test at least weekly. Whenever a patient is unexpectedly absent from clinic, a special urine specimen is obtained at the next clinic visit.

The procedures for supervising urine collection are not very satisfactory. An incentive to cheat is provided by the relationship between take-home privileges and "being clean." This relationship is both logical and necessary, for one would certainly not give methadone into the hands of an active addict, still in the heroin subculture, who would probably regard the clinic methadone as just another commodity for the marketplace. However, given this relationship, an incorruptible and completely valid system of urine collection is probably an impossibility. We know that an addict whose future freedom or incarceration depends on being clean (as when he is on parole) can devise extraordinarily clever and complex cheating systems. We have known patients to try bribing the supervising staff member to accept a substituted urine, or to allow someone else to urinate instead of the patient, or to omit collecting the sample. Switching labels not only provides the patient a "clean" result, but also helps destroy faith in the laboratory, since some other patient, who has not used heroin, receives a positive report. If the staff supervisors are ex-addicts, there is strong appeal to in-group loyalty, which may make bribery unnecessary. If the program is large enough so that every staff supervisor does not know every patient by number, the patient may simply have a friend who is "clean" give the urine sample, and state the patient's number. The use of certain cheating systems cannot be detected unless the act of urination is truly observed. Regardless of instructions, supervising staff will rarely look directly at the urinary meatus to be sure it is the source of the urine sample. To do so is embarrassing to most people other than physicians and nurses, and the embarrassment can easily be exploited by a patient, through hints about homosexuality. Thus, even crude devices employing a rubber bulb in the pocket, leading to a polyethylene tube along the underside of the penis, can be fairly effective. A woman can conceal a latex or plastic container of urine in her vagina, and thus "urinate" convincingly under the not-too-close observation of the supervisor. Finally, a man could introduce "clean" urine into his own bladder by catheter, and then pass a seemingly valid specimen under even the most rigorous observation.

We conclude that as long as urine test results are tied to any privileges, cheating will occur. One way to avoid this would be to abolish all take-home privileges and to require the same 6- or 7-day attendance by all, regardless of whether they are abstinent or still using heroin. This seems a therapeutically counterproductive solution, for it would unquestionably repel many patients, interfere with legitimate employment, and effectively reduce the staff : patient ratio. An alternative is to adopt a form of methadone that would require less frequent clinic visits, and then to abolish take-home privileges. This is the solution we discuss in the next section of this chapter—the use of long-acting methadone.

Another way to deal with the problem would be to eliminate regular urine testing, retaining only occasional anonymous surprise tests to monitor program accomplishment. It is possible, however, that frequent urine testing serves a therapeutic purpose, by yielding information of value to the counselor, by reinforcing the patient's decision to remain abstinent, by symbolizing the fact that the staff are concerned about the patient's success (Nightingale *et al.*, 1972). We set out to determine experimentally whether or not urine testing had this sort of value.

The basic experimental design was carried out in three replications, at different clinics. Twenty patients were assigned randomly and concurrently to each of two groups—a monitored group and an unmonitored group. The monitored group was handled in routine fashion, with regular urine-testing procedures, as described above. The unmonitored group was told at the outset that they would be participating in research concerning urine testing. They were told to pay no attention to the posted random urine lists, and that no urine specimens would be required of or accepted from them. It was made clear that no loss of privileges would be suffered, i.e., that as long as they remained untested, they would be assumed to be "clean." Finally it was explained that "some time in the future" they would probably have to be tested in order to comply with state and federal regulations. The maximum number of patients not subjected to urine testing at any one time was 20. At the same time, the program census exceeded 500, all of whom were tested in strictest conformity with the regulations.

Since patients were assigned concurrently at admission to the moni-tored and unmonitored groups, these groups filled up only gradually. When the median time on the program was about 3 months, a sur-prise check was made on all members of both groups. The date of this check was known in advance to only one person (A.G.). On a Monday morning at 6 A.M., one of us appeared at the clinic as it opened, and gave instructions to the staff. Every patient in both groups was to provide an adequate urine sample before receiving methadone. Assistance was to be offered by staff, such as extending the regular clinic hours, visiting the patient at home later in the morning, driving the patient from work to clinic during the day, and providing free coffee or soft drinks. But no exceptions were to be made. The same surprise procedure was followed two days later, on Wednesday. All urine samples were tested for opiates, methadone, amphetamines, and barbiturates.

In the first and second replications of this experiment, information was obtained retrospectively as to the patients who were in a parole or probation status, which would subject them to urine testing out-side the methadone program. These were excluded from consider-ation, since such patients in the unmonitored group were really being tested after all. To avoid being misled by unknown variables associated with parole or probation status, we also excluded all such patients from the monitored group. In the third replication, patients on parole or probation were excluded from both groups at the outset.

Table I shows the initial composition of the groups in each of the three replications, and also the final sets on which the analyses were based. Altogether, 106 patients started the experiment, 54 in the monitored (M) group, and 52 in the unmonitored (U) group. After exclusion of those on parole or probation, the starting groups num-bered 49 in M and 40 in U. The numbers present and tested at the end of the experiment were 33 in M and 27 in U, or 67% of the start-ing number in both groups. Thus, survivorship was not affected by urine testing.

Table II shows the comparability of the final M and U groups with respect to days on the program as of the Wednesday test date, and the number of absences from clinic since admission. Program ex-posure was very similar for the two groups, except at Mountain View clinic, where the mean (or median) exposure was about a month longer for U than for M. There were no important differences in the days of absence or in the fraction of patients with a perfect atten-

Table I

Urine Study: Composition of the Groups

Clinic:	East Valley		Mountain View		Tenth Street	
Group:	M [a]	U [a]	M	U	M	U
Initial number	20	20	24	20	10	12
Parole/probation	2	5	3	7	0	0
Revised initial number	18	15	21	13	10	12
On test day:						
Jail	4	3	0	1	1	1
Suspended [b]	1	1	4	3	1	0
Withdrawing	1	1	1	0	0	0
Absent on test day	0	0	1	0	0	0
Off program	0	2	2	0	0	1
Resultant number	12	8	13	9	8	10

[a] M, monitored group; U, unmonitored group.
[b] For 4 or more absences in a single calendar month.

dance record, except again at Mountain View clinic, where all patients in U, as compared with only 9/13 in M, had a perfect attendance record. This difference at Mountain View falls just short of significance at the 5% level. It need not necessarily be attributed to the absence of urine monitoring; the disproportionate loss of patients with short program exposure from the U group (cf. Table II) might in part be responsible.

The Monday urine test results are given in Table III. In the first replication, at the East Valley clinic, the outcome favored the monitored group; the difference between M and U was significant at the 5% level. In the second replication, at Mountain View clinic, the outcome again favored M, but in the third replication, at Tenth Street clinic, the outcome favored U; neither difference was significant. Wednesday test results were (not surprisingly) virtually identical to the Monday results. Tests for amphetamines and barbiturates yielded only a few positive results at either test day, and these were scattered among all groups.

The outcome of this experiment was less conclusive than we had hoped for. Certainly there is evidence here that urine monitoring has some therapeutic value, at least in some patients. Had we been content with the first trial, at East Valley, the conclusion would have

Table II

Urine Study: Attendance Record and Total Exposure to Program

	East Valley				Mountain View				Tenth Street			
	M [a]		U [a]		M		U		M		U	
	Days absent	Days on program	Days absent	Days on program	Days absent	Days on program	Days absent	Days on program	Days absent	Days on program	Days absent	Days on program
	0	112	0	94	0	150	0	150	0	112	4	119
	4	105	0	91	0	129	0	143	1	98	2	119
	0	101	0	77	0	97	0	136	0	84	1	91
	1	94	0	77	0	81	0	129	0	75	0	84
	0	77	1	49	4	80	0	122	2	75	1	63
	0	77	1	49	0	80	0	90	2	42	5	62
	0	49	1	35	0	73	0	73	0	28	0	55
	1	49	0	35	3	73	0	73	3	14	0	54
	0	49			2	73	0	63			2	28
	0	49			0	38					0	14
	0	35			1	38						
	0	35			0	38						
					0	38						
Mean		69		63		76		109		66		69
Median		63		63		73		122		75		62

[a] M, monitored group; U, unmonitored group. Each line (containing two numbers) within each group represents a single patient.

Table III

Urine Study: Test Results for Opiates

Clinic	East Valley		Mountain View		Tenth Street	
Daily dose (mg)	80		50		50	
Monday test date	2/28/72		8/21/72		12/18/72	
Group	M [a]	U [a]	M	U	M	U
Number positive ("dirty")/total	0/12	3/8	3/13	4/9	6/8	5/10
P [b]	0.048		0.275		0.278	

[a] M, monitored group; U, unmonitored group.

[b] P is the probability of observing the given outcome when there is no real difference, as determined by Fisher's exact method (Goldstein, 1964).

been clear; but the result was not confirmed by the subsequent replications at other clinics. There are too many known and unknown variables between clinics, and over the 1-year period from inception to completion of the three replications, to warrant much speculation as to why the outcomes were different. As Table III shows, the "dirty rate" in the monitored group was very different at the three clinics—"cleanest" at East Valley, "dirtiest" at Tenth Street. Perhaps, in general, monitoring is most effective when the overall heroin-use rate is low. We suggest, in other words, that monitoring has a weak influence in encouraging abstinence, which is expressed when other factors operate effectively in the same direction, but is overwhelmed otherwise. It seems reasonable that monitoring should be viewed by the patient as a sign that the program staff really cares about his drug use. In this sense monitoring would be just one of the many program elements indicative of staff concern for patient welfare.

On the other hand, it is noteworthy that at least half of the patients in the unmonitored group at all three clinics had stopped using heroin by the time of the surprise tests. Even if this experiment had shown a clear advantage of monitoring in all three replications, one would have to ask if the cost, energy drain, and other disadvantages of urine testing are justified by the improvement in abstinence rate among the half of the patient population who would not have become abstinent otherwise. This question could be answered by an experiment in which an unmonitored group was given additional counseling and other services commensurate with the cost savings from not collecting and testing urine. A clear-cut conclusion will obviously require a starting sample very much larger than we used here.

It is important to arrive at a decision quickly about the therapeutic value of urine testing, because if a long-acting methadone is universally adopted, and take-home privileges are abolished or more drastically curtailed, the only remaining purpose of urine testing would be its asssumed therapeutic value. If the therapeutic value is slight or nonexistent, or if the same therapeutic outcome can be achieved at the same or lower cost through other program services, there would be no purpose in retaining federal and state requirements for urine testing (Edwards, 1972), except for anonymous sampling to measure program accomplishment.

Critical Issue 3: Can the Community Be Protected against the Hazards of Take-Home Methadone?

Take-home methadone is obviously a hazard to the community. Patients have to be instructed about the dangers of accidental methadone poisoning. This instruction is reinforced by the following absolutely inflexible rule: No methadone is given into a patient's custody unless it is locked in a secure box in the presence of the nurse. We have found it useful to prepare the methadone in a vehicle that cannot spoil, so that patients can be expressly forbidden to refrigerate it; the refrigerator is the most dangerous place to keep an attractive fruit drink! Unsweetened Kool-Aid (in contrast to Tang) meets this requirement. The Kool-Aid has added to it an approved preservative, 0.02% methylparaben–0.01% propylparaben (final concentration). We believe these precautions account for the fact that although over 900 patients have been admitted to our program over a period of 3 years, there have been no methadone deaths among the patients' families. In two instances, despite the precautions, children have drunk their parent's methadone, but timely treatment saved them. It is too optimistic to hope that any precautions would be completely effective in preventing this kind of accident.

Deliberate diversion of methadone is an ever-present problem. We know that some methadone from our clinics is to be found on the streets, and has come into the possession of unauthorized persons. Although only a small fraction of all patients may trade in methadone or give it away to friends, this constitutes a serious hazard to the community nonetheless. Nontolerant drug users have no realistic idea of the potency of the clinic methadone, and it is difficult for them to comprehend that a dose, which is without effect upon the tolerant patient, may easily kill them.

From the therapeutic standpoint, it is a disservice to an ex-addict, who has not yet severed himself from the drug culture, to place a narcotic in his possession. He is subjected to pressure from addict friends to rescue them from impending withdrawal (an appeal that can rarely be resisted) and from nonaddict drug-using friends to let them try a new narcotic.

Finally, the system of take-home privileges inevitably corrupts the urine-testing procedures, as described earlier. It gives rise to an adversary system (or "game"), in which the object is to deceive the staff in order to gain or retain the privileges. Surely this impedes progress toward rehabilitation.

Ideally, then, we would like to eliminate take-home privileges entirely, and have patients drink all their methadone under observation in the clinic. Attending the clinic 7 (or even 6) days a week, however, is probably an unreasonable demand, especially for patients who are trying to engage in full-time employment or other socially useful work. It is largely in this context that a long-acting methadone should prove useful. Preliminary studies with l-α-acetyl methadol (LAM) have shown considerable promise (Jaffe *et al.*, 1972; Zaks *et al.*, 1972; Senay *et al.*, 1973).

Our trial of LAM is still in progress. This report covers our first 3 months of experience. Patients were assigned randomly and concurrently to five groups of 20 patients each. Females were included intially, but then were switched to methadone and dropped from the study at the request of the Food and Drug Administration; thus, the data analyzed here are based on fewer than 20 patients per group. Three of the groups (M-1, M-2, M-3) were stablilized at 50 mg of methadone hydrochloride daily and maintained at that level. Two groups were started at 30 mg of LAM hydrochloride; subsequent doses were 40, 50, 60, 70, 75 mg, given only on Mondays, Wednesdays, and Fridays. One of the groups (L) came to clinic only on those mornings, and therefore understood from the start that they were receiving long-acting methadone. The other LAM group (L-P) attended clinic 6 mornings a week (as did all patients on methadone), but received a quinine placebo on Tuesdays, Thursdays, Saturdays, and Sundays. Sunday doses were taken home from the outset. Other placebo doses were taken home when the patient qualified for take-home privileges. Thus, the patients in the LAM-placebo group presumably believed they were receiving ordinary methadone. In some cases, however, patients noted and remarked on differences in the taste or apparent strength of the medications administered on different days. We present the data on this group, therefore, with some reservations as to whether or not the design was a valid one. LAM never was given as a take-home medication. In rare circumstances (e.g., a short trip or other authorized absence) in which a patient was to be absent on a LAM day, regular methadone (50 mg) was given to the patient, to be taken daily.

In our experience, the urine of LAM patients does not contain material giving the same color reactions as methadone in the standard thin-layer chromatographic procedure. Therefore, a positive methadone test in the urine of a LAM patient can probably be taken as evidence for illicit supplementation with methadone.

A special questionnaire (Fig. 1) was administered by the nurse every Monday morning to the patients in all five groups. This sought to determine how effectively the LAM lasted through the 72-hour weekend period, the longest interval between LAM doses.

Key data at week 13, the end of the first quarter, are summarized in Table IV. Patients who dropped out during the first 2 weeks, during the induction and stabilization phase, have been eliminated from the computations. There were only a few of these: 0 in M-1, 0 in M-2, 2 in M-3, 3 in L, and 1 in L-P. Survivorship tended to be very slightly lower in the LAM than in the methadone groups, but this difference was neither significant nor of real import. Attendance records and suspensions for excessive absences were variable between groups, with no indication favoring methadone or LAM, and the same was true of jailings. The urine test data show that heroin use had been discontinued by three-quarters of the patients in all groups by week 13. The record of amphetamine and barbiturate use during the entire quarter seems to favor the methadone groups by a small margin.

Date _____

SANTA CLARA COUNTY METHADONE PROGRAM – MOUNTAIN VIEW CLINIC

Checklist (BEFORE MEDICATION)

Patient's Number _____

Medication (last dose) _____

Circle YES or NO. No blanks.

NURSE IS TO ADMINISTER THIS CHECKLIST. "Sick" is used here in the addict's meaning: the discomforts associated with narcotic withdrawal.

1. Do you feel sick right now? . . . . YES   NO

2. Did you feel sick at bedtime last night? . . . . YES   NO

3. Did you feel sick when you first woke up yesterday? . . . . YES   NO

4. Do you think your methadone dose now is   about right _____

                                             too much _____

                                             too little _____

Fig. 1. LAM Study: Monday questionnaire.

Table IV

LAM Study: Summary of Key Data for the First Quarter

Group [a]	Survivorship [b]	Perfect attendance [c]	Ever jailed [d]	Ever suspended [e]	Patients with negative urine tests [f] for		
					Opiates (week 13)	Amphetamines (entire quarter)	Barbiturates (entire quarter)
M-1	12/14 (86%)	5/12 (42%)	2/12 (17%)	1/12 (8%)	9/12 (75%)	11/12 (92%)	12/12 (100%)
M-2	14/16 (88%)	9/14 (64%)	2/14 (14%)	0/14 (0%)	11/14 (79%)	12/14 (86%)	11/14 (79%)
M-3	11/14 (79%)	6/11 (55%)	0/11 (0%)	1/11 (9%)	7/11 (64%)	10/11 (91%)	11/11 (100%)
Pooled methadone	37/44 (84%)	20/37 (54%)	4/37 (11%)	2/37 (5%)	27/37 (73%)	33/37 (89%)	34/37 (92%)
L	11/14 (79%)	8/11 (73%)	0/11 (0%)	0/11 (0%)	8/11 (73%)	9/11 (82%)	8/11 (73%)
L-P	12/16 (75%)	5/12 (42%)	2/12 (17%)	0/12 (0%)	9/12 (75%)	8/12 (67%)	10/12 (83%)
Pooled LAM	23/30 (77%)	13/23 (57%)	2/23 (9%)	0/23 (0%)	17/23 (74%)	17/23 (74%)	18/23 (78%)

[a] M-1, M-2, M-3: randomly assigned groups on methadone; L, LAM group receiving LAM Monday, Wednesday, Friday; L-P, LAM group receiving LAM Monday, Wednesday, Friday as group L, but reporting to clinic daily, and receiving quinine placebo on remaining days. All data are numbers of patients meeting the given criterion (numerator) and total numbers of patients active and within 10% of the nominal dose on Monday of the thirteenth week after start of treatment. In this table dropouts prior to week 3 are not counted as having ever started the program, since 2 weeks are required for induction and build-up to the stable dose. Also, females, included in the experiment initially, were dropped (and switched to methadone if they were on LAM) later by order of the Food and Drug Administration. Of the groups of 20 initially admitted, there were the following numbers of females: M-1, 5; M-2, 4; M-3, 4; L, 3; L-P, 2.

[b] Survivorship: patients who attended clinic in week 13, regardless of dose, e.g., includes those at reduced dose during withdrawal from methadone.

[c] Perfect attendance: patients who did not miss a single clinic visit during the entire quarter.

[d] Ever jailed: patients who were ever jailed during the entire quarter.

[e] Ever suspended: patients who ever missed four clinic visits in a single calendar month and consequently were suspended for 2 weeks, after a 2-week withdrawal period.

[f] Urine tests: All patients gave urine specimens every Monday, which were tested for opiates, amphetamines, and barbiturates. Data for opiates represent patients who were "clean" at week 13. Data for amphetamines and barbiturates represent patients who were "clean" (i.e., not a single positive test) the entire quarter.

The urine test data for opiates during the entire quarter are shown in Fig. 2. In order to smooth the trend data, running weighted averages were computed for each 3-week period, by weighting each "percent clean" by the number of patients at that treatment week, and pooling these weighted averages for three successive weeks, to obtain a weighted running average. Each such result was plotted at the midpoint of the 3-week interval. The discontinuance of heroin use by about three-quarters of the patients occurred within the first few weeks. The L group emerged as superior by the fourth week. By weeks 11–13, both LAM groups were superior to all methadone groups.

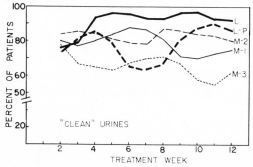

Fig. 2. LAM Study: Patients with opiate-negative urines by treatment week. Data are 3-week running weighted averages of the percent of active patients with "clean" urine at the Monday test of each treatment week. Treatment week refers to the Monday of each week after the start of medication for each patient; thus data at a given treatment week were collected on various Mondays, since patients started medication on the Mondays of various calendar weeks. Note break in vertical scale below 50.

A more rigorous test of sporadic heroin use is summarized in Table V. Here are listed only patients without a single opiate positive urine during an entire interval. Accordingly, the results are less favorable than those in Table IV for week 13 alone, but no consistent difference is seen between methadone and LAM groups. The generally better results in the first column are expected from the shorter interval—2 weeks instead of 4.

Results of the Monday morning questionnaire are shown in Fig. 3 for the questions dealing with "feeling sick." As in Fig. 2, running averages were computed. Complaint index is the percent of patients with the given complaint, i.e., "feeling sick." A pharmacological failure of LAM to sustain dependence sufficiently through the 72-hour weekend period from Friday morning to Monday morning would be expected to yield increasing "sickness" from Sunday morning to

Table V

LAM Study: Patients with Opiate-Negative Urines by Treatment Week Interval [a]

	Treatment week interval		
Group	3–5	5–9	9–13
M-1	11/14 (79%)	10/14 (71%)	8/13 (62%)
M-2	12/16 (75%)	10/16 (63%)	11/15 (73%)
M-3	7/14 (50%)	7/14 (50%)	4/13 (31%)
Pooled methadone	30/44 (68%)	27/44 (61%)	23/41 (56%)
L	12/13 (92%)	6/12 (50%)	7/12 (58%)
L-P	11/16 (69%)	7/16 (44%)	8/14 (57%)
Pooled LAM	23/29 (79%)	13/28 (46%)	15/26 (58%)

[a] Data represent numbers of patients without a single opiate-positive urine test during the given interval, divided by the total number of active patients on a dose within 10% of the nominal dose. (See legend to Table IV for abbreviations.)

Sunday evening to Monday morning. The methadone groups, receiving daily medication, should yield the same result Monday morning as Sunday morning. We expected a trend toward fewer complaints of "feeling sick" with increasing duration of treatment, in accord with our previous experiences. The figure shows that although there were large differences between the methadone groups in the early weeks, presumably due to the chances of random assignment, there was indeed a downward trend and a tendency for all three groups to converge by the end of the quarter. On the other hand, a pharmacological failure of LAM to sustain sufficient dependence through the 72-hour weekend period from Friday morning would be expected to yield a systematic increase in "feeling sick"

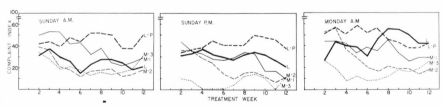

Fig. 3. LAM Study: Complaints of "feeling sick" by treatment week. The data are 3-week running weighted averages of complaint index for responses to the questionnaire administered before medication Monday mornings: "Did you feel sick yesterday morning (Sunday A.M.), last night (Sunday P.M.), this morning (Monday A.M.)?" Complaint index is percent of patients responding affirmatively. L, LAM group, no medication from Friday A.M. to Monday A.M.; L-P, LAM-placebo group, no medication from Friday to Monday A.M., but placebo take-home medication Saturday and Sunday mornings; M-1, M-2, M-3, methadone groups, daily morning medication. Note break in vertical scale at 70.

Sunday morning, Sunday evening, and Monday morning. The figure shows exactly such an effect in group L. Curiously, however, group L-P, which has a higher level of "feeling sick" at the outset, does not show this trend. A decisive interpretation cannot be given on the basis of these limited data. The simplest interpretation—that LAM does not quite "hold" about half the patients through the weekend— would be more tenable if the LAM-placebo group showed the same effect. That the L-P group showed no real increase in "feeling sick" between Sunday morning and Monday morning suggests that the problem in the L group may be more psychological than pharmacological. Unfortunately, more patients in L-P than in L felt "sick" even Sunday morning, so that the groups were not really as comparable as we should have liked.

In order to explore further whether the Monday morning "sickness" was primarily pharmacological or psychological, the following experiment was carried out. Three times, on alternate Fridays, the LAM dose was increased from 75 mg to 100 mg, on a blind basis. If the problem was pharmacological, complaints should have diminished on the following Monday mornings in both LAM groups as compared with other weekends, and also as compared with methadone groups (whose dosage was unchanged). Table VI shows that increasing the Friday dose had no consistent effect in reducing the complaint index in the LAM groups, or the ratio of complaint indices in the LAM and methadone groups. We are inclined to think, therefore, that patients who know they are receiving LAM may be excessively concerned about the medication "holding" them through

Table VI

LAM Study: Effect of Dose Increase on Complaint Index [a]

Group	10/2	10/9	10/16 *	10/23	10/30 *	11/16	11/13 *
Methadone (M-1, M-2, M-3)	32% (22)	45% (22)	53% (17)	32% (19)	19% (21)	47% (16)	24% (21)
LAM (L., L-P)	37% (19)	50% (16)	31% (16)	31% (16)	43% (14)	33% (11)	33% (12)
LAM/Methadone	1.2	1.1	0.6	1.0	2.3	0.7	1.4

[a] Data are complaint indices for all methadone groups combined and both LAM groups combined, by calendar week. Thus, each index includes patients at various treatment weeks. The shortest time in treatment at 10/2/72 was 7 weeks, the longest was 27 weeks. On the Friday prior to the Mondays indicated by (*), the LAM dose was increased blind from 75 to 100 mg. No dose change was carried out in the methadone groups. A beneficial effect would produce a decrease in complaint index on these marked Mondays in the LAM group, and a decrease in the LAM/methadone ratio. Numbers in parentheses are numbers of active patients on whom the complaint index is based. Only patients whose urine tests were negative for opiates at the given Monday were included. (See legend to Table IV for abbreviations.)

the weekend, and that this may be the major cause of the increased Monday morning complaint index in group L. We do not know if a larger dose increase on Friday would be tolerable or effective. This question deserves further investigation.

Dissatisfaction with the methadone or LAM dosage was expressed 51, 38, and 46% of the time by patients in groups M-1, M-2, and M-3, respectively (summational results for 11 Mondays following the 2-week induction period); and 36 and 51% of the time by patients in L and L-P, respectively.

No difficulties of importance were encountered during the induction and stabilization of patients on LAM. In some patients, however, during the induction phase, before tolerance developed, sedative actions of LAM appeared to develop after a delay of 4 to 6 hours. This could pose a problem of additive toxicity if a patient were to take another depressant drug because he felt the LAM "wasn't doing anything."

In summary, our findings with LAM indicate that by most of the important criteria such as survivorship in the program, attendance record, and cessation of drug use, this long-acting form of methadone is as useful as methadone itself. This broad conclusion is in agreement with those of other investigators (Jaffe *et al.*, 1972; Zaks *et al.*, 1972). There is suggestive evidence that LAM may not "hold" some patients well for the entire 72-hour period over the weekend, but this problem may be largely psychological in origin, and might yield to more intensive reassurance by staff.

ACKNOWLEDGMENTS

We are grateful to Dr. John Magistad and Dr. Vivian Olshen for statistical advice and analysis; and to Joshua Goldstein, Melissa Austin, and Linda Crouse for computer programming and data retrieval. These investigations could not have been carried out without the faithful cooperation and assistance of the counseling and nursing staffs of the Santa Clara County Methadone Program. Key responsible roles were played by Patricia Donnelly, R.N., Penelope Trelstad, R.N., June Hodsoll, R.N., and Pamela Craig, R.N. The work was supported by grant DA-00249 from the National Institute of Mental Health, and by a grant from the Drug Abuse Council.

References

Andrews, H. L., and Himmelsbach, C. K. (1944). Relation of the intensity of the morphine abstinence syndrome to dosage. *J. Pharmacol. Exp. Ther.* **81**, 288–293.
Aronow, R., Paul, S. D., and Woolley, P. V. (1972). Childhood poisoning: an unfortunate consequence of methadone availability. *J. Amer. Med. Ass.* **219**, 321–324.

Blatman, S., and Lipsitz, P. J. (1972). Children of women maintained on methadone: accidental poisoning of children. *Proc. Nat. Conf. Methadone Treatment, 4th 1972* pp. 175–176.

Cranley, W. R., and Haddow, J. E. (1971). Methadone overdosage in children. *N. Engl. J. Med.* **284**, 792.

Dole, V. P., and Nyswander, M. (1967). Heroin addiction—a metabolic disease. *Arch. Intern. Med.* **120**, 19–24.

Dole, V. P., Kim, W. K., and Eglitis, I. (1966). Detection of narcotic drugs, tranquilizers, amphetamines, and barbiturates in urine. *J. Amer. Med. Ass.* **168**, 349–352.

Dole, V. P., Foldes, F. F., Trigg, H., Robinson, J. W., and Blatman, S. (1971). Methadone poisoning. *N.Y. State J. Med.* **71**, 541–543.

Edwards, C. C. (1972). Methadone (listing as new drug with special requirements and opportunity for hearing.) *Fed. Regist.* **37**, 26790–26807.

Garbutt, G. D., and Goldstein, A. (1972). Blind comparison of three methadone maintenance dosages in 180 patients. *Proc. Nat. Conf. Methadone Treatment, 4th 1972*, pp. 411–414.

Goldstein, A. (1964). "Biostatistics: An Introductory Text," p. 110. Macmillan, New York.

Goldstein, A. (1972a). The pharmacologic basis of methadone treatment. *Proc. Nat. Conf. Methadone Treatment, 4th 1972* pp. 27–32.

Goldstein, A. (1972b). Heroin addiction and the role of methadone in its treatment. *Arch. Gen. Psychiat.* **26**, 291–297.

Goldstein, A., and Brown, B. W., Jr. (1970). Urine testing schedules in methadone maintenance treatment of heroin addiction. *J. Amer. Med. Ass.* **214**, 311–315.

Goldstein, A., and Judson, B. A. (1973). Efficacy and side effects of three widely different methadone doses. *Proc. Nat. Conf. Methadone Treatment, 5th 1973*, pp. 21–44.

Jaffe, J. H., Senay, E. C., Schuster, C. R., Renault, P. F., Smith, B., and diMenza, S. (1972). Methadyl acetate vs. methadone. A double blind study in heroin users. *J. Amer. Med. Ass.* **222**, 437–442.

Leute, R. K., Ullman, E. F., and Goldstein, A. (1972). Spin immunoassay of opiate narcotics in urine and saliva. *J. Amer. Med. Ass.* **221**, 1231–1234.

Mulé, S. J. (1969). Identification of narcotics, barbiturates, amphetamines, tranquilizers, and psychotomimetics in human urine. *J. Chromatogr.* **39**, 302.

Nightingale, S. L., Michaux, W. W., and Platt, P. C. (1972). Clinical implications of urine surveillance in a methadone maintenance program. *Int. J. Addict.* **7**, 403–414.

Zaks, A., Fink, M., and Freedman, A. M. (1972). Levo-methadyl in opiate dependence. *J. Amer. Med. Ass.* **220**, 811–813.

9

The Search for Rational
Approaches to Heroin Use

NORMAN E. ZINBERG

Almost any discussion of nonmedical drug use in this country stirs up powerful and often irrational emotionalism. This instant, pointless passion may well constitute the most severe aspect of dealing with the problem. Of course, one man's excessive emotionalism is another man's rational statement, and we may have to plunge on at high decibel levels for some time to come because we can document as truth very little about nonmedical drug, especially opiate, use. However, perhaps by noticing that the excessive fear and hysteria that surround the issue significantly complicate and distort the problem, we can begin by searching for areas on which people with different points of view can agree.

In this chapter, I will report my experience with the English system of heroin control and its implications for the arguments against the establishment of an experimental heroin induction clinic with the hope that areas of agreement can emerge.

In order to begin to have an argument, there must be mutual agreement about at least one basic premise. I am presupposing that heroin addiction is not a monolithic syndrome. That is, no single group of people exists who all choose this drug for roughly the same reason. Rather, several groups of people with widely differing motives have selected the same answer. Different types need different treatments, so we will have to isolate the groups and find out what is the most felicitous manner of working with each. This assumption per se is not highly controversial. Dr. Jerome H. Jaffe, Director of the Special Action Office for Drug Abuse Prevention, and a powerful advocate of this idea, has insisted that most of the addiction treatment programs supported by his agency have a multiplicity of services available. This means that the program must provide a variety of treatment and rehabilitation resources so that addicts can expect individualized responses to their problems.

We might hope that such a rational position would demand that all preventive, treatment, and rehabilitative possibilities be explored. Then multi-modal, the term in use for a variety of services, would include every approach that has shown itself to be useful. Unfortunately, it has not turned out this way. Different experts have anathematized different approaches, and our basic, rational premise has been thus ignored.

Among the many difficulties in conveying how programs with addicts work is the use of jargon to standardize treatment. "Give methadone to addicts," for example, deindividualizes and dehumanizes both the person who receives the drug and the dispenser. Anyone who has worked with drug users can tell you, usually with some despair, how different in his values, idiosyncrasies, troubles, and itches each is. Nevertheless, the public continues to think in monolithic terms. Besides the extent to which this attitude degrades the individual addict, it gives credence to the feelings of low-skilled working-class people that "they," the dominant white middle class and their official representatives, want to control and debase the minority groups with drugs. These underprivileged peoples fear that methadone, or any maintenance program, exists for the convenience of the middle class. Then the complexity and individualization of a good working maintenance program gets lost.

Although Dr. Jaffe supports methadone maintenance along with drug-free proposals, he is highly suspicious of any thought of either heroin maintenance or heroin induction. Later on in this chapter I will discuss the Howard Samuels/Vera Proposal (Samuels, 1972) and its critics. Dr. Vincent Dole, pioneer and advocate of methadone maintenance, finds the emphasis on multi-modality almost as difficult to bear as the idea of heroin maintenance. Dr. Judy Densen-Gerber of Odyssey House passionately supports drug-free proposals and equally strongly opposes methadone maintenance; she will accept heroin maintenance. David Roderick, representing many of the ex-addicts who are a powerful political force in the drug field, damns all maintenance proposals as "copouts." Some minority group spokesmen agree with Roderick and contend that "maintenance is a diabolic and systematic plan of extermination of the Black and Puerto Rican people." Operation Helping Hand wrote that accusation.

Before trying to discuss these sharply differing views, I want to describe a recent experience of mine in England. In the 1930's, the U.S. Treasury Department used the Harrison Narcotic Act, a tax measure, as a vehicle to repress opiate use. The Department began by prosecuting physicians whom it contended were largely responsible for the problem of addiction. At the same time, England, under the Rolleston Act (Zinberg and Robertson, 1972), treated the issue as a medical problem and permitted individual doctors to prescribe heroin as they thought the drug was indicated.

For years heroin users were few in England, so the issue prompted few headlines.

Then by the middle 1960's English heroin use began to increase. Although the number of registered users remained small (1530 in 1968—the peak), the percent of increment was great, resulting in gloomy headlines and national anxiety. The Brain Commission was formed. Since overprescribing by a few doctors was seen as the root cause of increased use, the Commission recommended heroin control clinics, which recommendation was implemented in July 1968. Although individual doctors no longer prescribed heroin, its use remained a *medical* problem. It was simply more closely controlled and regulated by the state.

Because this new system forced many unregistered addicts out into the open, the 1968 figures showed a large increase. This sudden exposure aroused enormous fears. British newspaper accounts reflected this apprehension. By extrapolating from the rise between 1967 and 1968, one story in April 1969 predicted 100,000 heroin addicts by 1973 or 1974. But the cries were premature. By 1969 no further rise was reported, and 1970 showed a significant drop in both total number of addicts and number of new addicts (Ford Foundation, 1972). There was general concession in England that the program was working. Even the police, who are notoriously afraid of any underestimation of the issue, agreed. Inspector Spears, Assistant Head of Scotland Yard's drug squad, said: "The problem now seems under control" (*London Times*, 1971).

"Experts" in the United States have watched this saga with great interest. Predictably, they have disagreed about everything: why the number rose in the first place; why it then declined; whether there is anything at all in this that can be applied to the United States experience. During this same 6-year-period, heroin addiction in the United States became an issue of national concern second only to war, with the estimates of rise in number of addicts going from a mean of 150,000 in 1966 to 350,000 in 1972.

In 1968–1969 I went to England to study the new clinic setup.

After pondering those same questions, it was hard for me then and it is hard for me now to imagine that we can learn nothing from the British experience. I gathered a number of second-hand reports during 1968–1969 about the transaction between addicts and doctors in charge of the new clinics. Although I had interviews with both, I never sat in on the actual interaction in the clinic setting.

In July 1972, Dr. Martin Mitcheson of the University College Hospital Drug Dependency Clinic kindly permitted me, as a visiting physician, with the agreement of his patients, to accompany him throughout his clinic day. This included observation of his patient interviews. The interchanges began in the traditional fashion of a follow-up medical interview and was characteristic of all the interviews: "How are you doing?"

"Well, Doc, it's been a hard two weeks. My sister had to go away suddenly and I had to see that her kid got into a home. It was rough, Doc, and that last script wasn't enough. It didn't hold me through all that bloody trouble."

Such beginning remarks would set the stage for the rest of the interview. In this case, Dr. Mitcheson probed into the details of how the patient had managed over the fortnight. He emphasized the positive, i.e., he pointed out that since the patient had managed to function in a difficult situation, this would indicate that he needed less heroin for an ordinary time. Mitcheson also asked whether the patient had supplemented his need with street heroin or barbiturates. This the patient stoutly denied. The doctor was particularly severe about barbiturate supplementation and reminded the patient that barbs made him aggressive, which led him into fights and other troubles. The patient described his anxiety during this period and his growing fear that he couldn't make it without more heroin. Mitcheson reassured him on that count, gave him a script for the same amount of heroin he had been getting (60 mg/day) and told him to discuss his problems concerning his sister and her child with the social worker.

Although many directors of drug clinics use Dr. Mitcheson's technique, there are several other methods. One doctor I talked to insisted that he never even mentions the drug during his discussions with patients. He only talks about their feelings and life style. One feature remained constant, however: both patient and doctor regarded the drug problem as a health issue. All of the traditional social rituals, the role differentials, the respective responsibilities of the patient to more or less correctly describe his symptoms and of the doctor to do his part to alleviate them were accepted. I do *not* mean that addicts in England do not consciously or unconsciously lie to their doctors. Anyone working with addicts anywhere would recognize the naiveté in such an assumption. But the lying, or "distorting," occurs within an accepted social framework that permits a degree of manipulation on both sides. Mitcheson was also manipulating when he pointed out that if the patient made it with 60 mg/day of heroin during a crisis, he might make it with less during an average week. These mutual manipulations do not undermine the sense of trust. The ongoing conflict did not erode this framework. Mitcheson's patient under the English system believed that the doctor wanted to help him despite their mutual awareness of their basic disagreement over how much heroin the patient really needed.

I was reminded at this time of a discussion I overheard between an allergist and a patient in this country about antihistamine intake. It was an almost identical discussion: How much drug are you taking? Does it control the symptoms? If you take too much, does it make it hard to function? Does too little result in discomfort? In this case the patient wanted to try a little less but the physician, fearful of a self-cycling increase in out-of-control symptoms, wanted him to use more: a reversal of the positions in the English interview, but an identical acceptance of the social roles and rituals involved.

Think about what trust means in the doctor/patient relationship to us in the United States. We let doctors stick needles and pills in us all the time. Suppose the physician were sadistic or crazy. Suppose there were no medical ethics or tradition of confidence in his wish to do what he can to help with the presenting complaint. If we did not have a socially regulated understanding between doctor and patient, we would not have a viable health system. A doctor may lecture to a patient for overeating or oversmoking or for not taking the prescribed potion. But outside of this area, he is neither a moralist nor a policeman except where nonmedical drug use is concerned. Here, U.S. physicians dogmatically support the reigning cultural outlook and turn sufferers away. And the basic traditional trusting relationship is permanently undermined.

Look at the history of the free clinics such as David Smith's in Haight–Ashbury (Smith, 1972). Although that group of patients had lost their confidence in the benevolence of our social institutions, including *organized* medicine, they could reestablish the traditional, socially supported relationship with an individual physician. But first they had to go outside the feared institutional setting. The health-oriented specialist made a special effort to reach people who could no longer trust or tolerate any of the institutions that saw them as enemy deviants.

The mutual trust that was taken for granted in our English interview could not exist between an American junkie and his doctor in a normal social setting. The junkie is seen and sees himself as an enemy deviant. He is, once an addict, at war with society. This includes doctors, social workers, ex-addicts, and everybody else. Whether he was at war before he became an addict is a moot, much debated, point. Probably some addicts were but many were not, including some returned Vietnam veterans.

Since we presently lack the underlying trust that permits the addict a confident relationship with a doctor or a doctor surrogate, we cannot adopt the English system. Much of that system is actually inadequate. The English have too few services for rehabilitation and counseling; drug-free situations are more poorly financed (as are most services there); and oral methadone has been underexploited. But certainly *all* addicts should have someone in this society with whom they can confidently, if not openly, interact. Whether this someone is a doctor or not is immaterial. We have made a few great advances: The addict who is sufficiently motivated to make it on methadone can feel comfortable in a methadone clinic; those who wish to strive to be drug free have a place to turn. In New York City, the methadone and drug-free facilities are approaching sufficiency, that is, they can care for those who wish to or are able to use these forms of treatment. Yet no one believes that all or even most addicts have any place to turn to keep them related to society. What about this hooked majority? To reach all the rest of these addicts we need more and different approaches, one of which may well turn out to be the use of heroin itself.

Some segments of the black and Puerto Rican communities will neither discuss nor consider the implementation of any use of heroin. This is obviously powerful and important opposition. On July 20, 1972 (*New York Times*, 1972a) Congressman Rangel, an acknowledged spokesman for this point of view, said that heroin maintenance was "an effective technique for keeping Spanish-speaking and black youth immobilized." Most of the statements on this issue have the same hyperemotional quality. They are full of words such as enslavement and genocide, and they are very serious. It is, after all, an inescapable fact that for at least the last 40 years these communities have suffered grievously from addiction. Yet the history of opiate addiction in this country does not bear out a convincing conspiracy theory against either blacks or Puerto Ricans. Meritricious references such as the one in the movie, "The Godfather," wherein white thugs set out knowingly to addict blacks for profit, but decide to protect the white community, badly distort the facts.

Until the unexpectedly vigorous enforcement of the Harrison Narcotic Act, opiate addiction in the United States was a rural problem. That enforcement dried up opium supplies in the rural United States (O'Donnell, 1969). Then those poor souls who could not easily make the shift to alcohol headed for urban seaports where they could obtain an illegal supply of heroin. The rural drug users quickly merged with the poorest, most deprived and suffering parts of the urban population, which included the immigrants. The population most at risk has always been the children of immigrants. Blacks moving from the South to urban seaports became part of that frightened, dispossessed group. Blacks then constituted the largest single group until the Puerto Ricans arrived. The lure of heroin and the resulting oblivion are natural temptations for this underprivileged potpourri of people. The conspiracy theory is a myth.

If no conspiracy exists, why do these groups fight tooth and nail against proposals that are in fact intended for their chief benefit? They are terrified of an epidemic theory. This view equates addiction to an inevitable spreading disease, its seductive attraction as inescapable as the plague bacillus. It sees the rise in the rate of British addicts during the mid-1960's as directly related to drug availability because of overprescribing. That is, the deadly "germ" was put into the air.

The proponents of the infectious disease theory reason as follows: Yes, the English clinic system offers greater controls in that almost all addicts and the amount of drugs prescribed are now known. However (at least until the last few months), it has knowingly shut its eyes to a limited oversupply in order to keep a "gray" market going that would preclude the development of a black market. Most of the clinic doctors knew that many addicts, when things were tough, needed a little more. Then when things were easier, the addicts could spare a little. The doctors also recognized that this wheeling and dealing among the addicts was not pushing in the classical sense, but was a kind of group activity, almost occupational therapy. Because under the clinic system some illicit heroin, or later, methadone, was still available in England, proponents of the epidemic theory would expect to see a continued rise in overall use and particularly in new addicts. They cannot explain the subsequent *drop* in British heroin use under the clinic system. Today, some British research projects on drug use are even being held up because not enough new addicts are available to form a sample.

There is no consistency to the ratio of heroin availability and its resultant use. In Vietnam heroin use spread rapidly among servicemen; yet in Thailand, where it was even more readily available and cheaper, the rate of use was very low. *The New York Times Mag-*

azine recently quoted Dr. Nils Bejerot (Markham, 1972), a Swedish psychiatrist, whose prescription for addicts was published in August 1971 in the *Israel Annals of Psychiatry*. He would "arrange for them in the best possible way, on some pleasant 'drug island' where they are allowed to live in peace with their addiction." Dr. Bejerot managed to discuss the Swedish amphetamine problem without once mentioning the continuous Swedish struggle with addiction, particularly with alcohol, which is one of the worst in the world despite considerable repression and a welfare state. The infectious disease thesis is insoluble. Different social and psychological reasons account for the rise or fall of a drug in a particular country at a particular time. It is impossible to "prove" anything.

We must try to understand the myriad "why's." Does everyone wish to be an addict? Is heroin so powerful or so pleasurable that it is irresistible to most youngsters? The answer yes does not fit what we know about opiates and about addicts.

About 10 years ago and long before the present panic, Dr. David C. Lewis and I published a study of opiate use in the *New England Journal of Medicine* (Zinberg and Lewis, 1964; Lewis and Zinberg, 1964). This study examined six groups of repeated users. One group used little or no opiates but pretended to be addicts because they cared about the life style. A second was addicted to needles rather than the drug; they liked to stick things in themselves. A third was addicted to a particular person, sometimes a doctor, lover, or relative; the drug was secondary. A fourth was severely self-destructive and developed serious physical symptoms or depression. To them the drug was important only as an alleviation. Although a fifth used opiates regularly, they continued to function and did *not* develop overwhelming tolerance or an abstinence syndrome. It was relatively easy for this group to be self-regulating and to keep their doses low because many were doctors, doctors' wives, or nurses, and had easy access to their drug. Only the sixth group exhibited the stereotyped addict career complete with craving, growing tolerance, and a great fear of withdrawal. The great increase in addicts over the last few years has not refuted this work. In fact, the confirmation that addicts differ in personality and motivation is growing. Although most of the people in our study were in serious trouble, little of it was directly related to the drug. If their favorite—heroin, morphine, demerol, methadone, barbiturate, or amphetamine—was not available to them, they could and would use another.

Of course a fraction of our population is in serious trouble. But this has little to do with a drug epidemic. Although that fraction will drug itself with something, the drugs are not the problem. Why do we persist in the belief that most of us are at risk? Why do we so overestimate the charismatic power of these drugs?

I recently collected a sample of 100 patients who entered a general hospital with a serious *specific* (i.e., not psychological) medical or surgical problem that required regular dosing of opiates for 10 days or longer with doses far higher than can be obtained using street drugs. Once their pain receded, only *one* recalled having any wish for an injection of the drug and that happened when he thought his condition had recurred.

And why do we so overestimate the extent of the pleasures from drugs? Is the effect of heroin as euphoric or orgiastic as we have been led to believe? Let us approach this issue in reverse. We were told in the past that a drugged state was completely enthralling both physiologically and psychologically. Withdrawal, therefore, was almost unbearable. "The Man with the Golden Arm" substantiated this thinking. Addicts were terribly *fearful* of withdrawal. But this myth began to be exploded once any group paid serious attention to addicts. "The Concept," a play put on by residents of Daytop Village, all severe ex-addicts, stated sharply that much of heroin withdrawal (barbiturate withdrawal is another matter and deadly) is psychological. Drug withdrawal in Vietnam then proved beyond doubt just how exaggerated was our previous view of the stranglehold heroin had on people. Many enlisted men withdrew themselves before leaving that sad country. Formal rehabilitation units withdrew men cold turkey on an outpatient basis. Some of these had enormous heroin habits. We already knew from the work of John O'Donnell (O'Donnell, 1969) and others that many heroin addicts at some point give up their drug voluntarily. Then they turn to alcohol. Even during their addictive period when they spend their time in jail or hospital, or have to cope with the problem of being broke, it is more on-again off-again than we had supposed.

We have surely overestimated the seductive power of heroin. We have also given it more credit for pleasure production than it deserves. I think that most straight people cannot understand the motives of addicts. In an attempt to comprehend, they imagine reasons that would be true for them but are probably not true for addicts. Straights know that it would take something incredibly wonderful to make them stick needles in themselves and risk their health and freedom. But these straights do not become addicts.

When I was discussing the heroin high with an enlisted man in Vietnam (Zinberg, 1972a, b) who used a great deal of heroin, I told him that I did not think I would like the experience. He said, "That's because you can leave. You're not in pain." Since then many soldiers and other addicts have echoed those same words. The truth is that heroin is not a drug of pleasure. It reminds me of that old joke: "Why do you beat your head against the wall?" "Because it feels so good when I stop." Under the influence of heroin, a person goes a long way away in his head. He sinks down a long tunnel where he can watch people, including himself, moving around swiftly and rather aimlessly. Sometimes the user loses interest. Then he slips away, drifts off, from all that activity. But if he wishes, he can pay attention. He can tell the foolish experimenter whether an object is sharp, very sharp, blunt, or a feather. The "pleasure" comes from the drug's capacity to move a person away from pain. In the case of an I.V. (intravenous) shot, the "tunnel" entrance appears almost at once. Hospital patients as well as junkies describe the blessed relief from physiological or psychological pain that comes from derivatives of the poppy. But this relief is not pleasure; it is cessation of pain.

How can we therefore preclude the infectious disease theory? After all, are not many of our people, particularly our poor, in pain? Yes, they are, but they are *in life* too. And heroin's metaphorical thickening of the walls, the erection of that long tunnel between the user and life, including the people in life, is a price too lonely for most people to pay.

The proponents of the infectious disease and conspiracy theories are still with us, however. One of their myths used to surround an evil pusher who hung around schoolyards seducing youngsters by a free sample into the hideous thrall of addiction. This facet of the conspiracy theory has been astonishingly tenacious without any evidence for it. I think it has survived so long because straights have wanted *personally* to understand why anyone would take this drug. Hence, they dream up ignorance and seduction. The modern version of the same myth lurks in the amoral peer who cannot wait to induct his ignorant friend into the mysteries.

It is true that most new addicts do become so through the ministrations of a friend. It is harder to get and use heroin than straights imagine. Many returned Vietnam veterans have discovered this fact. Certainly a kid in the ghetto has more access to drugs than a middle-class kid who has to go to an unfamiliar and hostile part of town to make a connection. But even the ghetto kid needs more "scratch" than he usually possesses and he must find out what the going price is. Then he must learn how to use the paraphernalia of injections, to cook up a shot (even for skinpopping), and to find veins. Although these are not overwhelmingly difficult procedures, a supportive mentor is generally required.

Certain charismatic types naturally make better teachers than others and these are sought out by neophytes. I have interviewed several such addicts who have admitted starting people off on the junkie trail. Without exception, they spoke of their reluctance and told me how many they had talked out of continuing. At first, I thought such tales reflected most addicts' inability to face reality and their own lives. They would wish to invent a less destructive world. And addicts are often terribly guilt-ridden people. I have been following up a sample of "chippers" (occasional users), however, and I find that more addicts try to talk them off heroin than on. A standard horror tale concerns the wife or girlfriend who more or less unwillingly becomes an addict and then a prostitute simply to be close to her addict consort. But my work shows a greater number of couples where only one is an addict—this is true of alcohol addiction as well—and the other strives valiantly and unsuccessfully to help. How can the contagion theory explain these couples?

A recent study by Leon Hunt (Hunt, 1972) goes even further. Hunt suggests that only during the first flush of drug use, perhaps even before addiction, will an addict act as mentor. If this is true, as I believe it is, using civil commitment, quarantine, preventive detention, or whatever to isolate addicts may help with crime. But isolation will *not* help contain the spread of addiction, which is, after all, the chief aim of the quarantine concept.

The next move would be early detection of addicts, which means compulsory urine testing in the schools, on the job, or in the vestry. Analogies to smallpox vaccination and tuberculin tests assume an infectious disease model of addiction. This model ignores the complex social and psychological considerations that are inherent in the victim who seeks out the drug "disease." Should this disease model be accepted, the problems of assembling on a national scale the apparatus for such testing and the implementing of it seem insurmountable.

Of course, we could select high-risk areas to try out these procedures. Such areas would not only have to endure the loss of civil liberty and the self-incrimination that is implicit in the existence of compulsory urine testing, but also they would have to deal with the issues of confidentiality, hassles about the correctness of the urine findings (at this stage, at least, they are often inaccurate). And finally, what would we do with "tainted" urines, once found? Would we automatically quarantine *all* people thus identified? For how long? Should we differentiate between exposed heroin addicts and barbiturate users? How many antagonists to how many drugs should they receive? This last is no trivial question. So far the toxicity of antagonists may be greater than the initial drug, and in themselves habit forming. Are all or any of the proposed "treatments" involuntary at all stages? And so on.

One of our greatest misconceptions lies in the belief that users and pushers are legally, morally, and socially separate. The key question is who seeks out whom; the key word is "ignorant." In my interviews with opiate users, both here and in Vietnam (Zinberg, 1972), the users have acknowledged that they sought out someone to teach them. They wanted to use heroin and in most cases outside Vietnam, despite some half-hearted denials, knew that they wanted to get hooked. Almost all of these users admitted that *they* had pushed their mentor to teach them. They were not ignorant about the drug, but hoped to learn more. One of the army's more naive educational campaigns in Vietnam was built on its belief that soldiers did not know that the white powder being offered them was heroin and not cocaine. When I asked soldiers if they had ever thought it was cocaine, both users and nonusers guffawed. This campaign was based on the typical straight belief that nobody would knowingly seek out "shit."

If they had no faith in either the conspiracy or infectious disease theory, the minority groups would lead the participants and exponents of treatment diversity. On every count minorities are most injured by addiction. According to arrest figures, individual black, Puerto Rican, and Chicano users are consistently more harassed by police agencies (*New York Times*, 1972d). Although heroin causes little if any primary physiological damage, hepatitis, infections, and debilitation come from dirty needles and the other derivatives of its criminal status. Minority groups are physically more harmed by these secondary physiological consequences of addiction and have less access to good medical care. Psychologically, it is harder to measure the harm that results from addiction for we know so little about the various psychic states that drive someone to crave it. If we could calm the minorities' irrational fears of epidemics and contagion, both the individual and his community would surely treasure any treatment that offered addicts a chance for a functional life that avoids the constant harassment of police and illness.

In the meantime, as this interminable discussion continues, the age of users sinks lower and lower. Again, in such a charged atmosphere, even this terrifying fact is not dealt with rationally. First, many investigators have found that it is exaggerated. For example, when a proposed adolescent treatment program in New York considered beginning their operation in collaboration with one high school, it was assumed that most of the dropouts left because of drugs. When 25 dropouts were followed up—no easy matter to track them down—it turned out that 4 had a drug problem (Danaceau, 1973).

Although this is a high percentage, it is nothing like what had been expected. The other 21 had serious troubles with the school and chose truancy for social and cultural reasons. It is true that many of those 21 are at risk as far as drugs are concerned. But to label them already drug users implicitly or explicitly, by way of newspaper headlines or what have you, surely increases their risk. Comparing their friends to a plague and giving the dropouts little hope of escaping the disease opens the psychological door to heroin for some of those 21. Furthermore, it discourages rational and realistic approaches to their real difficulty, which is connecting with a school that does not understand their language, perspectives, or values. Labeling them all carriers of an infectious disease gives the problem a false clarity that can easily become a self-fulfilling prophecy.

We know that the heroin trade thrives on economic exploitation. As a result of the illegality of the drug, a small group who are willing to chance getting caught are granted a virtual monopoly. And the law enforcement agencies "cooperate." They restrict the supply so that the illegal operators can set an exploitative and inelastic price that guarantees them enormous profits. Given the powerful addict-consumer drive and the restricted, expensive supply, the result is not surprising: customers turn criminal to pay the price.

How much addiction is directly responsible for how much crime is another area of great disagreement. The extent of the influence of addiction on police corruption, however, certainly hurts the minority groups most (*New York Times*, 1972e). The numbers game in all these matters leads inevitably to the "liar's figger" reaction. Each side quotes figures that are diametrically opposed. And both are partly right. Undeniably, addicts steal to support their habit. A recent Massachusetts survey estimated that addicts were responsible for 88%, or $127,500,000, of the property stolen in that state (Buckley, 1972). The extent to which they are responsible for terrifying, assaultive crimes is far less documented. But many addicts were surely stealing before they chose addiction. And we cannot assume that they would stop once they were off drugs or stabilized through some inexpensive legal regulatory dosage.

Although we cannot gauge the potential drop in the quantity of crime if the direct link between crime and addiction were severed, the nature of the crimes would almost certainly change. Generally speaking, addict stealing is uncontrolled and irrational. I picked up the Monday, August 28, 1972 New York *Daily News* (*New York Daily News*, 1972) at random. In that paper one story told of a subway assault by an addict for no profit and another of an assault by a 17-year-old user on a 76-year-old woman for her handbag within sight of a policeman. Of course, addicts try to take things they can resell, but they do so helter-skelter, as quickly as possible. And they take extraordinary risks because they care little for themselves and a great deal for the few quick bucks that can be translated into a fix. It may seem strange to speak of stealing as rational or irrational. But rational crime carefully balances the risk against the gain. This type of crime can be guarded against and can be understood by its victims. Irrational addict crime leaves chaos in its wake. Its victims see this frantic rampaging as senseless representative of a growing breakdown in the structure of society and its institutions of social control, such as the police and the courts. They cannot understand such crimes.

This is particularly true in the black communities where addict crime is common. Addicts like neither to travel nor to take the time for the fattest pickings. They usually operate close to where they live and to where they can make a connection. Hence, ghetto communities are terrorized. One of the saddest byproducts of this victimization surfaced recently. Residents of a black community were asked what prevented them from attending community meetings aimed at improving a variety of local conditions including the use of the neighborhood as a "shooting gallery." Many stayed home because of their fear that junkies would either break in, if they were out to an advertised meeting, or mug them in the street (Packer, 1972).

If addiction is an infectious disease, its victims must be quarantined to prevent its spread. So reason the adherents of the epidemic theory. Then this false concept of prevention drains all the energy and money from valid clinical research or treatment programs. In fact, it operates ideologically against them. For who can consider supporting small, carefully structured programs such as the Vera proposal when a plague threatens society? Advocates of the epidemic idea wish to remove the diseased victims from our vulnerable, healthy atmosphere. Quarantine is a euphemism for the arrest and confinement of addicts simply because they are addicts. Were it not so serious a matter, it would be amusing to hear Senator James Buckley complain to the Senate about heroin maintenance: ". . . thousands of persons being totally dependent on the Government" (Congressional Record, 1972). Would he, I wonder, support incredibly expensive detention centers such as have cost New York state over three-quarters of a billion dollars since 1967 for handling approximately 20,000 addicts altogether and with a census as of this writing of 368? (New York Times, 1972f)

Their expense is a small part of the detention centers issue. If and how they would work are the major questions. So far, all of the accumulated evidence confirms a relapse rate of between 80 and 90% following any sort of commitment for treatment, whether to jails, civil commitment programs, or hospitals. Richard Stephens and

Emily Cottrell of the National Institute of Mental Health at Lexington, Kentucky, recently published a comprehensive study that reported an 87% relapse rate (Stephens and Cottrell, 1972). They observed that this rate was identical to the findings of earlier studies. Long-term, continued surveillance involving parole or outpatient treatment cuts that figure only a little.

To understand this persistent relapse rate, we must further explore the nature of addiction in the light of two popular explanations. The first relies on a biochemical concept, which assumes that the individual had a preexisting defect of some sort, such as a thyroid deficiency. This defect is corrected by opiates and allows the user, for the first time in his life, to feel whole.

Followers of the second explanation, a metabolic disorder concept, think that a cycle of heroin addiction somehow changes the body metabolism either permanently or for a much longer time than any usual idea of detoxification. To rebalance the metabolism, heroin or another opiate is the only relief. Vincent Dole and Marie Nyswander (Goldstein, 1972) developed the methadone maintenance procedure based on the idea that this long-acting, orally effective drug would "correct" the metabolic deficiency without the many accompanying problems of heroin: illegality, need for injection, highs and lows, and so on. As my initial premise stated, addiction should be looked at in many ways, so the above descriptions may well apply for some addicts. The English addicts who bargain for more heroin "medicine" and who insist then and only then can they function "normally" make beguiling examples to reinforce the metabolic disorder theory.

Nevertheless, most addicts do not seem to fit in the metabolic mold. A surprising number of addicts, when put into a protective environment, such as a hospital, jail, or a therapeutic community, once detoxified, do not report the overwhelming drug craving that exponents of the metabolic disorder theory would expect. Indeed, this resultant comfortable functioning is one of the arguments advanced by believers in the infectious disease theory who want to lock addicts up.

Avram Goldstein of Stanford, an outstanding pharmacologist, is now working exclusively on the psychopharmacology of opiates. Dr. Goldstein supports a behavioral conditioning theory which, for once, does not conflict with a dynamic psychological explanation of addiction and of how opiate maintenance works (Goldstein, 1972). He points out the similarity between a withdrawal syndrome and a classical anxiety attack: sweating, weakness, chills, gooseflesh, nausea, and vomiting. Dr. Goldstein has observed addicts self-administer the drug after experimenting with many other ways of extinguishing anxiety. These individuals use it to quell an overwhelmingly painful stimulus. A set is thus developed. Certain specific behavior, i.e., the atmosphere of a certain neighborhood, certain people, or a specific act (the fixing ritual and injection), stands for relief of the painful stimulus. Notice that it is the behavior within a given set that essentially relieves the anxiety. The drug is secondary. This explanation thus deflates the metabolic theory.

Many addicts, observed by police and others, report that they develop a withdrawal syndrome immediately after using heroin if they find themselves in a situation, such as a jail, which they *associate* with withdrawal. And conversely, in a hospital setting many addicts declare that the opiates there do not "work." I have seen addicts after a while become paranoid and insist that they are being fooled and are receiving a placebo. (Unfortunately, their suspicions are sometimes true. Fooling addicts is a game that some doctors play in order to test addicts' powers of observation.) I am referring to situations where the addict does receive what he is told he is being given. The addict soon discovers that the "cure" for his disease, anxiety, is only temporary. The anxiety returns after the medicine wears off. What is worse, his response to the loss of his medicine is a redoubling or more likely, multiplying of the original anxiety symptoms. It is thus only reasonable for him to experience a compulsion to seek and use heroin.

Goldstein postulates the possibility, chiefly based on animal experiments, that heroin reaches a specific reward center in the brain (Goldstein, 1972). Although that may be a part of the explanation, it is not a necessary one. Anxiety hurts. Those unfortunates who either live in the anxiety pit or who are unusually sensitive to the bite of its snakes know how much anxiety hurts. The extent of their discomfort causes them to seek out the heroin "cure." Leon Wurmser of Johns Hopkins (Wurmser, 1972) and Edward Khantzian of Harvard (Khantzian *et al.* 1973) have recently agreed that many addicts in this country use heroin as a form of self-treatment, and not at all as a vice or for antisocial purposes.

Most humans have the capacity to tolerate a good deal of anxiety. Animals may or may not have such a capacity. Some people do not have adaptive mechanisms at their disposal (animals in captivity certainly do not). They therefore arrange life situations that are less likely to stimulate pain or they select activities whose positive attributes balance it. Methadone, like heroin, reduces intolerable anxiety. When injected, it apparently works as well as heroin *although* it lasts longer (more about the although later). When taken orally, methadone may not be quite as effective in reducing anxiety. This may account for the heroin-seeking forays by some persons in methadone programs. They quickly learn, however, that methadone will stave off the secondary anxiety-like withdrawal syndrome.

Without the protection of maintenance, individuals who cannot deal with anxiety invariably relapse into heroin use. Those who have not been thoroughly detoxified, and Goldstein suggests the total process may take from 6 months to a year (Goldstein, 1972), can be frightened of an impending withdrawal syndrome or set off by any stressful incident. Then they blindly seek a fix, often without forethought or previous motive. But what about those who, under our current system of punishing addicts, have been incarcerated for a long period of time and are to the extent of our present knowledge entirely detoxified? They, too, return to their heroin use in an astonishingly short time after release either from jail or a U.S. Public Health Service hospital. This can be explained by a simple behavioral conditioning model. The detoxified addicts leave the protected atmosphere to return to a less structured life filled with potential dangers. The sight of a friend or a familiar atmosphere revives powerful old memories and sets in motion the series of conditioned acts that ends in shooting up. A dynamic psychological explanation would also take into account the extent to which the addict feels that society sees him as an enemy. When he emerges from incarceration, he therefore enters combat. Also most addicts envision their incarceration as an unjust punishment. They feel "entitled" to their beloved/hated medicine and act accordingly, no matter how irrational this progression of thought may appear to the straight observer.

Let us agree that both the metabolic and psychological explanations are applicable to at least some addicts. Quarantine would surely not work for them. How long would we keep them in "camps" simply for being addicts? Could we lock them up long enough for them to "get over" heroin? Addicts who have remained in jail 5 to 10 years return to their habit within a single day. How would we "cure" them in the camp? Addicts are unrepentant deviants, a group notoriously untouched by any form of therapy. Once we discover a narcotic antagonist that is long-acting, nontoxic, and itself not dependency producing, we will have another form of maintenance therapy. This is supposed to take the "pleasure" out of the high and decondition the addict. But will it "cure" this person's inability to tolerate anxiety? And if it does not, will he not probably seek out other drugs? Barbiturates and amphetamines are both far more deadly than heroin. Alcohol used as a substitute for heroin may also carry greater risks than heroin.

The total cost to the individual of any social policy must be considered. We must first calculate the cost of our current policy. We must then assess the cost of future plans whether these involve the maintenance or quarantine of users.

Until we introduced the concept of maintenance, the current policy of attempted total repression of users was extremely costly to individuals and to society. And it was not working. To buttress our current program, official agencies, led originally by the old Federal Bureau of Narcotics, have constructed myth after myth. When pushers in schoolyards, drug progression, drugs turning brains to jelly, and other tales of horror are not supported by facts, they postulate and publicize others: drugs affect chromosomes; drugs are a contagious disease. Officials go on manufacturing myths such as the chromosome scare long after they are disproved on the self-righteous assumption that "if they have scared one kid off using drugs, it was worth the lie." This blindness to the costs of business-as-usual is unfortunately absolutely typical. The current hope of the new Federal Bureau of Narcotics and Dangerous Drugs is to restrict the drugs at their source; buy up the Turkish poppy fields and thus limit availability of heroin in the United States by interfering with the growth of the necessary plants. This naive plan in our modern world was finally exploded by the report "World Opium Survey 1972," prepared by President Nixon's Cabinet Committee on International Narcotics Control and reported in the *New York Times* (*New York Times*, 1972c). The report declared that, in spite of our greatly improved and expanded police surveillance, only a "small fraction" of the illicit flow is seized. Since only a few square miles of poppy are necessary to supply all illegal United States needs, the report acknowledges that there are several areas of the world ready, willing, and able to step in as suppliers should we succeed in curtailing the Turkish trade.

Has there been any change in policy as the result of this list of standbys? Of course not. In fact, the money and energy that should support the reassessment of such outmoded policies instead support the fight to maintain the status quo and to squash any efforts at innovation. Maintenance with oral methadone is no panacea, and indeed the need to improve most existing "gas stations" (methadone programs without supporting services, which just hand out the drug) is enormous. Also the issue of how to control the drug used so that it does not leak back to the community as a black market item is important and difficult. But, in general, methadone has resulted in some success. Although figures vary from program to program, they all reflect the progress of individual addicts. Many of those who were previously incapacitated are now functioning in work and life with a concomitant reduction in their criminal activity. Even some programs, such as Phoenix House, which have been totally committed to a drug-free ideology are now considering methadone maintenance as a stepping stone to a drug-free state.

Opponents of any form of drug maintenance fear that the addict will be drug dependent for his lifetime and that addiction will increase rather than decrease. It is easy to understand how some people who fear maintenance and are aware that our present repressive policy has failed offer greater repression as the answer. Our policy has failed, they argue, not because of the repression but because there was not enough of it. Permissiveness (the worst of bad words) will, according to them, create millions of addicts overnight. Now we must round up our addicts, fence them outside society for as long as necessary, and brand them (one plan envisions taking distinctive footprints which, like fingerprints, provide positive individual identification). Not only will this plan not work, but it can be accomplished only through a serious curtailment of individual human liberty. And such a curtailment of liberty will repress the poorest fraction of the population. How can the minority communities consider supporting such political action? It could deprive some of them of their rights to a trial by peers and deny them protection from what is now unlawful search. And it could recognize and possibly punish some addicts for what is essentially a life style or a personality orientation. Yet some of the strongest support for a quarantine program comes from the unlikely alliance of extremely conservative politicians, such as James Buckley, who oppose busing, guaranteed annual wage, and the like, and blacks such as Charles Rangel, who is against everything else Buckley is for.

Those minority group supporters of quarantine must be aware of what the Knapp Commission hearings in New York have shown. Herbert Packer, Stanford Law School professor, pointed out before the hearings that police corruption and discriminatory police practices go hand in hand with criminal laws that try to regulate morality, such as abortion, homosexuality, gambling, prostitution, and drug use (Packer, 1972). Packer used the Knapp hearing findings to show that our intertwining of criminal law with morality precepts in our treatment of heroin use has already led to serious problems for civil liberties. Nine-tenths of the cases that come before the Supreme Court involving an alleged illegal search and seizure are narcotics cases. Proponents of the Omnibus Crime Control and Safe Streets Acts of 1968 and John Mitchell's Organized Crime Act of 1970 relied heavily on the legislators' fears of a heroin epidemic to get the more repressive features of those acts passed. To pass the no-knock entry section of the 1970 law, for example, they claimed pushers could flush the white powder down the toilet if the law's invaders warned them by knocking before entering. Heroin traffickers vied with the Mafia to justify the need for electronic surveillance. Incidentally, these two groups are often wrongly connected. There is little or no evidence of organized crime's direct participation in heroin trafficking. Another potent assault on civil liberties can be found in John Kaplan's (another Stanford Law School professor) estimate that over 50% of those incarcerated under California's commitment laws were Chicanos, who make up only 12% of the state's population (Kaplan, 1971).

Hence, it seems reasonable to expect that if we were to make urine testing for narcotic use compulsory, the schools or districts first in line to receive this honor would be densely populated with minority group members. The proponents of quarantine have assured the public that the control of narcotic use is their sole aim and that the urine testing and footprinting would never be used for any other program of social control. This still sets a dangerous precedent. The decision of an individual to use drugs is a complex physiological, psychological, and social phenomenon. If we can view this as a plague that justifies the suspension of his liberties, it does not seem a great step to the curtailment of other like political and social activities.

Most of the black leaders who rail at the use of heroin in any treatment program also fear that maintenance would divert attention from the root social causes of addiction. Yet they want detention camps, or in public health terms, quarantine, to deal with what they regard as a social problem. Let us imagine that these camps would work, and authorities agree to isolate rather than treat this "infected" minority. Why should this "success" reinforce the desire to alleviate the social conditions that are at least partly responsible for the troublesome minority? It would seem equally plausible that once we found this "solution," we could apply it to other troublesome minorities. Does not political radicalism spread from one convinced advocate to others? And this would let us minimize the "waste" of money to remedy social ills. After all, if things get bad again, "we know where we stand," a marvelously ambiguous phrase made popular by a Massachusetts politician to convey opposition to racial integration without overtly declaring her bigoted policy.

The use of the concept of quarantines threatens both the civil liberties and social advancements of minority groups. A maintenance program offers them chiefly benefits. The addict who willingly chooses maintenance relieves himself of the frantic search for a connection and for the scratch to buy it. If he has any preexisting skills or is personally motivated to learn to do some kind of work, he can make more consistent and regular relationships with people. As straights understand this process of love and work, he should gain in confidence and self-esteem. Society would certify the drug as God's medicine rather than the devil's potion. The reformed sinner would be accepted back into the social fold. Because he is drug dependent, he is still, in my view unfortunately, seen as weak. But he is not "bad."

Since the individual on maintenance is treated humanely, he is less likely to steal from his neighbors, which, of course, helps the surrounding community and the larger society, but in addition, illegal wealth is no longer plowed back into other crime and corruption. Addicts on street dope suffer numerous health problems from adulterants, unsterile needles, and the like. These secondary problems crowd local hospital facilities and spread more prosaic bacterial infections. Maintenance would minimize these mundane health costs. Police would be freed from searching for drugs and pushers to protect communities from non-drug-related crimes. Scarce public monies could be put to other use. In Massachusetts it was estimated that in 1971 the criminal justice system itself spent $9,457,833 on drug-law violators and drug-related property crimes instead of on better lighting, patrolling, faster trials, and more rehabilitation facilities (Buckley, 1972). And it is ironic that all of these are more necessary in the areas where drug use flourishes than in any other. Were we to change our current, expensive, repressive system and put the funds saved into these improvements, think what profit poor communities would reap. And maintenance involves no risk to individual liberty, which risk is inherent in the so-called preventive measures of compulsory urine testing, footprinting, and quarantine.

If we accept the principle of maintenance, then why only oral methadone? From the point of view of the straights, the answers are obvious: no more horrible sticking with needles; one long-lasting dose replaces many disappointingly short ones; the fear of withdrawal abates; and adequate functioning is possible. Since some lethargy accompanies methadone maintenance, this last is a bit questionable. Of course, no straight would become an addict in the first place unless, according to his myth, he were unwittingly seduced into it in the first place. The most avid proponents of oral methadone estimate that no more than 40–50% would willingly stick with that regimen. They recognize that many addicts are attached to the needle as well as the drug and that many *crave* the quick highs and lows. Remember the British addict who did not "like" methadone even when it was injected? We know that the flirting with withdrawal and the self-destructive life style are immensely seductive for some, particularly if these activities are shared with a special person. And, finally, the addict is justified in feeling that our society has declared him an enemy deviant. How can he trust us to give him a drug that would help him with his pain? Whether he was suspicious of and at war with society before his addiction or whether these feelings resulted from his experience after he chose to use heroin is academic. Many American addicts will so suspect any clinic that represents straight society that they will automatically reject it. But maybe they could trust a clinic that permits them *their* drug and *their* needle.

Let us now examine the modest heroin maintenance research experiment proposed by Howard Samuels and the Vera Institute of Justice, and dissect the objections to it. Perhaps in this way we can find a base of rational agreement that will let workers in the field bury their small arms and get on with the job. This proposal is extremely modest (Samuels, 1972). It is intended strictly for clinical research and begins with 30 addicts to determine feasibility. If these results are encouraging, at its height it would only study 100. Only addicts who have demonstrably failed at other treatment modalities including oral methadone maintenance will be accepted into the program. The drug will be made available solely on the premises. The research aims to discover if an American addict can be stabilized on heroin so that he can feel relatively comfortable on a determined dose and can function both psychologically and physiologically. Longer-lasting injectable methadone, when possible, will be substituted for heroin. If he can be initially stabilized, as over 50% of British addicts are, he will be moved within a year from injectable opiates to either oral methadone or a drug-free state. Ergo, this is actually a heroin induction program; it is not simply heroin maintenance.

The money for this experiment will be obtained from research funds. It will not interfere with a single penny of support for existing treatment programs. We need this kind of small-scale expensive research to tell us what is possible with a small group. To quote the Vera proposal, those selected will be ". . . that group for whom every effort at rehabilitation has been exhausted." Although it is true that the results of this experiment will not necessarily help us to understand how heroin induction would work on a large scale using hundreds or thousands of addicts, many of the objections raised to the Vera program criticize the research for not doing what it has not set out to do. The proposal recognizes that there are two problems: to find out what, if anything, can be done with heroin induction with any number of addicts at all; then to apply on a large scale what has been learned from the first research. One of the most frequent objections to this experiment is that it would not work on a large scale. This may well be true, but it is not a relevant point.

The current overemotional atmosphere lends itself to internecine war over how best to cope with drug users. Opponents of the Vera proposal want something to fight about. If they can find no appropriate objections in the proposal, their commitment to controversy will manufacture some. In exactly the same way, many persons have responded to the Vera proposal as if it proposed full-scale heroin maintenance, which it does not. For example, the Committee on Youth and Correction has stated that "there is no justification for adopting heroin maintenance even on a limited basis as public policy at this time" (*New York Times*, 1972b). Some persons who really favor heroin maintenance either also oppose the Vera proposal or support it for the wrong reason. It is generally frustrating to have to tell opponents or proponents of the proposal that they oppose or support something that is not proposed. At its worst, this irrational reading of the proposal will prevent this or any other desperately needed effort to develop valid research with carefully evaluated, clinical information about the treatment of addiction. Indeed, it can defeat the whole problem.

James Buckley in the Senate and Congressmen Peyser, Rangel, and Biaggi in the House introduced a bill in 1972 barring any research that would involve dispensing heroin (*Congressional Record*, 1972). They regard such research as sufficiently dangerous to warrant full-fledged Congressional action. They fear that the government agencies that approve such research, i.e., Federal Bureau of Narcotics and Dangerous Drugs, Food and Drug Administration, Justice Department, National Institute of Mental Health, and the White House Special Action Office for Drug Abuse Prevention, cannot be trusted to safeguard the interests of our individual citizens and our social institutions. It is exactly this sort of hysterical response that makes up the social setting in which drug use takes place. Each escalation of emotionalism inhibits the search for rational approaches; the enemy deviant label attached to the user becomes more real for him and for those sticking on labels; and around we go in a vicious circle. This destructive circle makes it harder and harder to get addicts and citizens to relate within the programs.

At present, the pervasiveness of this varied opposition to any change in the social status quo of heroin and its users is hard to see because many who might react to it are caught up in the struggle for more and better drug-free, methadone maintenance, and other modalities of treatment. The wish to use optimally what is currently avail-

able occupies the Special Action Office for Drug Abuse Prevention
and other agencies, and offers hope for more addicts than are now
under treatment. But remember, no one estimates that more than
50% of addicts can be reached by existing modalities. When this
limit is reached, more comprehensive efforts will be expended in
desperation. Meanwhile, the unreached 50% may have become more
intransigent because of the current limited concept of what is possible. The desperate need to cope with them could result in poor
treatment and worse evaluation. The decision *not* to find out what is
possible is not a neutral decision. It is a significant part of the heroin
problem.

Any heroin induction experiment must consider what it asks of the
addict. Must he suddenly change his life the moment he seeks treatment? The difficulty in giving up everything that has been his life,
peculiar as this problem may seem to straights, on the day he enters
a clinic door seems to many addicts a vast and impossible undertaking. In theory, heroin induction permits a transaction. This must be
tested. Give up some things: the hustling for heroin; but keep the
beloved/hated drug and needle. Then if a reasonable human relationship can be established, more withdrawal can follow. The more
entrenched in war are addict and society, the harder it is for them to
establish such reasonable relationships.

The persistent misreading of the purposes inherent in the Vera or
any such proposal leads to other dangers even should the research
get under way (which seems very unlikely at the moment). For there
are plenty of problems involved in such research. Considering their
alienation from straight society, can this intransigent group of addicts
be induced into a treatment situation with injected heroin at all? In
fact, some of the most important questions this kind of program
would answer would be whether such research is possible and, if so,
how do we execute it. Will addicts restrict themselves to the limited,
stabilizing doses available at the clinic when there are readily available, unlimited supplies on the street? In England, virtually all
heroin is clinic heroin so that the country need not contend with this
serious question. Will the addicts forego the hustling, crime, and
other potent excitements in addict life style? Even if the experiment
establishes results similar to England's, which show that technically
addicts can function and work on heroin, will American addicts be
motivated to do so? How will the addict respond to taking heroin in a
clinic setting as opposed to the street surroundings he is used to?
Which is more important to most addicts: the drug or the street ritual? What sort of personnel will be most effective in establishing
relationships with which addicts? That is, can we discover any con-

sistent differences among those addicts who want to deal with a doctor, those who prefer a nurse, and those who seek out nonprofessional, perhaps ex-addict, clinic workers?

These are some of the questions that will be considered by the Samuels/Vera proposal. It is true that the researchers do not know in advance the answers to the questions to be studied. Although this hardly seems a reasonable objection, every question listed above has been raised as an objection to beginning the proposal.

The principles behind the Vera proposal are, first, to find out more about traditional and innovative treatment of addicts. The affected individual must be involved in deciding which combination of methods works best for him because, after all, he knows the most about his relationship with drugs and life. But the addict will *not* make the final decision about his treatment method. His relationship with drugs naturally affects his judgment. No drugs or treatment method should be offered out of context or proposed as the only treatment that is possible or efficacious. Ancillary services for rehabilitation should be available. These services should employ only people with whom the afflicted can form a dignified relationship, not a manipulative one. The nature of the problem of addicts and addiction will be presented reasonably, non-controversially, and factually to the public. This may well include facing unpleasant realities, i.e., the experiment at heroin induction may fail completely. This would squash that treatment idea. If the induction succeeded, but not the transfer to modalities other than heroin, we would have more knotty problems to unsnare. The transfer may succeed but be inoperable on a large scale, and so on. If we wish to consider these issues in a factual context, obviously, we must first carry out the experiment. Above all, the goal is for the addict to find a way to personal freedom as an individual who can function constructively and with a comfortable degree of acceptance in this society.

At this writing, I doubt that the United States will ever exactly apply the English system of controlling and regulating heroin use. Perhaps we should not even strive for such a parallel. I am sure, however, that we should accept our addicts into some aspect of our social system in the same way that the addicts in the English Dr. Mitcheson's office felt included. Anyone who has been part of a nonrepressive system recoils with horror from our repressive, punitive approach. And these like reactions come from diverse sources as, for example, veterans of the 1919 clinics such as Leroy Street and the addicts I talked to in England. We all agree that total repression makes a bad situation worse.

References

The Congressional Record—Senate, August 17, 1972.

Danaceau, P. (1973). "A Study of Methadone Maintenance Clinics." Prepared for The Drug Abuse Council, Inc., Washington, D.C.

Delong, J. (1972). "Dealing with Drug Abuse," a report to the Ford Foundation. Praeger, New York.

Goldstein, A. (1972). Heroin addiction and the role of methadone in its treatment. *Arch. Gen. Psych.* **26**, 78–94.

Hunt, Leon G. (1972). "Heroin Epidemics: A Quantitative Study of Current Empirical Data." Prepared for the Drug Abuse Council, Inc., Washington, D.C.

Kaplan, J. (1971). The role of the law in drug control. *Duke Law J.*, No. 6.

Khantzian, E. J., Mack, J. E., and Schatzberg, A. F. (1973). "Heroin Use as an Attempt to Cope: Clinical Observations." Presented at Annual Methadone Maintenance Conference, Washington, D.C.

Lewis, D. C., and Zinberg, N. E. (1964). Narcotics usage II. A historical perspective on a difficult medical problem. *New Eng. J. Med.* **270**, 1045–1050.

Markham, J. M., What's all this talk. *N. Y. Times Mag.* July 2, 1972.

New York Daily News, August 28, 1972.

Rangel, D. D., *New York Times,* July 20, 1972a.

New York Times, August 9, 1972b.

New York Times, August 17, 1972c.

New York Times, August 18, 1972d.

New York Times, September 7, 1972e.

New York Times, September 7, 1972f.

O'Donnell, J. A. (1969). "Narcotic Addicts in Kentucky." U.S. Public Health Serivce, Publ. No. 1881. U.S. GPO, Washington, D.C.

Packer, H. (1972). "Damn With Faint Praise (Or Praise With Faint Damn)." *The New Republic,* July 14.

Samuels, H. (1972). "Proposal for the Use of Diacetyl Morphine (Heroin) in the Treatment of Heroin Dependent Individuals." Vera Institute of Justice, New York.

Smith, D. E. (1972). "Love Needs Care." Little, Brown, Boston, Massachusetts.

Spears, D. D., *London Times,* August 17, 1971.

Stephens, R., and Cottrell, E. (1972). A follow-up study of 200 narcotic addicts committed for treatment under the narcotic addict rehabilitation act (NARA). *Brit. J. Addict.* **67**, 45–53.

Wurmser, L. (1972). Drug abuse: Nemesis of psychiatry. *Amer. Scholar,* **41**, No. 3.

Zinberg, N. E. (1972a). Rehabilitation of heroin users in Vietnam. *Contemp. Drug Probl.* **1**, 263–294.

Zinberg, N. E. (1972b). "Heroin use in Vietnam and the United States: A contrast and a critique." *Arch. Gen. Psych.* **26**, 486–488.

Zinberg, N. E., and Lewis, D. C. (1964). Narcotics usage I. A spectrum of a difficult medical problem. *New Eng. J. Med.* **270**, 989–993.

Zinberg, N. E., and Robertson, J. A. (1972). "Drugs and the Public." Simon and Schuster, New York.

(1972). "Research Report on Heroin Use." Presented to John J. Buckley, Sheriff of Middlesex County, Massachusetts.

10

Early History of Heroin
in the United States *

DAVID F. MUSTO

Since antibiotics were unavailable in the late nineteenth century, respiratory ailments claimed many victims. In the United States, for example, tuberculosis and pneumonia were the two leading causes of death. Understandably, pharmaceutical research concentrated on treatment of respiratory diseases and their symptoms. Thus, the Bayer Pharmaceutical Company of Elberfeld, Germany, sought substitutes for powerful opiates whose use in combating these ailments was limited by inconvenient or dangerous side effects. In 1898 the Bayer Company's search for an effective remedy to morphine's side effects, chiefly nausea and constipation, led its researchers to add two acetyl groups to the morphine molecule: Bayer adopted "Heroin" as the trade name for diacetylmorphine.[1] The firm believed that heroin would be a more effective cough suppressant than morphine. Yet within a decade of its introduction, doubts and fears began to spread about the new drug. Within 20 years of its discovery, the word heroin denoted great danger and folly to American society.

Heroin's transition from palliative to curse can be noted in the

* This investigation was supported by the Drug Abuse Council, Inc. © David F. Musto, 1973.

[1] H. Dreser, Pharmakologisches ueber einige morphinderivate. *Deut. Med. Wochenschr.* **24**, 185–186 (1898). Earlier, C. R. A. Wright of St. Mary's Hospital Medical School, London, had isolated the same substance and named it tetracetylmorphine in accordance with current nomenclature [On the action of organic acids and their anhydrides on the natural alkaloids. Part I. *J. Chem. Soc.* **12**, 1031–1043 (1874)]. A useful "History of heroin" can be found in the *Bull. Narcotics* [**5**, 3–16 (1953)].

medical press. Like so many substances, heroin was seized upon by some physicians as a possible cure for morphine addiction, and a rash of successful reports appeared in the first few years after 1898. Doctors in this era generally treated patients with purges (to eliminate toxins or morphine), sedatives, or drugs similar to the addicting opiate, and then, following withdrawal, pronounced their patients cured. Heroin was occasionally used as one of these substitute drugs.[2] Yet simultaneous doubts, warnings, and reports of "heroin-mania" soon balanced the accounts of heroin as an addiction cure. Professor H. C. Wood, Jr. of the University of Pennsylvania warned against the drug's possible addictiveness as early as 1899.[3] His words of caution were repeated the following year in the "American Yearbook of Medicine." While the Yearbook did report favorably on heroin's use in treating coughs and relieving the sensation of air-hunger, it admonished readers that "for the present, small doses should be used and administered with some care, as the toxic properties of the drug are not thoroughly well known." [4] By 1906, the *Journal of the American Medical Association* published a more detailed and ominous account of heroin in its series on "New and Non-official Remedies." It was still recommended that physicians prescribe the drug for a wide range of respiratory ailments: bronchitis, pneumonia, consumption, asthma, whooping cough, laryngitis, and certain forms of hay fever. But a stern warning added that ". . . the habit is readily formed and leads to the most deplorable results." [5] While a few individual writers continued to submit letters or articles to medical journals praising heroin, the bulk of medical opinion acknowledged heroin's dangers. Thus, 8 years after heroin's commercial distribution, hope faded that an ideal cough medicine had been discovered.

Heroin Abuse Recognized and Studied: 1910–1917

While the image of heroin no longer suggested a fully safe cough suppressant, neither had it reached the totally fearful picture later ac-

[2] For an American example see, M. B. Ahlborn, Heroine in the Morphine Habit. *N.Y. Med. J.* **74**, 235–236 (1901).

[3] H. C. Wood, Jr. The newer substitutes for morphine. *Merck's Arch.* **1**, 89–90 (1899).

[4] G. M. Gould (ed.), "The American Yearbook of Medicine and Surgery: Medicine." Philadelphia, W. B. Saunders, p. 180 (1900).

[5] *J. Amer. Med. Ass.* **47**, 1303 (1906).

cepted. Dr. Pearce Bailey, a leading American physician and later the army's chief neuropsychiatrist during World War I, examined for a weekly journal, *The New Republic*, the popularity of heroin among New York City's youth in 1915–1916. He estimated that three-fourths of the city's drug takers used heroin, mostly by sniffing. He described the typical heroin user as about 20 years old and male, who had become addicted through "force of imitation and suggestion," rather than from any physician's prescriptions. About one-fourth of the men studied had become addicts within a few months of starting heroin use. Dr. Bailey added that after the habit had been formed, the addict often turned to crime against property in order to raise money for the drug. Few wanted to be cured and most would enter treatment only under pressure. Dr. Bailey continued his findings [6]:

The heroin habit is essentially a matter of city life . . . It would seem that heroin taking is closely allied with the factors which make inebriety in some form inevitable in the poorer classes in large cities. Boys and young men seem to want something that promises to make life gayer and more enjoyable and the particular "fillip" they hit upon depends on their personal temperament and their surroundings. Often one choice excludes others. The heroin addicts are rarely given to drink, and under the use of the drug their sexual appetites dwindle rapidly so they are not often offenders in sexual matters . . . Few are married. They are generally healthy and able to work and are fairly intelligent. Many are of engaging personality but, as often happens with personalities who are engaging, they are all unstable, suggestible and easily led.

While regret over the heroin habit infused Dr. Bailey's article, it is obvious that there is little of the extravagant fear of heroin users that would very shortly become commonplace in America.

Dr. Bailey further estimated that heroin usage had rapidly increased around 1911, five years before his study. Other evidence confirms that this was the period when heroin replaced morphine as the favored drug employed by young opiate users in New York City and, to a lesser degree, in several other major eastern cities.

Similar conclusions were reached by Dr. W. A. Bloedorn, a Naval officer, who published his findings in the *U.S. Naval Medical Bulletin* shortly after American entry into World War I.[7] Bloedorn, concerned with the drug problem in the armed services, had contacted Dr. M. S. Gregory of Bellevue Hospital. With his help, Bloedorn examined addict admission records for the 1905–1916 period inclusive. These records prove most instructive, for they show an attempt to quantify the reality behind heroin addiction. The statistics gathered from the records were employed in an elementary way, yet are so

[6] P. Bailey, The heroin habit. *New Republic*, pp. 314–316 (1916).
[7] W. A. Bloedorn, Studies of drug addicts. *U.S. Nav. Med. Bull.* **11**, 305–318 (1917).

rare in the whole debate over heroin that they are indeed of great significance.

Bloedorn's data covered the years before and after the Boylan Act, passed in New York State in 1914.[8] This act permitted the maintenance of addicts, but restricted the practice to physicians. The Boylan Act furthermore permitted commitment of individuals regularly using habit-forming drugs to "a state, county, or city hospital or institutions licensed under the State Lunacy Commission." Moreover, the year 1914 also witnessed the passage of a federal antinarcotic law, the Harrison Act, which aimed at elimination of narcotics except for strictly medical purposes. Both acts helped create the later group of addicts studied by Bloedorn although neither had been enacted when heroin use began to be noted about 1911. Table I indicates that 13 years after its introduction in 1898, heroin overcame morphine in popularity. While pressures like the Boylan Act might have increased hospital admissions for all opiate addicts after July 1914, there is a striking rise of heroin users in admissions recorded after 1913, followed by a rapid drop in morphine admissions a year later. By 1916, heroin was the drug used by the vast majority of those admitted for treatment at Bellevue. The average age of the addicts admitted was about 20.

Table I

Annual Admissions for Heroin and Morphine Addiction to Bellevue Hospital, New York, 1905–1916 [a]

Year	Heroin admissions	Morphine admissions
1905	0	4
1906	0	9
1907	0	2
1908	0	3
1909	0	2
1910	1	25
1911	3	59
1912	9	83
1913	21	393
1914	149	398
1915	425	265
1916	649	129

[a] From Bloedorn.[7]

[8] For a more detailed discussion of New York State narcotic legislation see D. F. Musto, "The American Disease: Origins of Narcotic Control," p. 102 ff. Yale Univ. Press, New Haven, Connecticut, 1973.

Observers of New York City's drug problem were not alone in their conclusions of heroin's rising popularity shortly after 1910. The *Journal of the American Pharmaceutical Association* quoted in 1913 an account from Syracuse, New York, which reported heroin's growing appeal in the last 18 months [9]:

> Dope users who found that police surveillance made it very difficult to secure opium, morphine and cocaine, soon learned that heroin could be easily obtained. No prescription is necessary. As a result they began using this drug, and the habit grew by leaps and bounds. It started in the poorer districts, but soon spread to the better portions of the city.

Philadelphia General Hospital also conducted an examination of records shortly after the Harrison Act, only to discover a pattern similar to the one found at Bellevue, although the number of addicts in Philadelphia was fewer. The rise in heroin-related drug admissions to PGH (Table II) and interviews conducted with patients led Dr.

Table II

Annual Admissions for Opium and Opiate Addiction to Philadelphia General Hospital, 1911–1915 [a]

Year	Opium and opiates (includes heroin)	Heroin only
1911	29	1
1912	64	1
1913	40	14
1914	66	28
1915 (first 68 days)	136	86

[a] From Farr.[10]

Clifford B. Farr to suggest that heroin was a recent drug of dissipation, first noticed in Philadelphia about 1913. Dr. Farr suggested that the impetus behind heroin's rising popularity was a recent and effective crackdown on opium and cocaine.[10] He thought that drug users were looking for a more accessible and easily used drug than opium. Nor was this only one man's opinion. Dr. Bailey concurred in 1916 after he compared the equipment necessary for opium smoking and the custom of frequenting "dens" with the ease of sniffing or injecting heroin. Thus, contemporary writers voiced their opinion that

[9] Growth of the heroin habit. *J. Amer. Pharm. Ass.* **2**, 627 (1913).

[10] C. B. Farr, The relative frequency of the morphine and heroine habits. *N.Y. Med. J.* **101**, 892–895 (1915).

heroin's popularity was in part due to being one of the last habit-forming drugs to be controlled. The complications of opium smoking plus more rigorous law enforcement against opium and cocaine may well have led their habitués to heroin.

Nor was the problem of addiction found solely in civilian life. Indeed, World War I can be seen as a rough dividing line for American attitudes toward heroin misuse. This was to be the era when heroin achieved a truly infamous reputation. The use of heroin was first noted as a problem in the military in 1912–1913: some in the Army called the drug "happy dust," and took it by sniffing.[11] During mobilization, however, after April 1917, rumors began to spread rapidly about growing numbers of addicts. Government agencies such as the Internal Revenue Bureau, which had been advocating a stronger Harrison Act since 1915, reported to newspapers that in New York City alone thousands of draftees were rejected from the service because of drug addiction.

Individuals in responsible positions took up the cry: Representative Henry Rainey, later to head the Treasury Department's Special Committee on the Narcotics Traffic, stated that 80,000 draftees had been rejected due to drug addiction. This assertion later led Daniel C. Roper, head of the Bureau of Internal Revenue, to initiate a campaign against drug addiction. These estimates appear to be in error, for only about 3000 nonalcohol drug users were ultimately located at the examining stations, the camps, and in France. Yet by the time these more accurate statistics caught up with the melodramatic announcements, they were too late to restrain fear over drug use in the services and in the returning servicemen.

Dr. Royal S. Copeland, Health Commissioner of New York City, warned of the danger of addicts to the city. The Commissioner estimated that there were 150,000 to 200,000 addicts there, of whom many were "recently discharged soldiers." Heroin was the favored drug, he declared, and 70% of the heroin users were under age 25.[12]

---

[11] R. M. Blanchard, Heroin and soldiers. *Mil. Sur.* **33**, 140–143 (1913). Additional information on the use of drugs in the Army includes: The use of habit-forming drugs by soldiers. Editorial, *Med. Rec.* **90**, 683–684 (1916); J. M. W. Scott, Drug addiction, *Med. Clin. N. Amer.* **2**, 607–615 (1918); and, G. E. McPherson and J. Cohen, A survey of 100 cases of drug addiction entering Camp Upton, N.Y. via draft, *Boston Med. Surg. J.* **180**, 636–641 (1919).

[12] *New York Times*, Sept. 13, 1918; see also Musto, footnote 8, pp. 142, 156, 295, 299 and 300; see also, P. Bailey, The drug habit in the United States. *The New Republic*, March 16, 1921, p. 67.

Transformation of Heroin Use into
a Major Social Problem: 1917–1919

Heroin had begun its rapid elevation to the status of a major public evil beginning about 1917. The growth of the heroin habit and its predilection for city youth, already the target of concern because of urban crime, resulted in a strong reaction. Yet not until a national emergency created a fearful and intolerant atmosphere did heroin use among the young result in dramatic exaggeration of its effect. Heroin abuse became an enemy of the state.

The crucial factor in heroin's transformation does not seem to have been the incidence or character of heroin use in 1917, but rather the context in which this phenomenon was interpreted. In 1917, the United States harbored a climate of ambiguous fears, which coexisted with the nation's desire to react unanimously in order to preserve the world's freedom. The battle was not against an enemy of the United States, but the enemy of mankind. A national frenzy helped sanction an enforced conformity. Zealousness sought simple causes for complex problems, and drug abuse was a convenient object for concern. Prohibition of substances inimical to young soldiers occurred within weeks of the declaration of war. Alcohol was banned at the camps, and Congress permitted the President to stop the use of grain for beer production. After insulating the military from alcohol, drugs then became the focal point of concern. From examinations held at recruiting stations, it appeared that there were more drug users than alcoholics. Heroin seemed to take its toll on the younger city dweller to a greater degree than alcohol. Prohibitionists and other reformers picked up Dr. Bailey's suggestion in 1916 that urban life seemed to foster heroin use.

Exaggeration contributed to the image of heroin and other drugs as critical problems for the nation. If official propaganda could spread false stories of German atrocities in order to facilitate the war effort, then the Bureau of Internal Revenue could also exaggerate the number and dangers of addicts for an end of its own: strengthening the Harrison Act, a goal since 1915. War allowed the Bureau to dispense with some of the quieter and slower methods of peacetime persuasion. Heroin's image soon reached alarming proportions helped by a deliberate campaign inaugurated by Commissioner Roper. Roper was assisted by several circumstances: a concentration of the heroin problem in urban areas; public pressure to regulate other drugs of abuse, especially alcohol; and an existing bureaucracy enforcing federal drug control under the Harrison Act. The drug was one more convenient object on which to place the blame for social disorder.

The Response to Heroin after World War I (1918–1924)

Once acquired, the extreme image of heroin continued in the public mind. The postwar period of Bolshevik and anarchist agitation nurtured wartime worries. Reformers like Captain Richmond P. Hobson, the leading and highest paid platform speaker of the Anti-Saloon League and soon to be founder of the International Narcotic Educational Association, embellished upon heroin's dangers. He stated, "Most of the daylight robberies, daring holdups, cruel murders and similar crimes of violence are now known to be committed chiefly by drug addicts, who constitute the primary cause of our alarming crime wave." [13] Officials quickly seized heroin as an ideal explanation for the crime and murder rates or whenever unpalatable and antisocial acts were examined for the public's benefit.

In 1919 the Mayor of New York, John Hylan, appointed a special Committee on Public Safety to investigate two problems he saw as related, the heroin epidemic among the city's youth and bombings directed at institutions and national leaders. The evidence for a link between the two was meager, but his appointment of a prominent committee, and its consequent failure to set the record straight contributed to the protean image of heroin.[14] The citizens of New York City, the historic center of heroin use, and the American city with the largest number of narcotic addicts, found in heroin a ready-made explanation for almost any crime. It is small wonder that popular weeklies and newspapers held heroin a cause of public disorder.

Heroin and Crime

There were allegedly two links between heroin and crime: addicts stole in order to purchase drug supplies, and heroin stimulated a user to violent crime as a result of its physiological effect. Although

[13] Musto, footnote 8, p. 190.
[14] See Musto, footnote 8, p. 134.

the second assumption is incorrect, it was widely believed and became a persuasive argument against addiction maintenance programs, such as that operated by the New York State Narcotic Control Commission. Another argument against the state's maintenance program was that as the "contagion" spread through easy availability of the drug, more and more people would turn to crime to support their habit.[15] Heroin's convenient and plastic image was irresistible to public officials. In 1925, the City's Commissioner of Correction ascribed to opiates the high rate of murder and suicide in the city.[16]

Not only did the war unleash an atmosphere of intolerance for any deviance, but it also began what was termed a national "crime wave" by youth: bank robberies, other armed hold-ups, senseless murders, and aggravated mischief. In this context heroin provided a convenient explanation for disorder: the "crime wave" age group was similar to that noted as susceptible to heroin; the drug possessed fearful but vague effects; and an ascription of crime to its physiological stimulation was easily accepted, thus taking pressure off law enforcement in its efforts to curb violent crime. Heroin became a public enemy.

The link was further forged by crime statistics gathered from jails, prisons, and arrest records. With the enforcement of anti-drug laws or ordinances, the number of drug-using individuals in the statistics increased. Two conclusions were drawn from these records in order to support the link with crime. First, many or most of those arrested on anti-drug charges also had criminal or arrest records for other crimes; second, the increasing number of inmates or arrestees with drug habits suggested that the overall drug problem was rapidly growing worse. The fact that the inmates were in jail because of law infractions of recently enacted and increasingly enforced drug laws was seldom stressed. The implication left with the public was that drugs and crimes were linked and that the crisis was quickly growing. For example, an increase after 1919 of addicted prisoners in Sing Sing Prison from 1 to 9% was described not only by the chief physician of Sing Sing, but also for years by Captain Hobson as an increase of 900%, rather than put into the context of augmented drug law enforcement.[17] In another Congressional hearing an official of the New York City Police Department estimated that about three-quarters of crimes would be eliminated if drugs were controlled.[18]

---

[15] See Musto, footnote 8, pp. 119–120.

[16] F. A. Wallis, The menace of the drug addict. *Curr. Hist.* **21**, 741 (1925).

[17] See Musto, footnote 8, pp. 326–327.

[18] Testimony of G. Kuhne, Department of Correction, New York City, before Committee on Education, U.S. House of Representatives, *in* Conf. on Narcotic Education, (Hearings on HJR 65, 69th Congress, 1st Session), Dec. 16, 1925, p. 175.

Prohibition of Heroin Manufacture
in the United States: 1924

A national campaign begun in the early 1920's to prohibit the use
of heroin in the United States and its manufacture in foreign nations
reiterated these misleading statistics and opinions. Over a few years,
extravagant and virtually unchallenged statements regarding heroin
were pressed on Congress and the public. Wardens, police commis-
sioners, and medical associations eagerly dramatized heroin, acting
in what they felt to be the public interest. Those who opposed them
were either intimidated into silence or were unnoticed in the surge
of contrary public opinion.

With the transformation of heroin's image from that of a bad and
regrettable habit to a major public enemy came yet another target for
blame: the cause of the heroin problem lay in foreign nations, and
not in America. Presumably in this evil and underhanded way
foreign nations acted to undermine democracy and the American
way of life. If foreign nations were not susceptible to greed or ill-
disposed to the United States, so the argument ran, this terrible
scourge could easily be ended.

A strategem first used in the instance of the Harrison Act was again
employed: a strong federal law prohibiting heroin production from
imported opium would set a model for foreign nations and encourage
them to adopt a similar regulation. Once other nations prohibited
heroin manufacture, the American smuggling problem would vanish.
Thus argued Representative Stephen Porter, Chairman of the House
Foreign Affairs Committee, in 1924. Other major nations, however,
were not persuaded by Porter's arguments and failed to follow the
American precedent. This failure of the other nations did not surprise Porter, an opponent of foreign entanglements. It did, however,
justify for him American withdrawal from international narcotics discussion for the remaining years of the 1920's.[19]

Conclusion

In an effort to explain the rise in heroin use, authorities pointed to
the relative inconvenience of opium smoking and the easy availability and cheapness of heroin in a tightening drug market. As controls

---

[19] See Musto, footnote 8, pp. 197–209.

were further extended to substances such as morphine and cocaine, heroin won a temporary reprieve. The shift of morphine users to heroin and the latter's attraction to adolescents dramatized the drug as the most seductive and probably the ultimate in narcotic debauchery. Finally, this last resort of determined drug-users was assaulted with the whole armamentarium of social controls.

Persons who earlier had described heroin without alarm soon expressed themselves differently. For example, Dr. Bailey declared after the war that addicts were "suggestible, (and) easily become the tools of designing propagandists in spreading seditious doctrines, or in the commission of acts in defiance of law and order." [20] Even when informed students of drugs like Dr. Lawrence Kolb, Sr. argued that heroin did not stimulate violence, guardians of public safety ignored him. Certain voices, particularly that of Representative Porter, sought to blame America's heroin problem on foreign nations, an idea that gained credibility in the isolationist atmosphere of the 1920's.

The public response to heroin demonstrated that the social perception and actual effects of a drug need have little relationship. The link of heroin with violence illustrates the ease with which disparate social fears can be conjoined in an attempt to make sense out of a bewildering environment.

Perhaps the most somber lesson drawn from heroin's transformation into a major public enemy is the realization that the social institutions with special responsibility to inform public opinion and to guide official actions were as caught up in the distortions as anyone else. One might have expected the American Medical Association to have supported the reasonable positions advocated by Dr. Kolb or wondered why the legal institutions did not vigorously challenge the statistics of heroin use and exaggeration of its link with violent crime. When, however, a belief is a convenient explanation for so many problems in society and the only victims of the belief are a vague, elusive collection of pariahs, a change in official and public attitudes may come slowly, if at all.

---

[20] P. Bailey, Applicability of the findings of the neuropsychiatric examinations in the army to civil problems. *Ment. Hyg.* **4**, 303 (1920).

11

Drug Abuse:
Changing Perspectives
in Long-Term Social
and Political Strategies

RAYBURN F. HESSE

Programmatic strategies to control narcotic addiction must encompass and consistently address the universe of drug abuse and dependence—narcotic and nonnarcotic—and must assess and, by preordainment of new circumstance, give credence and substantiation to emerging *social strategies* that focus simultaneously upon the nonuser, who is at risk in our drug-taking society, the experimenter, the casual or recreational user, the involved user, and the dysfunctional user, the latter including but not limited to the narcotic addict.

Such approaches, programmatic or social, must accept certain multiple truths, hard-won by trial and error during the tumultuous rush to programming in the late 1960's.

The truth is that there is no such universal as the addict. Instead, there are a variety of individuals who use drugs, licit and illicit, narcotic and nonnarcotic. There are persons who are infrequent users, habitual users, dependent users, and addicted users. There are persons who are dysfunctional without the use of drugs and persons who cope and adapt and become relatively more functional with the application of drugs. There are persons who use drugs for different reasons and with different effects, individuals who are of varying ages and ethnic and economic backgrounds, who have differing so-

187

cial and psychological characteristics, persons who are simultaneously at different stages of involvement in the drug abuse process, and persons who are therefore at different states of readiness to receive and profit by our help.

The truth is that, while we place appropriate emphasis upon street addicts and the various drug cultures among our youth, we cannot forget that our drug abusers today are increasingly found among top corporate executives, middle management, clerks, salesmen, white and blue collar workers, and housewives.

The truth is that, like all epidemics and social crises, drug abuse will have its fallout—persons who will remain physically afflicted and socially dysfunctional—even when this problem has reached its peak, crested, and tapered down to manageable proportions. Long-term care for an undetermined number of persons who will not respond maximally to any treatment modality will apparently become a fact of life.

The truth is that, whereas our universe was dominated 4 years ago by a heroin addict who was a passive, dependent personality, predominantly a ghetto resident, today's drug abuser is younger on the average, more inclined to take risks, and importantly, he is a multiple drug abuser.

The truth is, as the Federal Strategy Council on Drug Abuse (1973) conceded, in a report so rigidly drug specific that this fundamental conclusion was overwhelmed: "There appears to have been an increase over the past several years in the number of drug users who can be described as multiple or polydrug users. Such drug use patterns emphasize the need to focus on the life style and the fundamental causes of drug use rather than on the elimination of the use of any one drug."

The truth is that our "escapist addict" has been largely replaced by persons who use drugs to cope and adapt, as well as persons who seek escape, and also by persons who choose drugs for recreational purposes.

The truth is that all of the major industrial nations are experiencing one or more forms of drug abuse, primarily nonnarcotic, while some of the developing nations are experiencing problems of narcotic addiction. We can dispense with the myth that drug abuse is an American phenomenon, resulting from or occasioned by some malaise within American society.

The truth is that there is not an international pandemic of narcotic addiction. Rather, as the World Health Organizations Expert Committee on Drug Dependence has observed, there are a series of national epidemics of drug abuse, which are best viewed collectively as a pandemic of drug misuse.

The truth is that the motivations for use, the drugs of preference, the extent of use and abuse, the effects of the various drugs, the responses to treatment, and the willingness to undergo treatment vary from user to user, from community to community, and nation to nation and can be altered by mood, setting, environment, the individual's physiological and psychological makeup, the dosage, the quality of the drug, the availability of certain drugs.

The truth is that the principal drugs of abuse for the majority of abusers are psychotropic substances legally manufactured in this country and only recently put under new, more effective controls.

The truth is that we have failed, as governments, as societies, as professionals, and as individuals concerned about the quality of life in our nation, to design, conduct, and provide primary, secondary, and tertiary prevention.

The truth is we have not had effective political, moral, or spiritual leadership at the national level, so far as drug abuse in concerned.

The findings of the National Commission on Marihuana and Drug Abuse (1973) give emphasis to this conclusion:

The Commission has carefully surveyed the social response to the contemporary drug problem, and has been struck by a persisting uneasiness which seems to color the entire effort. On the street and in the councils of government, increasing numbers of drug abuse experts wonder whether their commitment and efforts have had any actual impact on the problem. Many of them assume optimistic positions in public, while suspecting privately that no solution will be found. The Commission understands the reasons for this malaise.

We are convinced that public policy, as presently designed, is premised on incorrect assumptions, is aimed at the wrong targets, and if too often unresponsive to human needs and aspirations.

. . . American drug policy is almost seven years old, and not once during this period have the underlying assumptions been systematically evaluated and a broad, coherent foundation for policy-making established. As a result, each new occurrence in drug development and each new use pattern have been viewed as unfamiliar, with the unfamiliarity breeding a sense of crisis and the crisis precipitating ad hoc policy responses.

The Commission feels strongly that the present institutional response, despite sincere efforts to move it in the right direction, continues to be rooted in the mistakes of the past, and, indirectly, tends to perpetuate the problem.

Because of this confusion about objectives, the formal institutional response to the drug problem has been more reflexive than rational, more situation-oriented than strategic. The ad hoc responses to use of specific psychoactive drugs have interfered with examination of the fundamental questions relating to behavior patterns and the appropriate means of social control.

Research has provided us with an almost endless stream of psychoactive substances.

The tendency is to identify a new substance, determine its potential hazards as a chemical and then to insert it into the existing system. This procedure tends to perpetuate the public focus on the drugs rather than on the prevention of behavior about which society is concerned. When the drug appears in the streets, as it inevitably does, social institutions respond as if the behavior was unanticipated, and because they are ill-prepared to deal with the situation, an atmosphere of crisis is generated.

Because the focus has always been on the elimination of prohibited substances altogether and on the elimination of the street use of therapeutically useful drugs, social institutions have directed primary attention to the problem of use of specific drugs. Patterns of drug-using behavior have been ignored except as an after-thought of intervention.

When increases in prohibited drug use continue to escalate, policymakers respond, not by reassessing the problem from different perspectives, but rather by pressing for ever-more costly mechanisms of control; costly both in terms of resources and important social values. Drug policy can be thus summed up: increased use of disapproved drugs precipitates more spending, more programs, more arrests and more penalties, all with little positive effect in reducing use of these drugs.

Finally, the truth is that the single greatest deterrent to an effective solution to the problem of drug abuse has been and remains our failure as a society to determine, declare, and pursue a universally accepted drug abuse policy.

The explicit mandate given the government and the professions by the Drug Abuse Office and Treatment Act of 1972 is to devise new policies and strategies relating to the abuse of chemical substances.

Such policies and strategies will be most short-sighted and probably doomed to failure or nonimplementation if they deal only with the presence or absence of a drug.

In a societal context, we have an infinite number of social casualties, some of whom use drugs.

The critical need is for a new social policy that defines, establishes, and promotes a comprehensive network of support for all of our social casualties, a problem-specific policy that addresses cause as well as effect.

Any realistic and workable drug abuse policy of the 1970's must be phrased as a social policy and must project strategies in a societal, not a governmental, context.

Programmatic strategies must devolve from, pursue, and enforce these social strategies, which include among their diverse input elements, our public goals, political aspirations, and private fears.

The mandate for a new drug abuse policy is given various forms of expression and is met with diverse suggestions for resolution, but the element fundamental to all discussion is the public demand that we prevent the abuse of drugs. Most commonly, the debate over resolution revolves around technique and procedure—each modality of treatment and prevention having its cadre of advocates whose success all too often is the achievement of a polarity of opinion, which stifles real discussion and, therefore, progress.

The ultimate truth we must recognize is that neither society, nor government, nor the professions have made up their collective minds as to what they truly want done about drug abuse. Our failure to address the problem in the whole of its societal context has created confusion, contradiction, and frustrated our best efforts.

It is ironic that societies of men, operating within systems of law, demand that government be totally effective in controlling human behavior, failing to recognize in their outcry that the government and the law are mirror images of society and man.

This maxim was emphasized by Elliott Richardson in 1972, while testifying as Secretary of Health, Education, and Welfare, when he said any ultimate attack on this problem must address itself to the whole process by which a society derives and affirms values.

We were agreed, in the middle 1960's, before the problem became pandemic, that the major industrial nations have created, for a variety of reasons, an infinite number of social casualties, some of whom use drugs.

Our responses, unfortunately, then and now, reflected our virtually absolute lack of unanimity of opinion on how to cope with this phenomenon. Our dedication to institutional approaches resulted in a splintering of social effort, climaxing in a stand-off in which many capable resource organizations were sidelined, deliberately or by choice, while the fledgling elements of programming that emerged as the new responses were quickly cast into an equally institutionalized and increasingly entrenched new health industry.

The war on drug abuse most often featured internecine battles among drug abuse treatment agencies competing for funds and favor.

The approaches tried were scattershot—the law enforcement model, the medical model, the public health model—and, while each approach, like the individual modalities they spawned, could objectively claim some degree of success, none was singularly capable of responding to all of the diverse manifestations of the problem, let alone addressing its equally diverse causes.

At best, the system was inefficient, a system of programs jerry-rigged upon programs, built by men and women who piled public and social policies upon one another in a never-ending pursuit of the magic bullet that would quell rising public fears. Too often, these fears were our principal motivants.

An assessment of programs and program policy in Washington and most state capitols during the past decade would reveal a pattern of social and programmatic waffling—this year the law enforcement model in response to rising crime rates, next year renewed emphasis upon treatment as concern was directed for the drug user—vogue following fad, often the direct product of shifting funding and program priorities in Washington.

As we turned the decade, we found we had adopted the snowball model.

Thus, we appeared to have achieved a social as well as a legislative milestone in 1971 when President Nixon proposed and Congress concurred that treatment, prevention, and law enforcement, as well as their related disciplines, were not separate approaches but were closely interrelated and should therefore be coordinated at all levels of government. Public Law 92-255 was signed into law March 21, 1972.

Public Law 92-255

While it gains little to review extensively the policies and program approaches prior to the reorganization of the federal-state effort, it is useful and instructive, in contemplating development of new social strategies, to review the rationale and purpose of this Law as well as its implementation.

Not surprisingly, the Congress noted among its principal findings that "the effectiveness of efforts by State and local government and by the Federal government to control and treat drug abuse in the United States has been hampered by a lack of coordination among the States, between States and the localities, among the Federal government, States and localities, and throughout the Federal establishment."

Just as there were some 19 federal agencies involved in drug abuse programming, some states had as many as a dozen different agencies operating, funding, or directing programs at the state and local level, often without any established pattern of coordination or cooperation.

Comprehensive programming, close pursuit of established social goals, and effective delivery of services were not possible. The delivery system was a patchwork derelict whose structure promoted and ensured inefficiency.

Worse, drug abuse programming did not have a priority. At the time when the new Act was approved, the New York State program was larger than the total federal effort.

It is important to emphasize at this point that the critical decision reached by the Nixon Administration was to give drug abuse a very high priority. This decision has as much impact and became as important as any of the single provisions of the Act or any of the solitary changes in government procedure.

Indeed, as we will demonstrate later, the system created by the Administration and the Congress depends heavily upon the continued assertion and recognition of this priority.

The Administration and the Congress declared that a major goal of the government was to promote and improve drug abuse programs and to foster the development and implementation of a national strategy that would balance and give appropriate and proportionate priorities to education, treatment, rehabilitation, research, training, and law enforcement. The goal of this national strategy was to maximize and coordinate the resources of federal, state, and local governments, delineating and coordinating their responsibilities and relationships.

These concerns and rationales gave birth to two new entities: the Special Action Office for Drug Abuse Prevention (SAODAP) at the federal level, and the state drug abuse authority, which, like SAODAP, is a single agency responsible for all drug abuse prevention functions. The advent of SAODAP and the state drug abuse authority represented a major change, even upheaval, in the old order of federal-state operations.

The effect of Public Law 92-255 was to make the state, through this single state agency, the coordinate unit in the national strategy. Like SAODAP, the state drug abuse authority was charged, in Section 409, with the responsibility of planning for the coordinated development and implementation of programs and resources.

SAODAP

The Special Action Office, its progress, and its programs will not be assessed in depth here. The focus will be upon SAODAP and those policies and elements of its operations which have an impact upon strategy development and which provide background to this discussion of changing social perspectives and policies.

From the outset, the Special Action Office was a political curiosity. Not only did the Congress vest in the office and its director unprecedented powers for coordination—and reorganization—of the federal effort and its resource system, SAODAP by definition was a concentration of effort and power at a time when the Administration was moving apace to decentralize other federal approaches.

Moreover, SAODAP was an adolescent, requiring several months before it matured in the uses of its power and before it found its level in the political hierarchy of social systems. Certain misuses of power, like certain problems that arose during the necessary and rather successful process of reorganization, are important because their memory and their effects will influence the design and operations of the National Institute on Drug Abuse.

The great importance of the institute—to the field, to HEW, to SAODAP, and the state drug abuse authorities and local programs—is not readily apparent from the sparse language of the Act, which says the Institute shall administer the programs and authorities of the Secretary of HEW, and that the Secretary, acting through the institute, shall "develop and conduct comprehensive health, education, training, research, and planning programs for the prevention and treatment of drug abuse and for the rehabilitation of drug abusers."

The National Institute on Drug Abuse will in fact become the successor organization to the Special Action Office, to the current drug abuse prevention offices within NIMH, and to other organizations and offices within HEW and the government.

It is important in assessing the federal approach to drug abuse to review relevant history.

First, the initial effort to consolidate federal policy/program apparatus originated in the Senate, where key figures such as Senator Harold Hughes of Iowa advocated legislation to create a national institute for drug dependence.

Second, the Nixon Administration proposed the Special Action Office, with even broader powers than the Congress finally approved, such office to exist until 1975, but did not propose an institute nor did the Administration propose the creation of state drug abuse authorities, the consigning of major responsibilities and programs, or the federal–state planning process.

Third, the Senate, after approving SAODAP with some diminution of authority, still proposed the concurrent creation of an institute *within* NIMH that would virtually have rivalled SAODAP, the institute to conduct all HEW programs in accordance with the policies, priorities, objectives, guidelines and, where appropriate, the funding controls established by SAODAP.

The House, long cool to an institute, did not propose its creation. Yet, the House also favored terminating SAODAP a year earlier, the House version requiring SAODAP to expire on June 30, 1974.

The House position was critical in two respects. First, it stopped the simultaneous creation of the institute.

Second, it put the House on record as saying it did not believe this particular reorganization, redirection, and new program effort required 3 years, at least not 3 years of specialized program and policy control exercised by the White House. This break with purpose is seen as important and significant, given changes in approach now under consideration which could well shorten SAODAP's life span. These changes are discussed on page 215.

Also critical to that life span is the decision of the Senate–House conferees that the new institute would (1) be a unit *within* NIMH and (2) deliberately come into existence 6 months before SAODAP's statutory phase-out, i.e., the institute would become operational December 31, 1974.

Finally, there is this highly significant statement in the Senate–House Conference Report: "The postponement (to 1975) will give the Department (HEW) time to prepare for the establishment of the new Institute. The conferees anticipate that, in the consideration of other legislation in the field of mental health and drug abuse, scheduled for expiration in the future, further consideration will be given to the proper role and function of the new Institute."

The Congress thus opened the door to a continuing examination of SAODAP and relations among federal agencies, and of the federal strategy produced early in 1973 by the Federal Strategy Council with heavy SAODAP input, and the Congress also served notice that it had not decided the shape, content, or role of the new institute and did indeed reserve all of its options for further reconsideration.

Not to be overlooked in the Senate–House Conference Report is this explicit summary of SAODAP's statutory role: "The conferees reaffirm the intention of this legislation that the Special Action Office concentrate its efforts on interagency coordination and policy development. It must not attempt to manage or intervene in the routine operation of programs conducted by the departments and agencies. Such action would be contrary to the express purpose of the bill and would waste the resources of the office."

The temptation is to say that SAODAP violated this tenet in the breach, which is true. But the need for balance and perspective compels a further set of comments.

While there was broad, general agreement on objectives (and almost none on technique) certain agencies, certain units, and certain officials often frustrated the legitimate aspirations of SAODAP, some working rather assiduously at this goal. SAODAP officials cited this hindering as one rationale for their virtual insistence for much of the first 18 months following enactment of the law that states and local programs deal through SAODAP. Then, too, certain statutes and/or regulations prohibited some agencies and programs from responding as expeditiously as was needed and desired.

Another rationale was that SAODAP believed a major element of its mission was the initial development and testing of new concepts, e.g., the Treatment Alternatives to Street Crimes Program, the waiting list expansion contracts, and the 409 planning program for the state drug abuse authorities were run from SAODAP even though founded through other agencies. There was less dispute about the need for initial SAODAP supremacy over such programs as the Integrated Drug Abuse Reporting Process, the Client Oriented Data Acquisition Process, and the Unique Identifier (which no one else wanted footprinted on their image).

And, in truth, many potential recipients of federal largesse and those agencies and programs with a vital stake in federal decision making, such as the state drug abuse authority which went largely unrecognized by NIMH for several years, were generally pleased with many aspects of SAODAP's direct influence on day to day decisions.

Here was a new agency with new people, little or no legal impediments, virtually devoid of a body of regulatory law, which was more accessible than the tradition-bound departments and which could and did act as an ombudsman, traffic cop, court of last resort, and decision maker.

Officials in SAODAP and those in the departments will each claim that they were the true believers, i.e., they were up front with progressive proposals that were frustrated by the other side.

The purpose of this writing is not to chronicle the issues and then determine who was negative or who dragged their feet. Most observers contacted seem generally agreed that the entire process effected by SAODAP—alone and through interagency agreements—could have been conducted much more expeditiously and certainly without so much confusion, or changes and reverses in policy and purpose, a view especially shared by the states.

Yet it is not unreasonable to conclude that the state drug abuse authorities and local programs benefitted in very substantial ways from this competition between SAODAP and its partners—perhaps benefiting as much from this competition as from their direct efforts for nonfederal involvement in decision making. The states, for example, had strong advocates and supporters in both camps.

On balance, given the actions of the last few months (January to July 1973), the ultimate atmosphere was one of deliberate cooperation, which proved conclusive to progress.

How does this brief political history of SAODAP and other agencies relate to and affect strategy development and social policy? In a very simple but all-important way. SAODAP has been not unlike a Russian Tsar, simultaneously Emperor, Autocrat, and Father of all the Russias. Indeed, the analogy drawn by more than one congressman before 92-255 was that the United States needed a Drug Tsar.

Like an Emperor, SAODAP determined that the major (virtually exclusive) national priority would be the treatment of heroin addiction, a decision questioned by many professionals and the march of time, but SAODAP also determined that there would be quality controls and cost effectiveness measures applied to all programs.

Like an autocrat, SAODAP became quite imperious in its insistence upon the use of the footprint identification system, retreating finally in the face of an internal revolution.

Like a father, SAODAP could be accessible on many issues, regulations for methadone maintenance, the form and content of state plans, and the information base of the national data systems being good examples of issues on which SAODAP sought and observed consultation from within and outside the government. However, also like a father, SAODAP could be almost totally inaccessible, reserving unto itself to decide the fate of others (like children), such as when SAODAP was developing the formula grant distribution system for the states, or deciding who should receive grants and contracts according to its targeting system.

While none of us who participated in and survived those first steps and their attendant growing pains are suggesting that the accessibility given was uniform to all issues or even to certain issues on which independent thought was believed essential—the final thrust of the federal strategy, for example—the major point being attempted here is that, for the first time, the drug abuse professional in the field had an audience for his opinions. Moreover, the demand in the field is for an even greater influence on future decisions.

Stated forthright, the drug abuse professional not only wants to ensure that he loses none of the participatory influence he has gained, he wants that input mechanism structured to permit an even broader expression of thought.

Thus, there is concern over the form and structure of the new institute and the National Advisory Council on Drug Abuse which will advise its leaders.

Again, much of the input from the field was permitted by the pace of expansion and by the competition among the federal hierarchy. No field professional wants to have to depend upon that state of affairs; indeed, the structure being planned will eliminate that lever. And, as accessible as SAODAP finally became, it is doubtful that any professional wants to find himself—in the era of the institute—looking back and regarding SAODAP as that one brief, shining moment in which there was a Camelot.

To the contrary, the government can anticipate that the field professional and the other influence forces will strive to ensure that he does not encounter just such an experience by insisting upon a format and structure that provides direct access for him and for those in the federal system who are entrusted with program decisions affecting him.

And there is need for cautious efforts to ensure that the rewarding lessons of the SAODAP process are learned—and some others are not repeated—in developing the new institute. This too can be facilitated by deliberate efforts to seek and obtain outside opinion.

What did SAODAP and Company accomplish? How do these achievements impact upon the design and thrust of new strategies and policies?

The fact is that the federal government, under SAODAP direction, created more treatment capacity in 1972 and 1973 than had been created in the previous 50 years.

In April, 1973, one year after receiving its full complement of authorities (SAODAP existed for about 10 months on an Executive Order), SAODAP reported that 214 communities now had federally funded programs as opposed to 54 in June, 1971; that there were 63,382 clients in federally sponsored programs, as against 20,608 in October, 1971. The new federal–state–local system was, in April 1973, capable of servicing 120,000 clients at any given time, and had an annual turnover capacity of more than 200,000, a capacity level at which treatment would be available to all who wanted it, or so said SAODAP.

There were targeting problems, to be sure. Although SAODAP was saying that "in most parts of the country, we are no longer in a situation where many want treatment but cannot get it," SAODAP conceded that in some major areas there was not enough treatment capacity to meet demand. For example, while SAODAP was saying that the elimination of waiting lists was among its higher priorities for first-year operations, there were 21,000 persons on waiting lists in February 1973.

SAODAP, to be sure, responded to the problem, and the June reports indicated that targeting had improved, waiting lists were reduced, and new and improved measures were initiated or in planning stages to ensure greater accuracy of resource deployment.

An imaginative, long-needed criminal justice diversion program was launched, but it is too early to assess its impact. A very promising program of research, unprecedented in scope of funding, was initiated, including a program to develop new narcotic antagonists. If it could not, as conceded in the federal strategy, put precise parameters on the degree of drug abuse, SAODAP could number among its achievements its efforts to put parameters on the extent of federal programming effort and launched several ambitious programs to obtain client movement data, indicator data (deaths, overdoses, new admissions, arrests), performance data, and assessments of needs. The government, under SAODAP leadership, moved with dispatch and resolution to cope with the problem of drug abuse in the military and made effective inroads.

A national/regional training centers program was established. Top priority programs of technical assistance to state agencies and local programs were begun, using private contractors.

A principal effort, now achieving more of its designed potential, was the consolidation of grant/contract programs in NIMH, which became the lead agency for treatment with important responsibilities in prevention, education, and training. This major activity, which consumed considerable first-year effort, is also among the major endeavors that have an impact upon the institute and the future of federal policy and programming.

Again, waiting lists for treatment declined and in June, SAODAP was equating the expansion of treatment with an apparent decline in drug arrests, drug deaths, and drug-related crime.

At long last, SAODAP began to respond to the problem of nonnarcotic drug abuse, a delay in recognition and response that also has an impact upon the future of programming. By July, SAODAP was finally evidencing a departure from its previous drug-specific orientation, which had been challenged by many professionals.

In terms of the future, this change in focus ranks among the most critical of changing perspectives.

Equally critical to the future were the SAODAP involvements in the creation of state drug abuse authorities and the beginning of the federal–state planning process and the drafting and issuance of the first federal strategy.

Much of what else should be said about SAODAP emerges in succeeding sections below.

The summary comment that should be made here is that SAODAP, with major assistance from NIMH, which is now asserting leadership, has become involved with the field and set the program in motion, overcoming considerable obstacles and charting through many previously unexplored areas of programming and planning.

The States

Long before the legislation became final, the states began organizing to play a vital part in the planning and implementation of a national strategy, many of them working through a new organization that they founded to give themselves representation, but more importantly, to give themselves a vehicle for the interstate exchange of technical assistance. That organization became the National Association of State Drug Abuse Program Coordinators (NASDAPC).

The states reasoned that they, no less than SAODAP and the various federal agencies, must have the capability and capacity to plan for coordinate drug abuse programs and to have their interests, needs, and priorities reflected at the federal decision-making level, if the national strategy was to achieve maximum implementation. Thus, seeing themselves as working partners, not competitors, the states wholly supported the critical decision of the Nixon Administration and the Congress that policy and coordination should extend to all "drug abuse prevention functions," defined by the Congress to mean "any program or activity relating to drug abuse education, training, treatment, rehabilitation, or research, and including any such function even when performed by an organization whose primary mission is in the field of drug traffic prevention functions, and is unrelated to drugs."

The states declared, in testimony before the Congress, that the national program must reflect and involve the respective resources, needs, and priorities of each individual state and territory, as expressed in comprehensive state plans, which, collectively, would reflect the national problem, give relevance to national priorities, and provide structure to the national strategy.*

The Senate Committee on Labor and Public Welfare, recognizing the need for the total involvement of the states, made it expressly possible for the states to participate in the national strategy by offering amendments that provide for formula grants to the states, which would permit such comprehensive planning and enable them to launch new or improved projects.

Finally, Section 409, Title IV, Public Law 92-255 emerged. (The states, through the National Association, provided critically important support, protecting their new role during the House negotiations.)

Section 409 said that any state desiring a grant shall submit to the

---

* NASDAPC testimony before the Senate Appropriations Committee.

Secretary of the Department of Health, Education, and Welfare a state plan for "planning, establishing, conducting, and coordinating projects for the development of more effective drug abuse prevention functions in the state and for evaluating the conduct of such functions in the state."

The respective roles of the federal government, the states, and the localities assumed definite parameters, and the shape of programming for the future emerged through the far-reaching requirements for state plans.

Moreover, Public Law 92-255 required that all applications for federal funds from within a state be reviewed and coordinated by the state drug abuse authority; it required coordination of state drug abuse plans with other health and mental health plans; and, in a most important new provision drafted by Representative Paul Rogers, which assured the states the power to implement their policy decisions and to sustain quality control, the new law required the states to license or accredit all treatment programs.

The fundamental premise of the states, first given substance in National Association meetings in July and November 1971, was that direct administration, control, and operation of drug abuse programs should be vested in state and local governments, consistent with a truly national strategy that reflected the divergent problems and capabilities of the states, sustained by the technical resources, funds, and leadership of the federal government—all within a truly coordinated system where the participants would have a voice in decision making. Accordingly, the states agreed on the need for a planning mechanism to control the pell-mell expansion of programs and permit the development of new strategies, based upon empirical data and proven hypotheses.

The states' sense of their new role was heightened by the Administration's increasing emphasis upon revenue sharing and the decentralization of the federal establishment.

SAODAP held that the state plan is "intended to be a key tool in the management and targeting of total government resources." According to SAODAP, the state plan shall be used ". . . as a working action plan to administer drug abuse prevention services within the state and to upgrade and expand these services as necessary; as a basis for planning and implementing a drug abuse prevention management information system; to target state resources to priority needs; to target local resources to priority needs; to influence, via the approved plan and the review and comment procedure, the application of federal resources to priority needs; as the framework containing the criteria upon which proposal review and comments are made to the federal government; and to rationalize and integrate the delivery of allied human services."

SAODAP's "Implementation Concepts" reinforced the reality of citizen participation in the planning process, requiring specific representation on state advisory councils. Many states already had such councils and had themselves suggested language to make such bodies more representative of the people.

The concept of the states ultimately becoming the primary resource for technical assistance was given special emphasis because many officials at both the federal and state levels saw the ultimate role of the state as the provider of skills and resources rather than as an operator of programs.

Other sections of the SAODAP implementation concepts, which set policy for NIMH regulations, declared that the state drug abuse authority would set the standards on licensure and accreditation (as requested by the authorities) but need not operate the actual licensing system; authorized the state drug abuse authority to establish and enforce minimum standards of operations for all drug abuse projects within a state; encouraged the state drug abuse authority (commonly referred to as the single state agency) to review the regulations, guidelines, requirements criteria, and procedures of operating state agencies; and to otherwise coordinate and exercise policy control over drug abuse programming.

Finally, SAODAP corrected what most states considered the major abuse of their offices: the failure of federal agencies to consult state agencies before funding local programs. SAODAP said, "All federal agencies funding drug abuse programs will look to the state plan and the single state agency for guidance on whether or not to fund a grant request."

Moreover, the role of the states was reinforced and given prominence through SAODAP and NIMH activities on other fronts. SAODAP, NIMH, and other agencies have worked through the states in funding and implementing programs, in many instances contracting directly with the state drug abuse authority which has then contracted for services. Teams of state officials have been brought to Washington to consult with SAODAP, NIMH, and other agencies on issues ranging from CODAP to the evaluation of drug education programs. SAODAP provided each governor with a model executive order that urged each state to give even broader powers to its state drug abuse authority. And SAODAP, NIMH, and other agencies have assigned an increasing number of officials to field consultation, thus expanding the availability of federal assistance.

The New Federalism at Midpoint

There is no question that the combined efforts of federal and state officials, including key members of Congress, have effected a sorely needed, high-potential, integrated planning system. There is no question but that the federal–state partnership is beginning to work, giving optimism that remaining problems can be overcome with a minimum of discord.

There is no question that the drug abuse industry will advance by leagues if the integrated planning system, given its absolute reliance on coordination through policies governed by empirical data, produces the comprehensive strategies desired.

There is no question that federal and state officials and the staffs of major organizations such as the National Association are working together and constantly striving to achieve success with a new process.

There is no question that the states are assisting each other. To cite one example, the National Association has sponsored and conducted, with the cooperation of SAODAP, NIMH, and other agencies, 14 different regional, intersectional, and national workshops in which federal, state, and privately employed consultants have provided technical assistance. The systems used in New York, Illinois, Virginia, Colorado, Connecticut, Michigan, Minnesota, Indiana, South Carolina, and other states have been documented and presented to sister states for guidance. Through these meetings and others, officials from the several states have established relationships that carry over into daily activities and facilitate the exchange of guidance.

Organizations such as the National Commission on Marihuana and Drug Abuse, the Drug Abuse Council, the National Coordinating Council on Drug Education, the Alcohol and Drug Problems Association, the National Legislative Conference, the International City Managers Association, the Southern Regional Education Conference Board, and others have prepared guidance materials, conducted surveys, sponsored workshops, and initiated other activities that have contributed to the advancement of the states and the state-community planning process.

But, there are residual questions. There is the important question about the future structure of the federal mechanism, post-SAODAP, which we will discuss on page 215.

There is the very substantial question of the future of drug abuse program funding. Will revenue sharing be sufficient to sustain the programming level made possible in the past through SRS, NIMH, LEAA, OEO, OE, and SAODAP? Will the Administration and the Congress protect vital social service programs through specific block grants? Presently available information causes much uncertainty.

There is the equally substantial question about the impact of Governor Rockefeller's new war on drug abuse and New York State's new weapon, which has been called the strongest drug law on the books, providing much increased sentences for sellers of drugs. What effect will this and similar legislation have on the nature of programming? On the problem? On the individual?

The fact that 60 to 70% of the public polled about the Rockefeller position reported approval of this stringent position gives rise to a corollary question: Has time run out on the treatment/prevention industry? The public has been promised so much and apparently sees so little benefit that the conscientious, objective observer must wonder how much longer the public will tolerate vast expenditures for drug abuse prevention programs.

Can we generate new and more promising systems of care through primary, secondary, and tertiary prevention, which will succeed and thus garner renewed public support?

The question about the priorities of the federal government remains relevant. When truly and fully satisfied of its impact upon the problem of heroin addiction, will the Nixon Administration and the Congress withdraw, leaving unresolved the major problems of addressing the behavioral needs and life styles of so many thousands of drug-impacted people, including those heroin addicts now in treatment who require longer-term care for their real problems?

Finally, in fairness, there is the question about the abilities of the states to respond, to develop and channel new directions, to implement a truly national and concentrated effort.

The remainder of this chapter will try to give focus to these questions and will attempt some resolution of them.

The Federal Strategy

The federal strategy, *assessed in terms of the purpose conceived by the Strategy Council,* is an illuminating statement of federal policy. We have been able to extract from the strategy some 200 premises, beliefs, recommendations, strategies, conclusions, and statements of purpose.

Although we find the federal strategy to be much too general in some of its assessments, even within its limited mission, and while we believe the professionalism applied to certain assessments is uneven, the federal strategy stipulates, with more precision than some may find apparent at first reading, the goals and objectives being pursued by the government.

Given the extremely negative reception awarded the federal strategy by a special House subcommittee—and given the salient fact that the original strategy is currently being rewritten—there are those who would say that the only appropriate comment on the federal strategy is to note that it is being overhauled—extensively.

That course of action is neither fair to the strategy, the Strategy Council, nor the professionals who contributed to its development.

At minimum, the current federal strategy serves as a basis for noting progress and/or change in strategy when the new report is delivered this winter.

This document, the Strategy Council said, is an attempt to describe the federal government's efforts to achieve three major objectives:

1. To reduce drug abuse in America
2. To reduce the adverse social consequences of drug abuse
3. To concentrate federal government efforts on those forms of drug abuse which cause the greatest harm to society

The Strategy Council said its perspective permitted a focus on three basic concerns:

1. Concern for the individual who may need society's help to retain or regain his function, independence, and health
2. Protection for each citizen and every community from harm that might be caused by drug abusers
3. Concern for the overall effect of drug use, as well as of our response to it, on the values of our society

The federal strategy offers the following statements that are relevant to our understanding and assessment of it:

In order to formulate an appropriate public response, we must first consider the nature and extent of drug abuse problems in terms of how seriously they threaten the individual and the society.

Having taken the position that different drug abuse problems may require somewhat different approaches in order to reduce the social cost to an irreducible minimum, we must consider several factors for each drug: The extent and pattern of its use; its social cost in terms of adverse consequences to the individual user and society; our understanding of the reasons for is use or abuse; our capacity to alter the causal factors or repair the consequences; and, the alternative benefits that might be achieved by allocating Federal resources to reducing the social costs of a different drug abuse problem or indeed to another social problem entirely (Federal Strategy Council on Drug Abuse, 1973).

Like the federal program (through July 1973), the federal strategy concentrates on heroin use and addiction.

The strategy says there are no entirely satisfactory methods for estimating the number of heroin addicts in the United States, but gives a "best" estimate of between 500,000 and 600,000 users and addicts in 1972.

There is a note of qualified restraint throughout the strategy, with the council repeatedly offering assurances that the trend is down, i.e., the rising curve of new addicts each year is flattening out, but cautioning that this apparent reduction in rate of growth does not mean a peaking of the epidemic in every community, and warning that a decrease in the rate of growth does not necessarily mean that the pool of narcotic addicts who need treatment is decreasing.

Finally, the council asserts, "At present, however, we do not know the precise size of the population needing care, whether it is still growing or actually shrinking. We do know, however, that if it is still growing, it is doing so much less rapidly."

Moreover, the council observes that this population of 500,000 to 600,000 narcotics users and addicts includes ex-addicts, and addicts who are temporarily abstinent, concluding that the difficulty is in knowing how many people fall into each category.

Thus, the council is saying it does not know, with any real precision, the implications to treatment of this population.

Yet, the council immediately rejoins by saying that, in spite of the uncertainty about the precise numbers, "we are, in most parts of the country, no longer in a situation where many want treatment but cannot get it." That statement is variously phrased as "most parts of the country" and "in a number of communities" and "some cities" and "in many parts of the country."

Similarly, the strategy says that "in a number of communities" treatment is now immediately available to all who want it and, in some communities, programs have excess capacity. That too has been variously expressed as "in most cities."

In its summary, the council states, "This general policy (to first make treatment available to all who want it) has resulted in a very balanced—or multi-modality—treatment system for the country as a whole."

Perhaps it is an issue of report construction, but one wonders why the council indulged in seemingly contradictory superlatives. The fact is that the federal government has created more treatment capacity in the past 18 months than in the previous 50 years. But, you have to pick and cull through the report to get this information.

This was an admirable achievement and SAODAP, NIMH, and OEO are truly to be congratulated for their remarkable effort to expand treatment capacity.

Continuing with the strategy, the council says there are no satisfactory units to measure the true social cost of narcotics use. In another section, the council says that determining the extent and social costs of the barbiturate–sedative problem is as complex as estimating the costs of heroin addiction. In still another section, the council says that determining the extent and the social costs of amphetamine related drug abuse presents problems like those encountered with barbiturates and related sedatives. Continuing, the council says that the extent of the use of cocaine is hard to gauge accurately. Finally, the council says there are as yet no surveys to substantiate the impression that actual usage of hallucinogens has declined.

The council was most explicit in declaring how one assesses the social cost of marihuana use, but even that section concludes by the council saying, "We cannot tell at present whether the current widespread tendency to experiment with marihuana will continue, will stabilize at some low level, or, like other fads and fashions, will run its course and gradually subside."

The struggle of the federal government to posit answers to these questions is highly significant, given the federal emphasis upon measurements of social cost which the states must provide in their plans.

The strategy says, in effect: After a decade of government intervention, we still have not described, with any real sense of professional certainty, the universe of drug abuse. Finally, we are taking that first step, so critical to all those that must follow.

Significantly, that effort is now a federal–state partnership.

There is a rationale, not stated but accepted, for framing the strategy in terms of specific drugs—because it eases the problem of identifying the government's multiple approaches.

But the strategy needed a perspective, one that could have been fashioned at least in part by a more stimulating, more encompassing discussion of polydrug abuse. Instead, this new challenge was given just one page in the book.

That polydrug abuse is a major challenge was reinforced recently by Dr. Robert DuPont who succeeded Dr. Jerome Jaffe as Director of the Special Action Office. DuPont asserted recently that the government may be facing an even greater challenge (than heroin addiction) in the years ahead in the form of polydrug abuse, which he called a more subtle phenomenon than heroin, involving less predictable abusers who are harder to trace and more difficult to attract into treatment.

Still, for the immediate future, DuPont will continue the emphasis on heroin, but he does predict a shift of programs and resources in the future to nonopiate drug abuse.

The sense of purpose that exudes from DuPont's stewardship is one of greater awareness of the broad spectrum of abuse, an understanding of the problem we hope will be reinforced in the revised strategy.

We hope to see this strategy also address anew several other unresolved issues and to correct what are considered to be certain imbalances in the stated approach.

For example, while the government seemed to be straining to prove its point of having made inroads against heroin addiction, which indeed it had, the government was much less specific about resulting phenomena left in the wake of its effort. There are indications, for instance, that some heroin addicts have become polydrug abusers, including renewed use and abuse of alcohol, and, for this and other reasons, are not requiring treatment as before.

Jaffe had some difficulty in explaining to the Congress what had happened to all those addicts and abusers, a difficulty with which one could sympathize more if the government had been less insistent upon the scope of its successes.

The case could have been more blanced—and this too we hope to see in the next strategy—if there had been more exploration of the undeniable facts about drug abuse, such as the following gem:

We recognize the difficulty in reaching consensus on the best approach to drug problems in general and to the use of any one drug in particular. Part of the difficulty stems from our incomplete understanding of why certain drugs are used, what factors lead from use to addiction, and what the long-term consequences of use and abuse are likely to be.

The next strategy would be more of a strategical assessment if the council would begin with that future, address the present in the context of that anticipated future, and delineate current and proposed government action to prepare for and be productive in that future environment.

The council, for example, must pick up where Jaffe left off in his Congressional testimony. Jaffe eloquently and expertly questioned the role of government in developing and managing health delivery systems—a funding resource, a planning resource, a research resource, as he believed proper, or an operator of programs, a day-to-day administrator of funded programs, and so forth.

Jaffe and the council showed us one glimpse of that future when they reviewed alcoholism programming and addressed drug abuse in the context of substance abuse, an all-important discussion given the new approaches outlined on page 215.

The implications of the shift of power to OMB and the relationship of that assumption of authority in tandem with the moves made by Secretary Weinberger to create the Alcohol, Drug Abuse and Mental Health Administration are not clear, but should be explained by the council.

According to DuPont, the bureaucracy is already redefining its task—it is moving toward a federal role, within a single health institute, of research and demonstration program inception—the process which Jaffe argued wisely should be the concern of all in the field.

Our concern is that the professional in the field have an opportunity to render opinion on that future, just as we believe he must render his opinion on the federal strategy. Without his concurrence, it can never be more than a federal strategy; with his active support and involvement, the Federal Strategy could become a viable national plan.

The Marihuana Commission Strategy

The National Commission on Marihuana and Drug Abuse recommended in its second and final report that the Congress create a single federal agency, similar to the Atomic Energy Commission, which would establish, administer, and coordinate all drug policy at the federal level and which would be the principal, if not sole, contact with state drug abuse programs.

Unlike the Special Action Office, which comparatively has an overseer role on policy and programs relating to drug abuse prevention activities, the separate agency recommended by the Marihuana Commission would absorb the following agencies and their functions: the Special Action Office, the Bureau of Narcotics and Dangerous Drugs, the relevant units of the Bureau of Customs, the Office of National Narcotic Intelligence and the Office of Drug Abuse Law Enforcement in the Department of Justice, the Division of Narcotic Addiction and Drug Abuse at the National Institute of Mental Health, the drug-related functions of the Law Enforcement Assistance Administration and of the Office of Economic Opportunity, all research and control functions performed by the Food and Drug Administration, all related functions performed by the Office of Education and of the National Clearinghouse for Drug Abuse Information. (BNDD, the relevant units of Customs, and the mentioned units of Justice were merged, subsequent to the Commission Report, in a new Drug Enforcement Administration. A new alignment of agencies is in the offing; as this is being written, a new HEW alignment, factoring for the creation of the new Drug Abuse Institute, is being planned. See the last section for details.)

This total merger—drug abuse prevention and drug traffic prevention—would be time-specific, with a reexamination after 4 years and a disbanding of the agency within 5 years, surviving components being reassigned to their original agencies or integrated into other, perhaps more appropriate agencies.

Whereas the Executive Branch, through the Special Action Office and now OMB, has virtually dominant authority, the Marihuana Commission would vest certain oversight powers in the Congress, specifically recommending that Congress, after 4 years, establish a commission that would evaluate the social response to drug abuse during the preceding 4 years, consider the results of directed and undirected research, recommend whether the unified agency should, in fact, be disbanded, continued, or modified, propose new policies, programs, and techniques, and reexamine the basic issues and consider new departures/responses.

Moreover, the Commission recommended that similar agencies be created within each state, saying that each state agency should have sufficient powers, among other authorities, to coordinate all drug programs at the state level and to provide guidance and funding to community programs.

Concurring in the call for an extensive program of research covering all aspects of the problem, the Marihuana Commission said HEW should participate in the design of the research program "to avoid overlap and maximize the cost-effectiveness of Federal research efforts."

This research, the commission said, should deal not only with the immediate information needed, but also with requirements of future and long-term policy making; it should fund not only projects which produce quick results, but also those often overlooked, requiring several years to generate useful data. The commission also recommended appropriation of funds for nondirected research which would not be part of the formal federal research program.

The directed research plan, as envisioned by the Marihuana Commission, would include:

a. A continuing series of projects similar to the two commission-sponsored national surveys, as well as other studies to provide a longitudinal data base on public attitudes and drug-taking behavior.

b. Etiological research focused on populations exhibiting low as well as high incidence of use. "It is of equal importance for policy purposes to examine and understand those groups who explicitly disavow drug use and faithfully abide by this norm."

c. Continued support of the basic clinical research program at the NIMH Addiction Research Center.

d. Examination of how well drug offenders perform while on conditional release, including bail, parole, probation, and treatment, so that the criminal justice system can better design and implement diversion programs. "Also of importance are studies to determine the effects of incarceration for drug offenses on users, especially young users and first offenders."

e. Longitudinal studies of persons who have completed treatment, comparing them to those who left treatment programs before completion and those who never entered treatment.

f. Careful systematic study of the dynamics and consequences of systems in other countries where heroin is freely available.

g. Study of synergistic effects of various psychoactive substances currently used, whether licitly or illicitly. In particular, the National Institute of Alcohol Abuse and Alcoholism should perform ongoing research into the effects of taking alcohol with other drugs, since alcohol is legally available and often used this way.

h. Research on the effects of drug use on driving. For both research and traffic safety purposes, simple and quick methods for detecting presence of drugs in the body must be refined.

Additionally, the commission said the federal government should provide technical assistance and necessary funding to establish a uniform reporting system, together with necessary laboratory support, on drug morbidity and mortality statistics.

The Marihuana Commission said:

Drug use prevention strategy, rather than concentrating resources and efforts in persuading or educating people not to use drugs, should emphasize other means of obtaining what users seek from drugs, means that are better for the user and better for society.

The aim of prevention policy should be to foster the conditions of fulfillment and instill the necessary skills to cope with the problems of living, particularly the life concerns of adolescents.

Information about drugs and the disadvantages of their use should be incorporated into more general programs, stressing benefits with which drug consumption is largely inconsistent.

Drug dependent prevention services should include educational and informational guidance for all segments of the population; job training and career counseling; medical, psychiatric, psychological, and social services; family counseling; and recreational services.

The primary responsibility for designing a prevention strategy and operating appropriate programs should reside at the state and local level, the Marihuana Commission recommended, calling for state-wide, comprehensive drug dependence prevention programs—funded, at least in part, by federal block and formula grants.

The function-specific approach of the Marihuana Commission was continued in its discussions of treatment programming, the commission declaring that the federal government should have major responsibilities for funding—through block and formula grants to the states—treatment and rehabilitation services administered by the states, retaining discretionary funds for direct funding of demonstration and special projects.

The federal government should not have direct operating responsibility for providing treatment and rehabilitation, the commission said, such services being provided at the state level, except for offenders within federally operated correctional institutions.

While agreeing with the federal strategy on the federal role in civil commitment—none—the commission said persons charged with federal offenses should be serviced by states through state-operated programs on a reimbursable basis, a step beyond the Strategy.

The commission also recommended federal sponsorship of a program that is theoretically in existence, i.e., the evaluation of existing drug treatment and rehabilitation programs to see whether they are (1) cost effective, (2) designed to deal effectively with their clients, and (3) have established suitable criteria and objectives. And, the commission said the federal government should establish performance criteria for state drug treatment and rehabilitation programs, a point with which federal agencies largely agree, but one which is in some dispute at the state level.

The Marihuana Commission said opiate antagonists should not be administered involuntarily, either as a method of treatment or as a method of prevention.

The Marihuana Commission said, "As a matter of statutory or enforcement policy, assertion of control over the consumer should not be tied to concepts of criminal accountability but rather to concepts of assistance appropriate in the individual case. The primary purpose of enforcement of the possession laws should be detection and selection of those persons who would benefit by treatment or prevention services."

The Marihuana Commission said that one of the following dispositions should be mandatory for drug-dependent persons who are apprehended for consumption-related offenses, including possession: (1) diversion to a treatment program in lieu of prosecution, or (2) diversion to a treatment program after conviction but before entry of judgment. Failure to comply with the conditions of treatment would, by this recommendation, result in return to court for prosecution or sentencing, with additional levies of fines or imprisonment.

For non-drug-dependent persons apprehended for so-called consumption offenses, including possession, the Marihuana Commission said one of the following dispositions should be mandatory: (1) diversion to a prevention services program in lieu of prosecution; (2) diversion to a prevention services program after conviction but before entry of judgment; (3) a fine of up to $500; or (4) probation with appropriate conditions.

The Marihuana Commission recommended that federal criminal investigative agencies concentrate primarily at the top levels of the illegal drug distribution network—importation, exportation, and large-scale foreign and domestic diversion of drugs at the manufacturing and wholesale levels, leaving to the states primary responsibility for supervising retail pharmacies, hospitals, and physicians.

The Marihuana Commission said federal law enforcement agencies must develop long-range strategies; should form strike forces, abandoning the present system of regional offices; should have a separate anticorruption unit under the Attorney General; and should provide technical and funding assistance to state and local agencies.

State enforcement, the commission said, should concentrate on the lower levels of licit and illicit distribution networks.

On the other hand, local police were seen in a new role, cooperating and participating with other community institutions in the development of a preventive services program, including, as part of such a program, the development of precise guidelines for nonarrest dispositions of persons apprehended for consumption-related offenses and the referral of such persons to appropriate treatment or prevention programs.

Moreover, the commission recommended that local police units receive training in dealing with the medical needs of drug-dependent persons and alcoholics, climaxing this section with a recommendation that local police act as early-warning systems on emerging patterns of drug use in the community. In the latter effort, the Commission recommended police analysis of drugs, which the commission said could be extremely useful in preparing other community agencies to launch specifically targeted preventive efforts.

The Marihuana Commission went well beyond the Special Action Office position on in-school education, declaring that "policy makers, in recognition of ignorance about the impact of drug education, (should) seriously at least until programs already in operation have been evaluated and a coherent approach with realistic objectives has been developed. At the very least, state legislatures should repeal all statutes which now require drug education courses to be included in the public school curriculum."

The Marihuana Commission, which agreed with SAODAP on a moratorium on the production and dissemination of new drug information materials, pending development of standards and inventory/analysis of existing materials, recommended a federal procedure for screening all federally sponsored or funded information materials for accuracy.

According to the Marihuana Commission, which cited cost-benefit and philosophical–constitutional standpoints, the government role should be limited to assuring the availability of accurate information regarding the likely consequences of the different patterns of drug-using behavior.

The recommendations of the Marihuana Commission with respect to industry are of particular note; first, because they are intelligent observations, second, because they constitute an effective approach, and third because SAODAP and the Federal Strategy Council virtually ignored this new frontier.

1. Management and unions, supported by the Departments of Labor and Commerce, should cooperatively undertake a comprehensive study of employee drug use and related behavior.

2. The business community should not reject an applicant solely on the basis of prior drug use or dependence, unless the nature of the business compels doing so. When preemployment screening is necessary, companies should establish appropriate screening procedures, including physical examinations, for job applicants and keep the results confidential.

3. Industry should consider alternatives to termination of employment for employees involved with drugs. Where the nature of the business allows, employees should be referred to company-run or other public and private rehabilitation or counselling programs.

4. The business community should consider adopting employee programs patterned after the "troubled employee" or "employee assistance" concept. This program consists of a management control system based on impaired job performance, determined by minimum company standards. It seeks to determine and treat the underlying causes of poor performance, whatever they may be, rather than limiting itself to the standard responses.

5. The fact of treatment and rehabilitation should be confidential to encourage employees to accept counseling and other assistance. No

record of the employee's drug problem should be carried in any file which is open to routine inspection. If treatment requires a temporary absence, the company should attempt to keep the employee's job open for him.

The Shape of Things to Come

Somehow, as the product emerged from the deliberations, it was like watching your child play with his miniature extruder.

Using your ratchet-plunger, you add the forms: HEW, PHS, HSMHA, HSA, HRA, NIMH, DNDA. Then, for your mix, you blend SAODAP, NIAA, and NIDA. Result: ADAMHA. Or, as it will become known, well-known, in the near future, the Alcohol, Drugs, and Mental Health Administration.

The ranking of the units in the title, which respectively represent the National Institute of Alcohol and Alcoholism, the National Institute on Drug Abuse, and the National Institute of Mental Health, is not supposed to convey any sense of priority for any of the Institutes. (The alternative arrangements come out MHAD, DAMH, etc. and who wants to hang those possible nicknames on the newest child in the federal galaxy?)

ADAMHA was the selected (favored by NIMH) form for reorganization, being chosen over the alternative (favored by SAODAP) of a Substance Abuse Administration.

As announced by HEW Secretary Casper Weinberger on September 17, 1973, HEW was seeking an individual "with the necessary medical, scientific, and administrative skills" to head ADAMHA.

Weinberger announced that Dr. Robert DuPont, Director of SAODAP, would become head of NIDA, Dr. Morris Chafetz and Dr. Bertram Brown would remain as Directors of NIAA and NIMH, respectively.

Why ADAMHA? Why not a Substance Abuse Administration? The Special Task Force, which reported to Assistant Secretary for Health, Dr. Charles Edwards, was guided in major part by a previous decision to abolish the Health Services and Mental Health Administration, creating a Health Services Administration and Health Resources Administration. NIMH was destined to become part of the National Institutes of Health, because of its anticipated role as "primarily a research institute."

The question then became one of what to do with the service and training activities of NIMH, which could not properly be included in NIH. The corollary questions were what to do with the drug and alcohol institutes, which Congress had created as units within NIMH.

The summary conclusions of the Task Force, after almost 4 months of work and interviews in the field, were the following.

1. The problems of drug abuse and alcholism are high priority, and the federal response to them is still in its early stages of development.

2. The drug abuse and the alcoholism fields require continued visibility and leadership.

3. The drug abuse and alcohol fields should gradually be combined.

4. The mental health, drug abuse, and alcoholism fields appropriately relate both to the health and to the human service systems, although not exclusively to either.

5. The drug abuse and alcohol fields are related to the mental health field, but not exclusively.

6. The drug abuse and alcohol fields should gradually be integrated into the health field.

7. The mental health field is commonly operated along functional lines.

8. The mental health field generally receives low priority from other health professionals and programs.

9. The mental health field requires continued visibility and leadership at this time.

10. The mental health field should gradually be integrated with the health field.

It should be noted that the task force was concerned about the low priority which mental health would receive in health settings, but, while noting the relationships between mental health and substance abuse, the Task Force also observed that these fields "conflict with and extend beyond mental health" in many respects, noting also that there are "stereotypic attitudes, moralizing and reliance on a narrow clinical model by many mental health practitioners."

"All of these," the Task Force said, "have hindered the full development of drug abuse and alcohol programs."

Still, the Task Force concluded that the mental health field and substance abuse activities are "both legitimately concerned with man as a psycho-geo-social organism; both fields relate to health concerns; both make important contributions to the human service systems."

An operative finding was that mental health and substance abuse should ultimately be integrated into the health field, a finding that became more significant as the Task Force sorted organizational options based upon eight selection criteria.

Those criteria also tell us much about the shape of things to come.

1. Promote the maximum feasible integration of mental health and substance abuse activities with health policy and programmatic activities
2. Promote optimum coordination of mental health and substance abuse activities with other human service agencies
3. Provide needed leadership and visibility for both mental health and substance abuse activities
4. Remove training and service functions from NIH
5. Maximize integration of drug abuse and alcohol activities
6. Reduce the likelihood of continued organizational domination of the substance abuse areas by the mental health field, while maintaining their close relationship in other areas where desirable and necessary
7. Assure organizational and administrative feasibility of change, including minimal disruption of ongoing activities
8. Allow maximum flexibility for future change

Seven of the eight criteria virtually assured selection of ADAMHA over the Substance Abuse Administration. The eighth criteria (shown here as Number Six) was a principal argument against ADAMHA.

Indeed, in recommending ADAMHA, the Task Force noted only two "con" arguments: "(1) Does not promote rapid integration of mental health with the general health field; (2) risks some domination of drug abuse and alcohol programs by the mental health field."

However, in considering the Substance Abuse Administration, which would have integrated mental health services much more quickly, the Task Force noted these negatives: "(1) Fragments the mental health field at the Federal level and thereby loses its visibility and leadership; (2) compromises the ability at the Federal level of the mental health field to coordinate with the human services system; (3) potentially produces major disruption in ongoing mental health program activities; (4) contradicts the specific professional recommendations of mental health leaders interviewed."

On the other hand, the Task Force observed that an argument for a Substance Abuse Administration was that it would separate substance abuse activities from the mental health field.

Clearly, the dominant concerns were for the visibility, continuity, and continued priority for mental health.

Yet, it should be stated that drug abuse, like alcohol, would have been under a new administration, in either event, although the likelihood of having professional mental health field leadership commanding the new superstructure is conceded to be greater with ADAMHA.

Was ADAMHA what the Task Force really wanted? Not exactly. Recall the earlier findings with regard to integrating mental health and substance abuse activities into the health field.

There were five options, the two described above, two others that got scant mention, and a fifth that would have integrated mental health and substance abuse into the health field—immediately.

The Task Force reported, "This option was unanimously considered to be the most desirable eventual organizational structure because it represents a unified health system and ideal integration of the mental health, substance abuse, and health fields."

However, the Task Force said, this option was felt to be "politically infeasible" at the present time. "In addition," the Task Force said, "the leadership and visibility currently needed by mental health, drugs and alcohol would be severely compromised."

Therefore, the Task Force felt that "while Option 5 represents the goal of an integrated health system, it should not be recommended at the present time."

But, option 5 did not die aborning.

The Edwards report said,

The disagreement [between Option 1 and Option 2] centered primarily around the appropriate timing of the organizational change and which option would be more viable in moving toward the organizational structure proposed in Option 5.

Most Task Force members agreed that it would require at least 5 years for an orderly transition to achieve all of the facets of Option 5 but that some significant steps could be made in the next 2 years.

Thus, in presenting the two principal options, the Task Force provided Weinberger with stepwise progressions from both options to Option 5.

What is Option 5? Under that option, substance abuse and mental health research activities would be transferred to NIH; service programs would be transferred to HSA; and manpower and training activities, research and development activities, and data systems would be transferred to HRA. The three institutes would cease to exist.

That, with the exception of one other critical finding, is the shape of the future recommended by the Task Force and set into motion by Weinberger.

The other critical finding? Not unexpectedly, the Task Force said, "One problem . . . would be the continuing authority of SAODAP to establish all Federal policy for drug abuse. Consideration should be given to terminating the Special Action Office prior to its legislated termination on June 30, 1975, to avoid the existence of two potentially conflicting authorities in the drug abuse area."

Weinberger's announcement said, of course, that DuPont would continue to serve as SAODAP Director.

The next shots to be fired will be in front of the Rogers' subcommittee, which will hold hearings on its bill, H.R. 10019, which establishes ADAMHA.

Those hearings will provide, at least in part, an examination of the federal drug abuse effort, its past, its present and its future. They may also provide the touchstone for a new social/political policy.

Developing a New Social–Political Strategy

Strategy Summary

The trend in most programs is to address the problem of drug abuse in terms of the abuse of specific drugs and in terms of drug-specific programs and modalities.

Given the changes in the etiological nexus of the problem, those approaches are no longer acceptable.

If our principal problem, in a sociological context, is that our society generates an infinite number of social casualties, some of whom use drugs, then we must first view our every effort in terms of its relationship to our total system of providing support for those casualties.

We can then abandon the mental health model, the public health model, the law enforcement model, the medical model—and frame our approaches within a social health model.

This then permits us to view drug abuse as one of several societal problems, to give it appropriate rank, and to evaluate our efforts not as singular modalities but, having thus established our limited role within that system, we can call upon our own activities, and sharply increase our potential for success.

That, in a real sense, is the goal of the new federal–state approach to drug abuse programming. That interrelationship of programs was in fact a foundation stone of Public Law 92-255, which held that drug abuse prevention and law enforcement were not separate approaches, but were of necessity interrelated activities, which must function in tandem to achieve their singular and common goal of reducing the incidence and prevalence of drug abuse in our society.

A Functional Approach

We have, as stated earlier, five cohort groups:

1. The nonuser, at risk in a drug-taking society
2. The experimenter
3. The social or recreational user
4. The involved drug abuser
5. The dysfunctional abuser, including the addict

We can address them through systems of primary, secondary, and tertiary prevention, but there is another construct that is perhaps more conducive to the ultimate goal of interfacing these major response systems.

We can group our cohorts into: nonusers; abusers/users who are not involved with the criminal justice system.

This grouping then permits us to address three approach systems:

1. Alternatives to drug abuse
2. Alternatives to criminal justice
3. Alternatives within the criminal justice system

These three approaches can also accommodate our three traditional response systems of primary, secondary, and tertiary prevention.

Alternatives to Drug Abuse

We begin, not by some arbitrary alignment or deployment of the thrust/response mechanisms that can be employed as alternatives, but by assessing two principal factors: the behavioral life style of the individual and the fundamental causes of drug abuse.

To say that we can prevent someone from using drugs is a myth, if we take the word prevention literally. What we can do is help people make rational elections not to use drugs by (1) intelligently informing them of the hazards of drug misuse and abuse, (2) by providing them with the personal reinforcement mechanisms necessary to achieve a functional life style, and (3) by eliminating to the maximum extent possible those elements of their life which are contributive or conducive to drug use.

Thus, instead of the knee-jerk reflex of the past few years, which spawned a gaggle of drug education programs without purpose and some without real content, our first step is not to propose that we educate all of these people about drugs.

Functionally, our first step is to assess the universe of drug abuse, an assessment that defines the users in the general population, the users among our youth, the users currently in treatment, the users currently in jail.

A comprehensive epidemiological assessment will provide us with the characterological typologies of current users, in all four categories of use, their drug-taking habits, their drugs of preference, and other essential data, which we can then use to construct a profile of those persons who are at risk and those who are most vulnerable.

We can construct a matrix from one suburban high school in the Northeast and demonstrate that, of 100 students, 50 will experiment with drugs. Of the 50 experimenters, 30 will become social-recreational users. Of these 30 users, 5 will become involved drug abusers. And, 2 of the 5 will become dysfunctional, most likely addicted abusers.

Most of our research has focused upon the 5, with primary emphasis there upon the 2 dysfunctional abusers.

We need to go back to the 100 and find out why 50 students did not experiment, why 20 experimenters stopped at that level, why 25 social-recreational users did not become involved or dysfunctional. And, in asking why, we need to determine whether their characterological typologies differ from that of their cohorts, whether they had personal reinforcements, and so on.

A common method of acquiring such data and insights is to buttress general population assessments with specially designed in-school surveys that not only trace patterns of abuse and identify user typologies, but also provide data on attitudes toward and knowledge about drugs.

We provide essentially cognitive drug education, but we anticipate results achievable only from affective education or behavioral education programs.

If we recommend as a second step that we also acquire this essential information about a special population, we have greatly enhanced our capability to direct the most potentially effective messages and services to the appropriate target audiences.

While probing characterological typologies of nonusers and users, from which we select our at risk and vulnerable populations, we must also assess the life needs of all individuals. For example, there are alternatives programs of special assistance to the hard to employ, or enrichment programs for minority youth, or special youth business leadership programs that enable youth to own and operate small businesses.

In the past, we have created prevention programs based upon impressionistic insights of our drug abuse/behavioral problems. We can no longer afford that luxury. For a fraction of the cost of our mistakes, we can generate the data that allow us to separate chance from proven direction.

Armed with this knowledge, we can then devise a series of approaches: in-school formal educational programs, peer group guidance programs, affective education and behavioral education programs, community education programs, and such service programs as employment assistance, retraining, and special programs for known problem groups.

We can devise and employ such programs, satisfied that we no longer have to present lectures on narcotics addiction to youth who are involved with barbiturates and amphetamines.

And, while that process is occurring with users, we can focus major preventive efforts on the persons who meet the vulnerable typology but who do not yet use drugs.

Alternatives to Criminal Justice

The phrase itself requires some explanation. We are talking about drug abusers whose lives we hope to interdict before they become involved in the criminal justice system.

We are all familiar with the various modalities of treatment to which we can direct drug abusers.

Today's drug abuser is no longer the passive, dependent heroin addict who so dominated our thinking until recently. Today's drug abuser is younger on average, consumes a variety of drugs, each for its specific effect, and, is thus a polydrug user. A question related to the polydrug user is whether the drug abuse program designed for an older addict is responsive to his needs.

Before a community rushes to judgment about its needs for treatment, the community's leadership should ponder at some length the functional process that it wants to occur in the community.

Beyond treatment, what? For too many programs, and unfortunately too many of their clients, that major question has never been answered and is not being answered today.

We assume, by some magical process, that a person having gone through treatment has become a whole person. If we have a 21-year-old addict, semieducated, semiskilled, who has made a life style of petty crime, and we put that addict into treatment, what we have got at the end of the treatment process is a 21-year-old former addict (temporarily), semieducated, semiskilled, who makes a life style of petty crime.

We have assumed, and the public has graded treatment programs accordingly, that treatment programs cure people. No, they arrest the most obvious problem the patient manifests—his dependence upon drugs. And, unless and until other support mechanisms are provided, we will continue to render a limited service that has no guarantee other than that most drug abusers will return to the use of drugs. We must begin to speak to his need for drugs, i.e., his reason for using drugs.

Our functional approach to users, therefore, must also begin with an assessment of our drug-using population, again centering on characterological typologies and drugs of preference, education, work experience, life styles, patterns of behavior.

We need the kind of monitoring system of our treatment programs which will tell us, as quickly as possible, these differences in terms of changes in the drugs of preference, typologies of users, and other areas so that we can be alert to changes in the etiological nexus of our problem.

Again, we must focus upon the human needs of the drug user.

When we possess this body of data, our functional process through which we program the drug abuser requires a system of diagnosis and referral which permits us to direct patients toward those programs where we can predict the best possible outcome. All treatment programs succeed to different degrees with different kinds of clients. Thus, our functional process is also dependent upon good client/management information systems.

If we have successfully conducted outreach and intake, and have functionally processed the individual through a treatment modality that speaks to his drug-taking behavior, we then have our cardinal opportunity to develop a system of support which speaks to those human needs discussed earlier.

Functionally, we do not want an overly institutionalized drug abuse industry. This industry has the special expertise to provide certain services; other elements of the community, such as social service agencies, also have a major role to play—and the process we design for the individual must include and utilitze those resources.

Ironically, we then find ourselves utilizing many of the same resources that we opted for in developing a process of alternatives to drug abuse. Hopefully, that is precisely what we are doing. For some unknown reason, there has been a strongly held body of opinion that prevention programs, and their various resource mechanisms, were suitable only to the prevention of first use.

One of our major prevention failures has been the failure to prevent recidivism. Indeed, it can be argued that a critical need today is to provide prevention-style programming for the former user to ensure that he maintains that status.

Again, perhaps the best method of arraying these services is to talk about the process that must occur to reintegrate this individual into society, before we lose him permanently to a life style of crime.

Alternatives within Criminal Justice

For years, we have missed unique opportunities to assist society and its casualties by ignoring the person whose criminal habits and/or drug-taking behavior result in arrest and incarceration.

At minimum, we need to provide the alternative (to simple incarceration) of treatment while in custody or in prison.

At maximum, we need to address a whole series of issues relating to the role we want criminal justice to play in drug abuse. As the resource mechanisms discussed on page 222 indicate, there are many, many prevention programs that can be sponsored or operated by criminal justice agencies.

But criminal justice has other roles, equally significant in impact to its role of controlling the availability of drugs and enforcing the drug laws.

That other role consists principally of criminal justice acting as a key instrument of social policy, utilizing its resources to return individuals to society, without incarceration.

Many of the critical resource elements and programs which should be found in a truly comprehensive criminal justice/drug abuse prevention system have been promoted successfully by the Drug Enforcement Administration and by SAODAP.

These can be arrayed in terms of prearrest, postarrest, pretrial, postconviction, and postsentencing programs.

The processes that occur when intervention is effected at any of these points should be designed in terms of the impact upon the individual and upon his capacity and capability to function within society. Class sentences are not an effective social response to drug abuse.

Needs

There are almost as many "needs" in this field as there are needles.

We need to ask such questions as: Does our internal program really prepare the client for a work experience? What supportive services must we provide to augment manpower programs? Should we subcontract the whole of our vocational rehabilitation effort?

We need to draw more indelibly that narrow line between that drug education which properly acquaints the user and potential user of the hazards of drug use and that drug education which merely creates a morbid curiosity to experiment.

We need to rethink our approach to community and in-school education. Despite the efforts of the last few years, the ignorance about drugs is appalling.

We need special studies into the unusual problems related to multiple drug use.

We need to attract and involve more scientific, academic, medical, and other institutional resources.

We need, as a matter of highest priority, to provide high-caliber training for personnel, for new professionals entering the field, and for the thousands of paraprofessionals and laymen working in community projects.

We must seek out, identify, and plan to cope with different subcultures with only marginal cross-involvement.

We need to study acute drug reactions among youth, with important concentration on posttreatment activities. We need an intensive investigation of narcotic deaths among youths, with emphasis upon life styles, drug habits, and the incidents preceding death.

We must analyze the relationship of marihuana use and subsequent drug abuse, looking not only at transitional factors, but also at the phenomenon of association, especially among multiple drug users.

We must expand our knowledge of onset factors, particularly among young people, with special emphasis upon attitudinal studies.

We need to study the economics of narcotic addiction, and the patterns of drug abuse in the new underground. We should survey official attitudes on drugs and rehabilitation. We need to do follow-up studies on arrested addicts.

There is a need for a program that attacks the many facets of drug abuse as it specifically relates to business and industry. There is a need to enlist industry in a total effort to train and employ the rehabilitant. But there is an even greater need, which has precedence, and that is to examine the whole of our vocational rehabilitation effort, with special emphasis upon marketable job skills. There is also a need to assist industry with the on-board employee who abuses drugs.

There is a need to question our whole approach to institutional settings.

We especially need more effective programs oriented to youthful abusers of non-narcotic drugs. The industry's experience has been with narcotics and with an older client. We are dealing not just with a youth drug culture, but with a distinct youth culture.

We need tighter control over the quality and kinds of materials and films in distribution to our target populations. Much of the material in use today is far below any acceptable quality mark.

The Universe of Drug Abuse

What is the universe of drug abuse? As measured by some responses, it is a universe dominated by the narcotics addict, some 250,000 to 650,000 persons, depending on whose assessment you accept. Sadly, too many professionals and the general public focus exclusively upon the narcotics addict, directing their best-funded and most comprehensive efforts at treating his addiction, to the inevitable and sometimes total exclusion of not only other aspects of the drug problem, but also of other drug abusers.

The real world is one in which there has been a marked evolution on the drug scene, with changes occurring in drugs of preference, in patterns of abuse, and in the identity and character of the drug abuser—changes which require corresponding shifts in our thinking and in our program planning.

Again, we approach the problem accurately when we speak of drug abuse and drug dependence, narcotic and nonnarcotic. We demonstrate that we have learned lessons from the expenditure of millions of dollars and from our successes and failures when we make program differentiations for four distinct classes of drug abusers: the experimenters; the casual or recreational users; the involved users; and the dysfunctional abusers, this latter group including but not limited to the narcotics addict.

And, we approach an ultimate resolution of this problem when we program effectively for the nonuser who is at risk in a drug-taking society.

If we are to relate to today's user, from experimenter to addict, and especially to the multiple-drug abuser, we must speak in terms of what drugs do *for* him, not just *to* him. The multiple-drug abuser, who has been evolving for perhaps a decade, becomes involved in the concurrent use of as many as 32 different substances because he wants to receive a specific effect and reaction from each.

Whereas our universe a few short years ago was dominated by a heroin addict who was about 29 years of age, a passive, dependent personality, predominantly a ghetto resident, today's universe includes younger addicts, more inclined to take risks. This universe also includes the students in a ninth-grade class in upstate New York, boys and girls approximately age 15, of whom 27% have used either drugs or drugs combined with alcohol, another 24% reporting the use of alcohol only.

In 1944, only 8% of the patients admitted to the federal hospital at Lexington were concurrently using barbiturates. By 1966, 54% were concurrently using barbiturates and 35% were addicted to barbiturates.

While we place appropriate emphasis upon the various drug cultures among our youth, we must not forget that our drug abusers include top corporate executives, middle management, clerks, salesmen, white and blue collar workers, and housewives.

How widespread is this epidemic?

The New York State Narcotic Addiction Control Commission conducted what may be the most comprehensive survey of drug use undertaken to date. Of the 13.7 million people in New York State, age 14 and older, this survey disclosed the following.

Some 361,000 persons use barbiturates on a regular basis of at least 6 times per month, and some 10% obtain *none* of their drugs through legal prescription.

Some 187,000 persons regularly use the nonbaribturate sedative hypnotics, and some 15% obtain *none* of these drugs through legal prescription.

Some 525,000 persons regularly use the minor tranquilizers, and some 5% obtain *none* of these drugs through legal prescription.

Some 71,000 persons regularly use the major tranquilizers, and some 5% obtain *none* of these drugs through legal prescription.

There were 39,000 regular users of antidepressants; 110,000 regular users of pep pills; 222,000 regular users of diet pills; 17,000 regular users of controlled narcotics; 1.043 million persons who had smoked marihuana in the previous 6 months, including 487,000 regular users; 203,000 persons who had used LSD during the previous 6 months, including 45,000 regular users; 64,000 persons who had used heroin during the previous 6 months, including 32,000 regular users; and 101,000 persons who had used cocaine during the previous 6 months.

It should be noted that these figures represent a projection of the more stable drug users—those with fixed addresses—and in all instances, these figures constitute minimums. Go back three spaces and think again about the heroin data: 32,000 regular users who defy historic beliefs by maintaining fixed addresses and leading relatively stable lives, thus undermining more than one accepted truism about addicts.

Applying other data, these researchers conservatively estimated the New York State addict population at 147,000 persons.

In assessing our universe, there is another important dimension.

New York researchers found that some 293,000 regular users of marihuana were employed and that 26.6% used the drug on the job. Other related findings were: 25,000 employed regular users of LSD with 20% reporting use on the job; 10,000 regular users of methamphetamine and 60% reporting use on the job; and 34,000 employed regular users of heroin with 35% reporting use of the narcotic on the job.

Yet, this industry has yet to mount a major program to meet the needs of business and industry.

Our Lack of Knowledge

Before we rush to program, we must factor for the gaps in our knowledge and credibility. The Director of Research of the New York State Narcotic Addiction Control Commission gave this assessment of our knowledge about drug abuse in 1972; it is still valid.

The extent of our knowledge in the drug abuse field appears to be inversely related to the magnitude of the problem. While drug abuse has been a social and medical problem for over a hundred years, serious research by competent professionals is a relatively recent phenomenon. Historically, our knowledge has been contaminated with impressionistic insights, anecdotal case examples, and poorly designed small sample studies from which inaccurate generalizations were produced.

Drug abuse knowledge must serve four specific tasks. First, it must provide us with the techniques for preventing people from using drugs. Second, it must permit us to identify those persons who will elect to use drugs, to explain why they elect to do so, and to identify the drugs they elect to use. Third, it must provide us with the techniques and regimens necessary for the safe detoxification and rehabilitation of those persons who were abusing drugs. And fourth, it must provide us with the techniques of preventing the former abusers from relapsing to drug use.

Unfortunately, our current knowledge does not permit us to operate with any certainty in any of these areas. We are only now learning how we can more effectively prevent experimentation and to intervene into the experimentation process, terminating or at least directing the experimentation.

We know, for example, that we cannot make people afraid to try drugs but that they will rationally choose not to use drugs when presented with empirical evidence of the physiological damage that the use will produce.

When we attempt to identify those persons who will elect to use drugs, our present knowledge permits predictability only at the general level.*

While most professionals acknowledge the presence of social, psychological and biochemical–physiological factors within the drug abuse process, the experts do not agree on the role or relative prominence of these factors and their precise functions and interrelationships remain largely ill-defined.

Our knowledge is probably the most extensive in treatment. Our knowledge is not such, however, to prevent relapse with any certainty. Some persons appear to relapse regardless of what we do for them and some do not relapse regardless of what we do to them . . . Our current knowledge, therefore, limits our ability to place a specific abuser in that type of treatment situation where the predictability methodological strategies are being developed and an empirical base is being compiled which will permit validation of our theoretical assumptions and meaningful evaluations of our intervention efforts . . . (Chambers, 1972).

Policy Questions

The purpose of this discourse is to give background to several questions which must be answered ultimately by society, government, and the drug abuse professional:

Are we opposed to all self-selective use of drugs?

Do we oppose all use of drugs for pleasure?

What do we mean by prevention? What is it that we are trying to prevent?

Does an individual have the right to indulge in self-destructive behavior?

What is the real goal of our treatment programs—to rehabilitate the drug user, or to protect society from the effects of his deviant behavior by neutralizing those effects?

What is a successful treatment outcome? Total abstinence? Are we willing to concede that a treatment program has had an effective measure of success with a patient if he maintains a stable residence, holds a steady job, and remains free from arrest—but continues to use drugs?

What are our standards for normal behavior?

Is it realistic to view the family and schools as the major institutions whose cooperative actions hold the greatest potential for reducing drug use and abuse?

Are the legal and medical models of drug abuse prevention adaptable to effective preventive education programs?

---

* A major problem with saying that certain individuals with certain characteristics will use certain drugs is that we cannot explain expertly why other individuals in similar circumstances and possessing the same characteristics do not use drugs.

What should be the role of the federal government? The state? The community?

What changes in perspective, approach, and program are indicated by the emergence of polydrug abuse?

Can the knowledge that has been accumulated in the field of learning, communication, and innovation be applied to the development of effective preventive programs?

Can preventive programs based upon education expect to have an effect upon those who are already using and abusing drugs?

What is the relationship of drug information to drug education, and how do these elements relate to an individual's behavioral choices?

Can the community and its resources be organized into a comprehensive mechanism that has the capacity to meet the needs for prevention, treatment, and rehabilitation?

What elements of effective rehabilitation programs might be developed earlier in the interests of prevention?

What are appropriate prevention objectives for what age groups?

What are the most productive program strategies being used today, and what assumptions underlie them in treatment, education, intervention, rehabilitation, training, and research?

What assumptions underlie our approaches to nonnarcotic drug abusers, and do they respond accurately to this group's needs?

Are decision-making, coping, developing self-concept, and values the responsibility of the schools, and, if so, should they be the responsibility of the health curriculum program?

What process does a person employ in deciding whether or not to try drugs, and how does that process help him avoid problems?

What definition do you apply to primary, secondary, and tertiary prevention, and what strategies do you advocate that are most effective in obtaining the goals inherent in your definition?

How can we most effectively intervene with the following groups to prevent drug use or resumption of use: the nonuser, the experimental user, the recreational or social user, the involved drug user, and the dysfunctional user?

What are the principal differentiations in program strategy that should be effected among inner cities, suburbs, and rural areas?

Do we agree that dysfunctional drug abusers should be treated or should they be jailed? Are we willing to jail an entire generation of our children?

Do we agree, realistically, that the purpose of treatment should be to provide services to help relieve the physical disabilities and social pressures that bear upon dysfunctional drug abusers, and to help restore them to some level of acceptable functioning in society?

What should be our criminal justice policy? Will we provide alternative dispositions for users of narcotics as well as nonnarcotics; for user-offenders who commit crimes of selling as well as crimes of possession; for only youthful offenders; for only first-time offenders; for only those offenders who commit misdemeanor violations?

Where and how do we draw the lines that determine that one man goes to jail and another receives treatment and an opportunity for rehabilitation?

Each of us who has toiled in this vineyard for any period of time has a personal answer to all of these questions.

The issue is: When will we amass these opinions from the field, test them on the crucible of public and legislative opinion, and develop a universal policy that we can and will support?

Somehow, someday, these vital issues, many of them hovering over us from the day we admitted the first patient into treatment, must be answered.

References

Chambers, Carl D. (1972). Research report for Narcotic Addiction Control Commission. (Unpublished)

Federal Strategy Council on Drug Abuse. (1973). "Federal Strategy for Drug Abuse and Drug Traffic Prevention." Special Action Office, Washington, D.C.

National Commission on Marijuana and Drug Abuse. (1973). "Drug Use in America: Problem in Perspective." U.S. Govt. Printing Office, Washington, D.C.

Index